TURN IT UP!

(I CAN'T HEAR THE WORDS)

TURN IT UP!

(I CAN'T HEAR THE WORDS)

Singer/Songwriters Then & Now

BOB SARLIN

CITADEL PRESS
Published by Carol Publishing Group
New York

 CITADEL UNDERGROUND

First Citadel Underground Edition 1992

Copyright © 1973 by Robert Sarlin
Introduction copyright © 1992 by Robert Sarlin

A Citadel Press Book
Published by Carol Publishing Group
Citadel Press is a registered trademark of Carol Communications, Inc.

Editorial Offices	Sales & Distribution Offices
600 Madison Avenue	120 Enterprise Avenue
New York, NY 10022	Secaucus, NJ 07094

In Canada: Canadian Manda Group
P.O. Box 920, Station U
Toronto, Ontario M8Z 5P9

First published by Simon and Schuster, New York 1973

Manufactured in the United States of America
ISBN 0-806501315-2

10 9 8 7 6 5 4 3 2 1

Carol Publishing Group books are available at special discounts
for bulk purchases, for sales promotions, fund raising, or
educational purposes, Special editions can also be created to
specifications. For details contact: Special Sales Department,
Carol Publishing Group, 120 Enterprise Ave., Secaucus, NJ 07094

Grateful acknowledgment is extended to:

Crawdaddy, for permission to reprint "Randy Newman: 'I Never Give
Myself a Break,'" by Bob Sarlin (*Crawdaddy,* #3, Jan. 16, 1972).

Militant, for permission to quote from David Salner's review of *American
Pie* (*Militant,* March 17, 1972).

Unart Music Corporation, for permission to quote from "Everybody Loves
Me, Baby," "Three Flights Up," and "Vincent."

For Peggy, Kay, Benjy and Jonathan
"What is love for? Love is forever."

CONTENTS

TURN IT UP!

(I CAN'T HEAR THE WORDS)

Bob Dylan—
Newport 1963

Bob Dylan rehearsing with
the Butterfield Blues Band—Newport 1965

Van Morrison

Joni Mitchell

Laura Nyro

Randy Newman

Donald McLean

INTRODUCTION

I WAS RIGHT and I was wrong.

Right in that these singer/songwriters were the best representatives of a new movement in popular music. Wrong, in that I naïvely believed that all, or even some of them would continue to grow as artists—turning out one wondrous album after another. Alas, it was not to be.

Having recently reviewed the recorded output of my key subjects from the last twenty years, I came to an inescapable conclusion: not one of these songpoets has significantly improved upon the work he or she did before 1972, when this book first appeared, and some have gotten much worse.

I can only guess at the reasons for this mass failure. First, all this early work that attracted me was magnificent, and very hard to top.

Then it is also hard for young performers to handle all the changes exposure and success can bring. Success tends to both insulate and involve a performer. It surely deprives one of a certain artistic distance. Instead of standing outside the society looking critically (and often hungrily) at what's going on, you're suddenly thrust right into the middle of things. Old friends regard you differently and even your long-struggling spouse can get a little strange. Perhaps it's not coincidental that all of my married subjects (Dylan, Newman, Nyro, Morrison and McLean) have been divorced following their early success.

Finally, there's something to be said for the arrogant certainty of youth, the chutzpah that makes a twenty-one-year-old feel he can see what's wrong with the world and write a song to try and fix it. As this certainty fades, it becomes harder to deliver songpoems at full force.

All this is, of course, speculation. All we really know is that, for the songpoets the early 70's turned out to be a peak, rather than a foothill.

Let's take a look at my 1972 favorites one by one.

Of course, we've got to begin with Bob Dylan, the most enigmatic of the bunch. After one truly inspired album (*Blood on the Tracks*), Dylan lapsed into a sort of self-parody. Album after album raised hopes that he would once again achieve the power of the earlier work—and album after album proved to be pale imitations of his best. His lyrics suffered most—and his most recent album seems to steal much of its imagery from uninspired nursery rhymes.

The less said about his "Born-Again" period the better. Suffice it to say it was pretty scary to hear this master of uncomfortable truths thanking God for his Grammy. As to why Dylan found and lost Jesus, that's between Bob and his god or his analyst. What it did to his music is sad and demoralizing—one substandard dirge after another. There is not one memorable song from this period.

Dylan is still very active at fifty. He churns out yearly mediocre albums and tours constantly. His live performances are most inconsistent. I've seen him truly explode with energy at one concert, ripping into his lyrics, remaking even his earliest songs into new and more potent word weapons, serving up strong and chilling rock and roll, and then mumble his way listlessly through another. All within a year's span.

A recent release of previously unreleased tracks from throughout his long career only serves to highlight how much Dylan's work has declined since the early 70's. There are some outstanding pieces from his early years, including very moving alternate tracks from *Blood on the Tracks*, that convey a deep regret and an even deeper nostalgia for simpler times.

One must respect Bob Dylan for many things. For his incredible body of work, his wit, his truth-telling, his delightfully mysterious self-promotion. He has steadfastly refused to let the media exploit or trivialize his work or invade the privacy of his family. How many pictures of Bob Dylan's many children can you remember seeing during the last twenty years? How many commercials with Dylan tunes?

Van Morrison is another hard case to figure. Two things come clear when you review his work since 1972. First, good songpoetry and religious fervor just don't mix, "Amazing Grace" notwithstanding, and simple repetition does not constitute a style. Unfortunately, this man has repeated himself so many times he should sue himself for plagiarism. Of course, some songs are better than others, and every once in a while a better than average album will slip through, but, in general, there is nothing in Morrison's recent work that can come close to the power of "Astral Weeks," the sheer rock and roll whimsy of "Domino," or the delicious jazziness of "Moondance." There is no modern equivalent to the carefree nostalgia of "Brown Eyed Girl." There are seemingly endless "spiritual" ballads that resemble musical Möbius strips—they seem to promise they'll take you somewhere new but always seem to circle back upon themselves. His music is all foreplay—or impotence.

In concert, Morrison remains inconsistent. Unlike Dylan, who is either good or bad on a given night, Morrison can be compelling and distant on the very same night. This limits his live audience to devotees who eat up such idiosyncratic performances. On one recent album, where he joined forces with the lively and vital Irish traditionalists, the Chieftains, Morrison came alive again, and seemed focused for the first time in many years. But then one realized that his own compositions on the album were much weaker than the traditional songs he helped the Chieftains perform. One lives in hope that such a talent as this will rediscover his early edge and give us more of the kind of soul-stirring music that he is clearly capable of producing. But one sadly questions whether the wild Irish bard of "Astral Weeks" or the natural pop songwriter of "Brown Eyed Girl" will ever be heard from again.

Joni Mitchell is perhaps the greatest disappointment of all. Her 1991 album, *Night Ride Home*, shows that she can still stand up to the challenge of writing intriguing and moving songs. But it's taken nearly twenty years to get close to the quality of her early work.

In between is a jazz-influenced smorgasbord of albums that range from dull to almost unlistenable. It's one thing to watch somebody's talent fade, it's another to watch someone waste their gifts on feeble attempts at avant gardeism. A good portion of her work is impossible to hear without cringing. The fiery, intimate and often exquisitely lovely confessional songs have disappeared— replaced by distant and overwrought exercises in artiness. I know there are critics who eat this stuff up, and who loftily criticize those of us who mourn the loss of the early, intimate style. An appropriate punishment for them would be having to listen to *Mingus*, by Joni Mitchell, over and over again.

Don McLean is an interesting case. It seems as if he violated normal show business rules by consciously trying to cool his career after the wild success of *American Pie* in 1972. His follow-up album was a folksier attempt, and that, in turn, was followed by a collection of country classics. His career continued to thrive in the U.K., allowing him the best of all show biz worlds, anonymity at home and fantastic recognition abroad. That way you can satisfy your ego on a few profitable tours a year and still be able to go out to the supermarket when you get home.

McLean has done some classy and classic work with the Jordanaires, once Elvis's back-up singers, and even kicked off a Roy Orbison revival by recording a hit version of "Crying" during the early 80's. But McLean has not recorded a song to compare with "Vincent" or "American Pie," both of which are still heard quite frequently on the radio.

* * *

Laura Nyro nearly disappeared from the scene for almost a decade. She emerged as a proud lesbian whose best songs were clearly behind her. A recent live album, recorded at New York's Bottom Line, presents a woman of great voice with very little new to say. All the old songs on the album are exceptional and all the new ones are self-indulgent and unfocused. It's a little hard to hear the same woman who tore the head off the sucker with songs like "Stone Souled Picnic" singing a bright little ditty about taking her kids to a restaurant.

I believe that Laura Nyro could've been one of the great pop songwriters—a Carol King with class—if she hadn't gotten lost in quirkiness and lightheaded hippiedom.

On the bright side, Randy Newman has consistently turned out intelligent and adventurous albums over the last two decades. His "Short Prople" and "I Love L.A." became hits—and part of the language—and his movie scores and commercials are ubiquitous and always recognizable for their quirky style. But, in reviewing all his recorded work since 1972, I'd have to say that the best songs are still the old ones. Nothing in his later work can compare to the old combination of eclectric music, biting humor and stinging truth of those early songs. His work has not aged a minute, and it is still as emotionally stunning as ever to listen to the beautiful and bitter "I Think It's Going to Rain Today." Nobody but Randy Newman could get away with the casual horror of lines like "Tin can at my feet/ Think I'll kick it down the street/That's the way to treat a friend."

Finally, Robert Hunter, erstwhile lyricist for the Grateful Dead, has continued to turn out marvelous songpoems for that remarkable conglomeration. Who would've thought that the Dead would last this long—and not just last, but become the centerpiece of a near religious cult called Deadheads. Perhaps what attracts young followers to the Dead, besides four hour drug-soaked musical orgies, is the band's refusal to alter their music for commercial purposes. This is a trait shared by all my subjects—even as their talents have faded or become confused, they've continued down their own roads, without making desperate or feeble attempts at commercial currency.

As to Hunter, he has the great joy of having found an audience that both understands exactly what he has to say and worships him for saying it.

He has pursued a solo career, appearing in small clubs with just a guitar, and recently a collection of his lyrics, *A Box of Rain*, was published. It's not shabby, but a little hard to enjoy in one sitting. I'm sure Dead fans consider it a bit of a bible.

After having thoroughly depressed myself by reviewing the work of many of my original subjects, I just had to bring a positive note to these proceedings. I hit upon the idea of reviewing all my favorite singer-songwriter work of the last two decades and attempting to pick the best single LP—the album (or CD, as it were) that would definitely make it on to my proverbial desert island.

I considered the always wonderful work of James Taylor, but couldn't settle on any one album. I thought of the brittle and brilliant work of Richard Thompson, both with and without his ex-wife Linda. I listened again and again to the songs of John Hiatt, who, more than any other songpoet, has conveyed the angst of middle-age in his work. But a certain variety wasn't there. Suzanne Vega and Tracy Chapman left me cold, seeming like one-hit wonders of old.

Sting, primary songwriter for The Police and his own solo efforts, was a prime candidate, and his is clearly one of the commanding figures in this form. Bruce Springsteen is yet another eminently admirable songpoet. But I finally settled upon a gentlemen to whom I'd given polite but very short shrift in 1972—Paul Simon. I think he was too close to home for me to fully appreciate—we come from the same part of the world and attended the same college. Simon was the entertainment at my freshman orientation—he was paid $50 to sing his very folksy songs of 1963. I thought he was a very pale imitation of Bob Dylan and his cohorts. So much for my ability as a spotter of early talent.

Simon has emerged as a transcendentally talented singer of lyrics that can be compared to the best of today's poetry. And he is getting better all the time. At his worst he's way ahead of the crowd, and at his best, well, he is the best.

Now to choose the album. It turned into a horse race between the mid-70's classic *Still Crazy After All These Years*, and the late 80's masterpiece *Graceland*. Finally, I gave up—and chose both. It's easy when you're making up the rules.

What I didn't predict about the songpoets was that, as they grew older, the subjects of their songpoems would naturally change to match their altered circumstances. The old idea of the "love" song has now been expanded to include the "failed marriage" song or the "mid-life crisis" song or even the "sexual confusion" song. Simon is a prime example of this, and the concerns reflected in both these albums are those of a mature, sensitive observer of the world—in macrocosm and microcosm.

Still Crazy addresses adult problems from the first line of the first and title song. Here the singer sadly brags about his ennui and sense of detachment. He's grown philosophical, but deceptively so, for as he reveals in the last lyric, where he worries aloud about flipping out and "doing some damage/One fine day," all is not quite right. So our tone has been established—deceptive calm.

Simon's tribute to his origins in "My Little Town" is a true chiller. With telling images and breezy musical bed he paints a picture of a good place to get out of fast. A town where the very colors of the rainbow have disappeared for lack of imagination. And once again a song ends with the threat of violence—a young man "Twitching like a finger on the trigger of a gun." All this violence—repressed and otherwise—now seems to be prophetic. I think Simon sensed what was growing in society, and put it in the mouth of his narrator.

The death of love is the subject of "I Do It for Your Love," and once again the tragedy is presented sotto voce, yet with great power. "The sting of reason/the splash of tears/the Northern and Southern hemispheres/love emerges and it disappears." How sad and how inevitable. This is an anti-love song.

On we go to the jaunty "50 Ways to Leave Your Lover," a most cynical song. And a lot of fun, with its delicious internal rhymes and breezy drum track. I love the cleverness of "In the morning/you'll begin to see the light"—and the mysterious nature of his Dear-Abby-like adviser.

"Night Game" is a chilling song—with its cold moon and bone-white stars and winter setting. Death comes to Yankee Stadium, as it must come to us all. Thus the first side of the album passes away.

Side two opens with a gospel blast—"Gone At Last"—sung with Phoebe Snow. Here a couple down on their luck hook up at a truck stop—both hoping things are about to change. Here's a song about the power of love to "lift you higher," and who could argue with that.

Now everything's fine, and the title of the next tune, "Some Folks' Lives Roll Easy," lulls you into thinking that, with our marital and other troubles behind us, we're in for some good times. Not to be. This is one of Simon's greatest songs. Not just because it is achingly beautiful, but because it is an attempt at addressing one of the basic conundrums of life: the disparity between the rich and the poor, the lucky and the luckless, the blessed and the damned. And the narrator, who fears that he is about to join the less fortunate group, says a prayer in mid-song. With exquisite harmony he begs for compassion—"You said if I ever got so low I was busted/you could be trusted." To find a song this profound on a so-called pop album is a true testament to the rise of songpoetry.

Now, having raised doubts about the "good times" coming, and who will participate, Simon tells us of those for whom the whole subject is just too depressing to consider. These are the fun seekers of "Have a Good Time," who say, "Ah, what the hell," and "God bless our standard of living" while boogeying off into the sunset. You couldn't write a better prophecy of the 80's—or a more biting comment on how most people deal with the said question posed in "Some Folks' Lives."

And, then, his social consciousness stifled, our narrator comes on like a mentally deficient lover in "You're Kind." Once again the music is jaunty as he happily tells his lover good-bye, explaining lamely that "I like to sleep with the window open/And you keep the window closed.

Finally we go out with a bit of a hymn called "Silent Eyes" in which Simon reminds us that we shall all "stand before the eyes of God and speak what was done." Party on, he tells us, but someday the bill will come due.

Cut to 1987 and *Graceland*. Simon's career had grown cold and his songs had lost focus and gone a bit flabby. Writing intimate yet universal lyrics is no easy trick, and you can easily lose it in either direction. You can become too personal and lose the universality— or you can begin to write cold, distant and ultimately meaningless anthems. So a guy like Simon walks a fine line, but it's a line walked by all great artists.

Graceland is an album about musical fusion and intellectual and moral confusion. Once again Simon is unafraid of tackling big emotional issues. How does one keep the heart alive in a world where morality lags behind technology. How does one find love or "grace" in a world where certainty is as elusive and insubstantial as "moonlight sleeping on a midnight lake." With great joy, Simon tells us. With the companionship of a child, with the memory of a love lost and with sheer wonder at the pure intensity of life today. Finally, with a passion for life.

Simon's cool intellectual pose is deceptive—he is seeking the river of passion that runs below it all and when he finds it he dives right in and takes us with him. His cinematic counterpart is Woody Allen, another New York moral philosopher. Like Simon, Allen tries to make sense of life intellectually, while displaying an incredible passion and sensitivity. When the intellect can't solve things, he looks for joy in passionate couplings, with people and with the city he loves.

There's something Chaplinesque about both artists, and it's not just their shoe sizes. Their work boasts sophisticated (and sometimes raucous) humor, yet always carries with it a questioning of life and a touch of pathos. And finally, they are both true artists. Simon is one of the great record producers of our time. As I said twenty years ago, no one puts more care into every note of a recording than Simon. And no one synthesizes the world's musical repertoire quite the same way. Since his days with Simon and Garfunkel, when he recorded with Los Incas, Simon has sought out the best folk and pop musicians in the world and made them his collaborators.

In a very sad encounter after the release of *Graceland*, Simon was accused of plagiarism and cultural exploitation by a group of black students. How blind people can be. Simon does not exploit musicians like the Mighty Clouds of Joy or Ladysmith Black Mambazo. He enshrines them and exposes them to a vast audience they might not otherwise have reached.

From the very first sound on *Graceland*, a deep booming drum beat, Simon lets us know we will be hearing pop music unlike anything we've encountered before.

"The Boy in the Bubble" addresses another very basic conundrum of life in these strange times—how can a society so technologically advanced be in such moral disarray. In one song we go from the savagery of a car bomb attack to the "miracle and wonder" of "the baby with the baboon heart." from the "automatic earth" that creates a killing drought, to the "lasers in the jungle."

The music carries us along at a frantic pace, with the sounds of confusion frequently intruding on the powerful rhythm track.

Finally, there is the irony of recording a song about the Manichean nature of man with black South African musicians.

Next up, a little trip down the Missisip to "Graceland." A complex ditty, this one. Two strands weave together—a trip to Memphis to seek Elvis and possible salvation, and thoughts upon a dying love affair. But then again, there's the nine-year-old child buckled up on the seat next to the singer, and that delicious travelling music. And the final thought is optimistic, as Simon clings to the belief that someday "we will be received in Graceland."

In "I Know What I Know," Simon goes to a party accompanied by the delightful General M.D. Shirinda and the Gaza Sisters. In the midst of all this superficial chatter, the singer reminds himself of his job as an artist-to relate what he sees truthfully. There is much poetry loose in this song with lines as lovely as: "She loved so easily/ All I could think of was sunlight." But, all in all, this party is a mild affair and before you know it we're on our way home in a taxi having the discussion that forms the spine of "Gumboots." This is a very silly song, in which a fatuous character tries to talk himself out of his own pain.

Now we come to the high grade core of *Graceland*. The music is indescribably good—brimming over with sounds never heard before on an American pop album. And suddenly we are out strolling with the girl "with diamonds on the soles of her shoes." Here's a song about the exhilaration of new love, the high, easy feeling of strolling past the bodegas of Upper Broadway with a beautiful girl. As Simon tells us, this is one way to "lose these walking blues." And what a back-up troupe. This is the song that established Ladysmith Black Mambazo in the mind of the American public. They've subsequently made albums, toured and even provided the background for television commercials. Not bad for a township band from a South African ghetto. Their vocal music is full of mystery and touched with an almost classical dignity.

"You Can Call Me Al" was a hit for Paul Simon, aided no doubt by a truly silly music video featuring a deadpan Simon and wacky Chevy Chase.

The main character of this song, whom we can call Al, reminds me of a cross between Randy Newman's famous fool at the party in "Mama Told Me Not to Come" and Bob Dylan's "Mr. Jones." He has some self-awareness, but not much. He's trying to make sense of what's happening and where he is, but failing. Yet, even in this advanced state of middle-aged befuddlement he can still be moved to religious fervor by the "angels in the architecture." The poeticism of this lyric is delightful. One fresh and telling image pops up only to be quickly supplanted by another. My favorite passage comes when out narrator tells us that his role model has "ducked back down the alley/with some roly-poly little bat-faced girl." That image always makes me think of the politician who throws away his career for a pneumatic blonde. There goes another role model, heading down the alley.

Linda Ronstadt joins Simon for "Under African Skies," a song that examines the power of music, the "pulsing of love in the vein." There's a verse apparently written expressly for Ronstadt, in which a child from Tucson, Arizona, finds her wings through song.

What are "the roots of rhythm"? For me, this song is about how basic music is to people—how it draws on primitive emotions and touches parts of us rarely reached by other arts. We are one with Joseph the African, out in the desert, and with his music.

The only word for the next song, "Homeless," is sublime. Who but Simon could, in collaboration with Joseph Shabalala of Ladysmith Black Mambazo, tackle the task of conveying emotions as subtle and elusive as those expressed here. If there is a message to this songpoem, it is, "Many dead, tonight/it could be you." It truly conveys a feeling of being lost, surrounded by confusion, unable to find solid ground. The central image of "moonlight sleeping on a midnight lake" perfectly captures the emotions one feels when uncertain and afraid.

I live in New York City, surrounded by the homeless, and often when I see them I think of this song, and wonder about the anxiety and uncertainty they must feel. "Homeless," is a powerful humanistic statement—and part of its power is in its creator's refusal to take the obvious, political route in addressing this contemporary nightmare. And, finally, it is one hell of a beautiful piece of music—fresh and surprising and finally, breathtaking.

We move back down from the mountain top with "Crazy Love. Vol II." The voice of this song is akin to that in "You Can Call Me Al"—hapless, intimidated and a bit childlike. Talk about denial— this person says he doesn't want "part of this crazy love" more than twenty times. Of course, the narrator doth protest too much, and what we have here is a very sad song about a divorce that ends up on the "evening news." The music is ironically light and upbeat.

"That Was Your Mother" could well be a story the narrator of the song "Graceland" would tell his child as they drove toward Memphis. It's a fun song, with the deliciously spicy Cajun music of Good Rockin' Dopsie and the Twisters pumping right along. The best of today's singer-songwriters are addressing the issues of middle age—or, in this particular instance, what its like to be middle aged and divorced and have to explain yourself to your teenage son. Simon handles the task with good humor and truthfulness.

I must confess trying to "understand" the last song on this album leaves me feeling like the befuddled character of "You Can Call Me Al." "All Around the World or The Myth of the Fingerprints," featuring Los Lobos' musical talents, seems to be making fun of the kind of semi-spiritual paranoia one finds among cults. You know, the kind of group that believes extraterrestrials are drawing large pictures on high plateaus in Peru. Whatever, it's a light ending to a heavy album.

I can't wait to hear what Paul Simon has in store for us. And I can't wait to have that precious experience of discovery once again— to be turning the audio dial and to hear a snatch of a song that has something new and wonderful to say.

That's what the pioneering songpoets have left as their legacy. they expanded the very idea of the popular song, and every time a songwriter picks up a guitar or sits down at a synthesizer he or she owes a huge debt to these adventurous troubadours.

It's almost hard now to imagine a time when such songwriting was considered odd or inappropriate. When people were suspicious of a singer creating and performing his own sings. But there was such a time and it was plenty boring.

About ten years after the first publication of this book, a group of young South African students showed up at my door in New York wanting to discuss the lyrics of Bob Dylan. I laughed and told them the author of that book was long gone, but I'd be glad to chat with them. Sure enough, we had the greatest time, and I began to feel that old excitement, that sense of stumbling upon something so important one just had to share it with the world. It was a glorious feeling, and even now, when I hear a song that has something new and unique to tell me, I can still get a bit of that old feeling back. When that happens, I reach for the volume control and turn it up, so I can hear the words.

FROM NEWPORT ON

N EWPORT, 1963. Bright sun shining down over the sleepy millionaires' town filled with the bedlam of another folk festival. Thousands of kids on the roads into town—walking, hitchhiking, taking in each other and the summer air. Down in town, the police cars carried dogs in their back seats—a reminder to many of the civil rights struggle so much on the minds of the singers and the audience. This audience, however, was a gentle one.

We will never see another Newport summer like 1963, when innocence and idealism abounded and drugs were a definite scarcity. The young people had short hair and wore button-down shirts open at the collar. They carried banjos and guitars and many, many little harmonicas, and all over the city you could bump into small groups of people making music together, singing the old songs.

The winter had been long, following the political crisis of October when it seemed, for a few days, that all the nightmare predictions of the peace movement were about to become terrifying facts of life. But the Cuban missile crisis had not diminished a basic belief among most of the college kids that the government and President Kennedy were somehow watching over them and on their side.

A time of real innocence, a time of suntanned bodies stretching out on the grass of the Newport Casino to listen to ballad-makers and rediscovered bluesmen.

They held a "broadsides" workshop that summer at Newport, chaired by Pete Seeger and featuring the best of the young political songwriters—Bob Dylan, Tom Paxton and Phil Ochs.

The themes of the workshop were simple. Ban the bomb and free the Negro and feed the hungry. The songs were almost as simple as the causes they advocated. Simple chord progressions with easy words. Sing-along songs, and nobody seemed to object when they brought out the man who had written "The Talkin' Atomic Blues," way back in the early '50s.

I can remember hanging on to the railing of one of the Casino balconies and listening to Bob Dylan sing that day. His raspy, intentionally uglified voice seemed out of place in his small body, and it seemed incongruous that so much anger could come from this slight young man. Dylan was the hero of that year's festival, what with "Blowin' in the Wind" blowing out of every car radio in town, sung by Peter, Paul and Mary as if it were a fighting hymn.

The songs that were sung at that workshop were mostly political statements strung over a few unextraordinary guitar chords, but in some of the lyrics there was not only fire but a disarming self-awareness. When Paxton sang about his rambling boy, or Dylan about the pawn in their game, you could take the songs on two levels. They were not only political statements but also personal poems.

As the workshop was winding down, I got bored and wandered off into a concert of new performers. The area set aside for this affair was much larger than the one for the workshop, but there were far fewer people listening.

Up on the big stage, John Hammond, Jr., was making his Newport debut. It was an odd performance, for John—blond hair and WASP features, descendant of Commodore Vanderbilt—was singing the country blues, duplicating almost note for note the fierce performances that one can find on the scratched records of the '20s and '30s. The crowd was restless, maybe doubting sincerity in a technically perfect reproduction of those black blues. But then Hammond did something even stranger. He began to sing Chuck Berry's highway hymn "Maybelline," a rock hit of the '50s. The crowd perked up. A couple of kids began to move in their seats as the hard, sexy rock sounds thumped out of Hammond's acoustic guitar. Berry's song was about cars and girls and had some of the best of the early rock lyrics, strung out over the fast, humping beat of rock-and-roll.

If I had to pick a moment when the idea for this book was born, it was that moment, as I stood there stomping my foot and wondering what was making me feel so goddamn good inside. Then I tried to figure out why the workshop had bored me, and the reason came. This music had all the energy, all the joy and sexuality the other songs, with their intellectual lyrics and their political clichés, did not have. What if these two forms combined—now, wouldn't that be something?

This book is an attempt to answer that question. It is about the result of the integration of the intellectual and lyrical qualities of folk music and political folk songs with the simplicity and energy of good old rock-and-roll.

It wasn't until two summers later that someone attempted to compress these two forms into a new one. It was Bob Dylan at Forest Hills in August, 1965. And any resemblance between this sharp-suited, high-booted rocker and the kid who had chastised the playboys and playgirls of 1963 was purely coincidental.

First, the site was so different from that tiny workshop crowded with button-down folk fans. Forest Hills is a tennis stadium, and because the courts must be protected from the shoes of fifteen thousand fans, there is a distance of about two hundred feet between the stage and the audience, which sits in a semicircular set of stands. That night in August, Dylan needed the distance, for he was strolling straight into the face of a largely hostile audience. The objects of their anger, a set of big electric amplifiers, loomed behind Dylan as he did the first half of his program. It was quiet through most of the first set, for the fans had no quarrel with the old acoustic Dylan or with his songs of politics and personal distress.

After Dylan finished the set, he called for a short intermission and disappeared behind the huge amps as he headed for a backstage tent. It was a hot night, and the tension built during twenty minutes of intermission. Many had heard the rumors of an electric debacle at Newport, where Dylan had been booed off the stage while trying to perform some of his rock tunes with the Paul Butterfield Blues Band.

But this was New York, where Dylan had first emerged as the spokesman for his peers, with the voice that could say the things you had always wanted to say with ease and with music that added so much to the difficult words. His progress toward understanding had been made in public, and thousands of his contemporaries had shared the trip. And now Dylan had betrayed them, or so it seemed to so many who had rejected the raucous sounds of rock-and-roll for the quieter, more introspective sounds of "folk music"—the music of Peter, Paul and Mary and Baez and so many others.

Dylan returned to the stage, carrying his electric guitar and followed by a small group of musicians, and all hell broke loose. A small chorus of cheers was drowned out by boos, shouted insults and theatrical groans. It was as if every person in the stadium felt the need to take a stand there and then, and loudly. After a few seconds of plugging in and equipment checking, Dylan walked to the front of the stage, looked up at the crowd and took off on one of the most difficult journeys of his short life.

This book is about that journey, and about those who followed closely behind Bob Dylan to create a new and vibrant art—which I call songpoetry.

What Dylan did that night, and during many nights to follow, was to forcibly fuse the elements of his own music—close to the folk songs and political folk songs of the '40s and '50s—with those of rock-and-roll. It was no easy task.

Rock-and-roll, since its first intrusion on the public awareness in the early '50s, had been the paramount music of anti-intellectuality. It was a musical form in which the spoken lyric was usually a throwaway set of cliches directed at what the music-industry executives conceived of as the teen-age mentality. At the same time that rock became the joy of one generation, it became the object of almost universal derision among the rest of America, including the media and the schools.

The emotions expressed by early rock-and-roll were essentially sexual. It was an outlet for a very repressed, hitherto invisible portion of the populace, the teen-ager. Jacob Brackman of *Esquire* has written that the teen-ager of the '50s was highly visible and audible, and when his music was around it was hard to escape. The songs were loud and simple and aimed at the groin. They were dance tunes that called for new styles of dancing which drew more on the jitterbug than on the fox-trot, and more on black than on white style.

At the same time that this new form of music was making its way into the developing consciousness of millions of teen-agers, another form was beginning to draw a small but determined audience. This was "folk"—the music of Woody Guthrie and Leadbelly and the sounds of groups like the Weavers. Because of the kind of instruments that are used to strum out these songs, all acoustic, the lyrics were to be increasingly important. While it was easy to ignore a trite lyric in a screaming rock song, it was impossible to miss the words when the Weavers appeared, with their harmonies and guitars and banjos.

For some years, with few exceptions, the two forms remained separate. Each was refined: Rock became dominated by professionals and highly skilled studio musicians. "Folk" music became increasingly political until, at the end of the '50s, a folk-music boom developed, and with the increased airplay and use of television, nonpolitical folk musicians were in high demand.

But it was not until 1965 that Bob Dylan forged the two and created songpoetry. Since then, this form has shown itself capable of great growth, and it will last.

Rock-and-roll is high-energy music. It is music that can roll down your socks and lift your cap and set you singing and dancing and doing things you never thought you'd allow yourself to do. But rock-and-roll, born ignominiously in the sad and empty

'50s, has grown up now, and like anything close to adulthood, it has gotten complex, with subforms and categories and all those other little academic traps.

Most of these categorizations, like the death sentences some critics insist on imposing upon the entire form, are bullshit—the result of limited minds and souls confronting something too big for them to handle or understand. Thus, the categories flow: soft-rock, folk-rock, freak-rock, heavy-rock, jazz-rock and rock-rock. I don't know much about these categories, and the Lord and my close friends know I would never use them in public, but it does seem to me that rock, in all its current late-adolescent complexity, needs to be broken down, if only slightly, so that we can understand it better.

This book focuses on a group of artists who work in the medium of rock-and-roll. Yet something has happened to their work that separates them out from the mainstream. They have learned to apply their intelligent and artistic energies to the lyrics of their songs, and they have created a new form.

While many of the rock artists continued to rely primarily on the backbeat and the frenzy of rock-and-roll for the effect of their work, these artists—or songpoets, as I call them—learned to use the song lyric for more than filler. Many rock artists still feel that a lyric is simply for screaming unintelligibly over music so strong that nobody cares about, or can distinguish, the words anyway. This book is not a criticism of these artists, for rock-and-roll would surely be a limp and decaying form without their energies. But it is a recognition of those who have focused their attention on using the lyric to say something about being human.

Not all rock-and-roll writers are songpoets. Rock, like everything else, has a soft underbelly of mediocrity, and most particularly in the area of lyrics. First, there are groups who are purely and simply mediocre both musically and lyrically. But there are others who choose not to place much importance upon the lyric content of their songs, and this includes most of the groups now playing. At the outside, there will be one or two meaningful lines, and sometimes a chorus will stick in the mind, but on the whole these groups care little about songpoetry.

Another group of writers comes to mind here. This is the cult of singer/songwriters who have swamped the record market in the last few years, following up the success of writer/performers like James Taylor, Don McLean, Neil Young and many others. It seems that every record company has its little cast of these limp and often laughable ditty scribblers, each one less effective than the previous one. They are not in the same league with the best songpoets; not even in the same sport.

The people on whose work I will concentrate here are a rare bunch: the best at what they do; innovative and constantly creative. They have managed to combine elements of the best of rock-and-roll with a lyrical sophistication that has never been heard before in popular songs. Where, in the past, a Cole Porter might slickly line out his fantasies in a limited and often insincere manner, these songpoets are attempting, for the most part, to examine the kinds of emotional experience that have previously been untouched in this area. Their work has really only recently begun, and only the first fruits are available for analysis, but it is my belief that with the passage of years, and the growing acceptance of their music, they will explore even further.

Even a casual listener to rock will be struck by the fact that some of the most often heard names do not appear in this book. It is not the result of oversight. Popularity is not a sufficient basis on which to judge. The popular taste too often calls for the shining void, the highly stylized singer with little or nothing to say. This is well and good, and keeps radio stations busy and sells a great quantity of teen-age cosmetics, but it has little or nothing to do with songpoetry.

Yet many of those artists about whom I write have achieved a certain popularity. I certainly don't condemn the songpoets who stumble onto or intentionally seek the formula for a hit record or album. Often the public will latch on to a writer when he is young, and buy his hit records, and then abandon him when he begins to attempt more serious music. This was almost the fate of Van Morrison, one of the best.

Then again, the public is famous for ignoring a good writer

until he is on the verge of quitting the business in frustration, and then suddenly discovering his latest release and making it a whopping hit. This description can be loosely fitted to both Randy Newman and Don McLean, writers who worked for years before receiving any kind of real public attention.

As for the criteria I am using to judge these writers—well, you'll have to pick them out for yourself. I listen for a subtle, and perhaps subjective, combination of style and content. I treasure the few times I have come upon an artist who has found a unique way of rocking and rolling. It is this rare breed of artists who keep rock and songpoetry alive and well.

THE FOLK INFLUENCE

$\mathcal{S}$ONGPOETRY was the result of a gradual combination of some of the most vital elements of folk music and rock-and-roll. Over fifteen years a good part of the audience that was once attracted to folk music moved on to form the core of the audience for the songpoets, with good reason. The spirit of care and authenticity that was once found only in the songs of writers and performers like Pete Seeger and Woody Guthrie is now reaching out from the work of writers like Dylan and the other songpoets. They are deeply indebted to the work of men like Seeger and Guthrie, and freely admit it.

What was it that Seeger and Guthrie discovered and shared that so influenced those who were to find their mode only in the '6os?

It is hard to imagine now what a wasteland American popular music was in the early and middle '5os. The airwaves were dominated by Muzak-like compositions, limp material of limited aspiration. A few stations carried rock-and-roll, more often than not the more watered-down cuts that captured none of the real vitality of the form. Often, out of racism, major radio stations played castrated cover versions of black-originated rock-and-roll. Some stations played jazz, but they were few and very far between. Folk music was almost totally absent, for a variety of reasons—but mostly because of the political climate during the early '50s. The witch-hunters were out in full force, and the American entertainment industry had almost totally capitulated to their paranoid demands.

Publications like *Red Channels* circulated widely with lists of "tainted" performers who were suspected of having Communist affiliations of one kind or another. Pete Seeger and Woody Guthrie were both prominently featured in this kind of publication. For Guthrie it meant lack of airplay; for Seeger, no work. The Weavers, the group to which Seeger belonged, had been hounded out of existence by the Red Scare, even though they had been one of the most popular singing groups of the late '40s and early '50s. Their records of songs like "On Top of Old Smoky" and "Tsena, Tsena" had sold millions of copies, but by 1953 their managers could not get them a single date.

Despite this unofficial ban, Seeger persisted, and eventually, with his records and self-promoted engagements—many for politically sympathetic groups—he found an audience whose loyalty transcended the climate of the times. By the end of the decade, the Weavers had regrouped; folk music had entered into the popular music in great force, if not great quality, and Seeger had become a symbolic leader for a new generation of songwriters.

I can remember going to hear Seeger many times during the '50s, both with and without the Weavers. His concerts at Carnegie Hall, many called hootenannies and including other, less-known performers, were highlights of my adolescence. First, the long, eager trek up to the second balcony, to one of those rows so high that the management does the customers the favor of leaving the lights on so that they can read their programs, for there is little real hope of seeing clearly what is going on far below on the stage. The sight lines might not have been the best, but you could hear well, and there was a lot to hear. Seeger is one of the great concert performers of our time. His stage manner, with its informality and lack of condescension, established a standard for an entire generation of performers who followed him.

His concerts were easygoing affairs, but he demanded and got a tremendous, though subtle, emotional response from the crowd. Never a virtuoso instrumentalist, Seeger made up for what he lacked in technical polish with his contagious enthusiasm for his material and for his audiences. His material came from around the world, and much of it was political. The politics that once seemed radical were soon to become the politics of the entire Movement of the '60s. There were songs attacking racism, the glorification of war, social injustice; urging resistance and activism. And, of course, Seeger was important because he represented continuity. He sang songs of earlier struggles and of abiding faith in the good fight, and he taught a whole generation a lot, without seeming to jam it down their throats. A song might come from the Spanish Civil War—an event that was cloudy at best to his young listeners; but there were rousing choruses to sing along with, and great new guitar chords to learn. And lessons to be learned about perseverance and gentleness in strength.

Alternating on a variety of acoustic instruments, Seeger would introduce nearly every song with a short discussion of its history. He depended most on his guitars, twelve-string and six-string, and on his five-string banjo, but often played the recorder or sang a capella.

The spirit of Woody Guthrie was always present at these folk-music gatherings, even though he was in the hospital with a nerve disease throughout the '50s. Seeger often spoke of Guthrie on stage, reminiscing about their travels together and then singing the songs the troubador from Oklahoma had made famous.

Guthrie's songs are extremely important to the invention of songpoetry. During a time when much of American popular music was devoted to drawing attention away from the Depression and the catastrophic deprivation of a huge segment of the population, Guthrie was writing very personal songs that focused on those people and their suffering. He would lift tunes from the folk tradition and add his own words that related to the times. The result was an opus of more than a thousand songs that dealt with everything under the sun—from politics to sex, from dust storms to rushing rivers. What is most important about the work of this remarkable man is the extremely personal nature of it all. He had found a way to express, without compromise, exactly what he thought and felt about the world. Sitting here now, it is hard to imagine how unique an achievement that was.

During the '30s and '40s, and even later than that in some circles, it was considered sacrilegious to tamper with "traditional" folk music. At one point, the composer/collector John Jacob Niles felt it necessary to deny authorship of a number of his songs for fear that their lack of "authenticity" would cause an uproar among his audience of traditionalists. Popular music was then dominated by simplistic statements of safe ideas, usually concerned with one form or another of love.

Guthrie ignored the taboos, and it is preeminently for that reason that his work was, and remains, a crucial influence. Where once it seemed an act of great egocentricity to say what you really felt in your songs, now critics and audiences are quick to leap upon a singer/songwriter who does less.

Seeger's own songwriting was clearly influenced by Guthrie and others like him. It would have seemed absurd to a traditionalist of the '30s to hear Seeger sing about his personal experiences and beliefs in songs like "Where Have All the Flowers Gone?" and "Waist Deep in the Big Muddy." Much of his material, even his most recent compositions, focuses upon political struggles, but these are Seeger's most personal considerations, as much as Joni Mitchell finds her own love life her most symbolic and therefore a fit subject.

Seeger will most likely to be remembered for songs like "We Shall Overcome" and "Where Have All the Flowers Gone?" yet there is much else that he has written that is both tuneful and emotionally effective. My personal favorite of all his many compositions is the lilting "Turn, Turn, Turn," in which he borrowed from Ecclesiastes in the Bible to create a powerful statement for peace.

Although folk music "boomed" in the late '50s, with many songs on the charts and radios and numerous groups out strumming guitars and banjos, Seeger and his music have never found mass popular acceptance. His records sell poorly for an artist of such stature and fame, and he has never made any obvious attempt to change the situation. Instead he has focused his attention on ecology—particularly on the struggle to reverse the effects of man and industry upon his native Hudson Valley.

It is still difficult for any television producer to have Seeger on his show; the paranoia of the '50s has never completely disappeared. But Seeger's influence is wide and deep nonetheless, and some of the most popular performers of our time owe him a tremendous debt, as do we all. Each time someone steps out onto a stage to sing about his inner feelings, to sing to audiences who prefer lack of pretension, he carries on the work of Seeger and Guthrie as well as others who are less well known.

It is not by chance that people like Bob Dylan and Don McLean sought out Seeger. For a good long time, he was the only well-known American performer whose stage presence and musical aspirations matched the hopes of many of the younger generation. Even if they have now passed on into new forms based on the energy of rock and jazz, they are still continuing Seeger's work, just as Seeger had learned much from and built on the work of Woodrow Wilson Guthrie.

Some things that are present in Seeger's and Guthrie's writing and that later reappear in the work of some of the best songpoets are harsh self-criticism, a good bit of romanticism and humor and a taste for taking on the Establishment in the interest of the "little guy," the forgotten man. These have persisted in the work of writers as different as Randy Newman and Bob Hunter of the Grateful Dead. When Hunter writes his songs about fur trappers and hoboes, he continues a tradition that was kept alive by Guthrie writing about Okies and workers and those with whom they had to contend to earn their bread. When Randy Newman writes, "They sent her to low school/They sent her to high school/She just wouldn't go no further," he is very much in the anti-Establishment tradition of Guthrie and Seeger.

Guthrie was the true romantic who believed his songs could have an effect on what was happening around him. His love songs are passionate, and some of his lyrics explicit about love and lust. Seeger wrote "Kisses Sweeter Than Wine," about two people growing old together without losing their passion for each other. When Bob Dylan wrote "Sad-Eyed Lady of the Lowlands," his long, impassioned love song, he was writing more in the tradition of a Guthrie than in that of a popular songwriter schooled in self-censorship and stock imagery.

The humor in the work of Seeger and Guthrie is more often than not slightly self-deprecating. Guthrie often pictured himself as foolish, and often his characters had a wry and gentle humor. Think of the preacher in "So Long, It's Been Good to Know You," who takes up a collection before fleeing the dust storm. Or the unashamed silliness of a song like "Car, Car," which still delights children. If you think of Guthrie when you hear the early talking blues of Bob Dylan, you're on the right track, for not only did Dylan employ the talking-blues form that Guthrie so loved; he was to carry the humor into his more personal songs, even some of his most angry ones. In "Highway 61," Dylan tells of the promoter who is offered the job of putting on the Third World War. "I'm sure it can be easily done/We'll just put up some bleachers in the sun/And hold it out on Highway Sixty-one." Guthrie would have loved that verse.

The humor that flowed through the work of people like Seeger and Guthrie is everywhere in the best work of the song-poets.

This strain of anti-Establishment feeling, this affection for the wildly romantic and the presence of irony and humor that could as easily be directed at oneself as at other people—these are what Seeger and Guthrie kept alive when all around them songwriters and hacks were escaping into clichés and esoteric jazz poems.

ROCK-AND-ROLL!

$\mathbb{M}$OST of the early rock-and-roll was worthless as songpoetry. The music was all, and the lyrics were given short shrift. If the music pumped and throbbed and stabbed straight at the groin, who would listen to the lyrics anyhow?

Rock-and-roll was the only medium most of the teen-agers could empathize with. If it was crass at times, or most of the time, it perfectly matched their emergent feelings.

Still, there were aspects of early rock-and-roll that were greatly to influence the work of the songpoets, and these should be examined here, before we get on to the more sophisticated writing of the early '6os.

Rock-and-roll unintentionally guaranteed that there would never be an across-the-generations acceptance of the work of the songpoets. Body music was, and still is, alien to ears trained in the belief that popular music should be neutral and unobtrusive. While adults either chuckled at the inanity of early rock-and-roll or recoiled from its flamboyant sexuality, the youngsters who would later become the best of the songwriters of the '6os were listening like other teen-agers, with almost total acceptance.

What they heard on the rock-and-roll stations was a mixed

bag. Usually a station could be depended upon to play only a few, if any, black artists, and much diluted rock—music with many of the same intentions as the black rock-and-roll, but without the balls; castrated rock-and-roll, in which the lyrics diminished the sexuality, the beat was muffled and vocals sanitized. A good way to understand this might be for you to fish out some old rock-and-roll records and give a listen. First listen to Bo Diddley and then to the Everly Brothers. Both were categorized as rock-and-roll, but only one seems to be heavy with sensuality and power, while the other, the sanitized rock-and-roll records of the Everly Brothers, feature high, white, church-choir vocals over a beat that is at best subdued, sometimes missing.

Elvis Presley and Jerry Lee Lewis are both important exceptions to the rule that white cover versions of black songs were less sensual. Elvis, though covering the work of black artists like Arthur Crudup, still managed to convey something of the original intention of the raunchy music he was imitating. With his slobbering vocals and jerking hips, Elvis was immediately pounced upon by teen-agers as the raunchiest artist they'd ever seen or heard. Of course, they had not been exposed to the best of black rock-and-roll; but even so, Elvis was pretty hot stuff next to the Everly Brothers or Danny and the Juniors.

Jerry Lee Lewis, who first came to the attention of the general public with a fantastic rock-and-roll number titled "Great Balls of Fire," was an obvious madman, and as such he became an immediate hero to hordes of listeners, stifling under their adolescence in the Eisenhower years. Lewis would play his piano as if it were an opponent in a street fight, stomping and pounding it while he screamed out lyrics to songs like "Whole Lotta Shakin' Going On." He later went on to confirm the best suspicions his listeners had about him by marrying his thirteen-year-old cousin and then disappearing behind a boycott of disk jockeys, whose attitude toward much of rock-and-roll was calculated condescension. Lewis has since emerged as a country-and-western star, but has toned down his performances considerably for that audience.

The few black artists who did slip through the radio-station mentality were mostly so outrageous, or so brilliant, that they could not have their songs covered adequately. A good example of this is Little Richard Penniman, who sang his way out from a busboy job with his own composition "Tutti Frutti." When this song was covered by Pat Boone, it simply could not satisfy the teen-age audience, and the original version of "Tutti Frutti," with Little Richard squealing passionately, went on to become a successful record.

An understanding of the effect of covering a black single with a white version can be gained when one compares Little Richard and Pat Boone. Boone, clean-cut in the extreme, wore white buckskin shoes and sang with all the energy of a geriatric case. His music, unrelated to the groin, seemed aimed more at the elbows or some other neutral territory. Little Richard was an obvious rock-and roll genuine, with a frenetic stage act, a penchant for the loudest clothing and his hair piled at least ten inches above his clear black features. To this day, a full fifteen years later, no one has successfully imitated his style, and he is still selling records filled with wild rock-and-roll songs.

To a white teen-ager, perhaps a future songpoet, listening to the two versions of "Tutti Frutti," it must have become clear that someone was out to put a lid on rock-and-roll. Some listeners accepted this, but others, who would later form the vanguard of the rock of the '6os, turned increasingly to black artists for satisfaction.

One of the artists they turned to was Chuck Berry, who had been discovered and recorded in Chicago by Phil and Leonard Chess, the two brothers who were responsible for keeping the best of the black urban blues music in the public eye during the '50s. Berry was a rarity of his time: a full-blown singer/songwriter, equally gifted as a performer and as a composer of rock material.

Few of the rock artists of the '50s were writing their own material. Most of it was being churned out by urban writers who specialized in "follow-ups"—songs patterned after established hits. These songs would be pandered to A-and-R (Artists-and-

Repertory) men at record companies. Most of the decisions regarding material for an artist were made by these A-and-R men, often without consulting the performer.

Recording artists, eager to get their product on the market, would sign contracts that often gave away both artistic control and any possibility of financial success. Many of these exploitative practices were modified during the '60s, but there are still those who claim that record companies are never totally fair with their artists.

Chuck Berry, who is still active as a performer, was the best of the early rock-and-roll songwriters. He is a primitive songpoet, but a songpoet nonetheless. At a time when rock-and-roll lyrics were notably inane, Berry was composing songs that expressed in loud and clear terms the dilemma of being young and alive in the America of the '50s. His songs are filled with references to school and budding sexuality and to automobiles, the prime obsession of much of the teen-age audience. Each of his tunes featured a strong rock sound which stood out clearly among its imitations.

Perhaps the best of the Berry songs, "Maybelline," is about cars and cops. It expresses both an affection for speed and an arrogance toward authority, and its music is low-down, nasty and fast.

In 1963, in one of the first crossovers between the folk scene and rock-and-roll, John Hammond, Jr., son of one of the giants in the recording industry, sang "Maybelline" at the Newport Folk Festival. It was an interesting moment, for the audience's cheers made it clear that even Chuck Berry could be an appropriate addition to a festival devoted to the best of traditional and political folk music. "Maybelline," after all, is a very political song, and it is also in the best tradition of the blues, one of America's few native musical forms.

Few other early rock-and-rollers deserve mention. Most of them fade into a blur of anonymous sounds and sideburns, except for a small corps of aficionados who still cherish their collections of obscure singles.

It is necessary to mention Buddy Holly, who came to attention during the late '50s with a number of loose, country-oriented rock songs. Holly's image was not that of your typical '50s rock star. He wore huge horn-rimmed glasses over a thin face and sang with a sweet country voice. His reliance on a group sound (his group was called the Crickets) and on acoustic guitars was rare for the '50s, though it was to become routine in the '60s. He is one of the only '50s rock artists who might have succeeded in the more sophisticated '60s. He died in a plane crash in February, 1959.

Rock, of course, was viewed by most of the straight media as a fad kept alive by zany teen-agers. There was very little discussion of the merits of rock music in the press, but there were frequent debates on whether this throbbing, black-based music was immoral or harmless. Looking back, it is clear that the religious leaders and music teachers who painted rock as an immoral, revolutionary and probably Communist movement were, at least in the first two instances, essentially correct.

Rock was immoral not only in their eyes but also in the eyes of many of the teen-agers who so adored it. If the music seems innocent now, it is only because we have left those years so far behind. The '50s were a hellish time to be a teen-ager—not materially, but spiritually. And rock was about sex and sensuality and loud noise.

As for its being revolutionary music, I would agree only in part. While early rock-and-roll did succeed in contributing to the alienation of thousands of American teen-agers from their parents and the straight and narrow, it also was built on the youth market, and capitalism leaped on that market with alacrity. At the same time as one considers that rock and songpoetry have forced a change of consciousness upon the audience, one must also accept that every record library and expensive stereo system represents another victory for conspicuous consumption. Taking all this into account, it is still possible to see rock as a revolutionary movement, which helped create the setting for the struggles of the '60s.

It is also important to understand how badly rock waned by the end of the '50s. As more and more money was being made from the scene, the quality of the music was rapidly deteriorating. The artists themselves seemed to be getting blander and blander. Faceless and voiceless artists like Fabian Forte, Frankie Avalon and Sal Mineo were hits, and every month brought new gag records with names like "The Purple People Eater," to fill in where raunch rock had failed.

Many of rock's brighter fans deserted around this time, latching on to the folk movement, buying guitars and singing protest songs. If these young people had been speaking the vocabulary of the '60s they might have accused rock of selling out to the marketeers, but no such cry went up. Instead, they simply stopped buying records, and by 1962 singles sales had diminished considerably from the peak years of 1956 and 1957.

It was in early 1964 that the Beatles emerged in this country, after one of the biggest publicity campaigns in music-business history. It is no exaggeration to say that the Beatles saved rock-and-roll from an early and unnecessary death. Without their influence, rock might well now be viewed in the same way as Country-and-Western music, a harmless form with a limited audience.

But the Beatles appeared, with their odd haircuts and whitefied rhythm-and-blues music. It must be admitted now that they were a pretty bland bunch at the time, playing subdued music that, though it was a relief from the inanity that dominated American rock in the early '60s, was harmless stuff. If their versions of black rock songs outshouted and outclassed those of the Fabians, still they could not summon up the energy of the originals. I remember listening to the Beatles and then to Bob Dylan in 1964: the band bouncing its way through ersatz black music; Dylan just beginning to interject rock sounds into his weighty dissertations. I was convinced then that the Beatles could not last on the rock scene, that what they had to offer was simply too limited for an audience that could, if it looked just a bit harder, find its way to a Dylan or to any one of his gifted imitators.

The first real indication that the Beatles were more than just a fad band from the British Isles was their movie *A Hard Day's*

Night. The film presented each as a set personality: John the wisecracker, Paul the raucous good guy, George the silent one and Ringo the clown. Never before had rock stars appeared thus, and though the personalities were creations of a director and writer, they were believed and accepted.

The songs in *A Hard Day's Night* were not very good, but that wasn't important. The quality of the movie and the solidity of the characterizations were important in establishing the Beatles as human beings who had more to say than "I Want to Hold Your Hand." The film was funny and antiauthoritarian and a break from the traditional view of the rock star.

One scene sticks in my mind. The Beatles, ducking a rehearsal for a television show, run into a playground behind the studio and, to the music of "Can't Buy Me Love," frolic and romp like children. As the music fades, they are confronted by a burly, sour-faced caretaker who chases them from the private property. This on-screen confrontation between youthful exuberance and crabby adultdom was a breakthrough for a generation. Here were the music heroes taking on the authorities and winning, both financially and, it was assumed, morally.

The film's success guaranteed that the Beatles would be around for quite a while. Their next film, *Help,* a much more frantic and much less successful effort, featured music clearly influenced by Bob Dylan, the most important of the songpoets, and this ensured an even longer life for the group and its individual members.

What the Beatles represented to the postwar generation is, indeed, much more than their music. Although they took few overtly political stands, their antiauthoritarian streak soon became apparent to many teen-agers and college students feeling similarly about the world.

John Lennon's two iconoclastic little books, *In His Own Write* and *A Spaniard in the Works,* had raised suspicions that the Beatles were brainier than they seemed, and *Hard Day's Night,* the first rock film of any cinematic quality, was a confirmation.

Most of the early Beatles material is as worthless as song-poetry as '50s rock. Lennon has since stated that he saved his intellectual energy for his books. Only after hearing Dylan did the Beatles seem to realize the potential of the pop medium and begin to inject more than a modicum of intelligence into their albums. Still, this band of Liverpool scruffs managed to save rock-and-roll from sure death.

Other rock bands who followed approximately the same path as the Beatles are the Rolling Stones and the Animals. The Stones, by their dress and choice of music, quickly established themselves in this country as the band of outrageous attitudes and societal protest.

If you couldn't be quite sure what the Beatles were after, it was clear that the Rolling Stones were after your sister or, as some said, your ass. On stage Mick Jagger pranced his way through the best of raunchy, urban, black rock-and-roll, and the music the Stones provided was loud and nasty in a way in which rock had never been in America. What the Stones helped achieve was the acceptance of rock as a form of anti-Establishment protest. The Beatles, with their mod suits and smiling faces, could not have done this, but the Stones, so obviously at odds with the sedate society that fostered them, did.

Yet neither band was making any real statements with its lyrics at the same time; both chose instead to follow precedent and keep their lyrics banal and secondary.

With the arrival of the Stones, rock-and-roll was established as the most vital medium available to young people. Jagger's intentions with regard to the society in which he functioned were unmistakable. Where rock-and-roll musicians had once been satisfied to suggest, through beat and double-entendre lyrics, that their listeners might do well to look into sex as sport, Jagger threw out a challenge. He was not only a blatantly suggestive performer, but clearly committed to raising his middle finger to the Establishment. Although rock had long served this role for many of those who listened, now this one little British cat had made it clear once and for all that rock was the loudest and angriest protest music that had ever emerged. The Rolling Stones have never dropped this role in either their recorded music or their stage performances. The best evidence that the powers have taken note is the police harassment of the Stones on a variety of drug charges. The drug bust has turned out to be a favorite Establishment tactic. I don't know what Mick Jagger feels about this, but it seems to me that the arrests are comments on the power of the music.

Although it took the Beatles to save rock on the American scene in the early '60s, in less than three years the Beatles themselves began to stale, turning out albums that did not show any marked improvement over their early songs.

The key was not in the music, which had improved surprisingly as the Beatles began to take their roles as musical prophets with a little more care and seriousness, but in the lyric content. As late as *Rubber Soul*, the Beatles were still churning out pleasant songs that did not serve the intellectual needs of their community. Just as they had saved rock from burying itself in a sea of candy, they needed saving from their own sense of self-limitation regarding lyrics. Bob Dylan provided the key to the salvation and eventual triumph of the Beatles.

John Lennon recently told a national television audience that he had never even considered giving his full attention to the writing of lyrics until he heard Dylan, who proved to him that songs could say much more than "Love Me Do."

Lennon should not be surprised. It was happening to dozens of rock-and-roll musicians all over the world. They were listening to Dylan, and he was giving them all a new and precious freedom in their writing.

THE FIRST SONGPOET—BOB DYLAN

Wᴉᴛʜᴏᴜᴛ Bob Dylan there would be no reason for this book to exist. By himself, the slight refugee from the wastes of Minnesota forever changed popular songwriting. It is unlikely that the other important writers would have emerged if Dylan had not charged along before them.

When Dylan's name is spoken among many young people, it is with the reverence reserved for the uncompromised hero. There are a number of reasons—some based on the realities, others on the myths that have built up around this fiercely private man.

Until a couple of years ago it would have been impossible to write anything intelligent about Dylan's life. With Anthony Scaduto's brilliant biography of the singer, we can begin to trace the many influences upon the native genius. Before Scaduto's study there had been nothing in print or on film that could begin to capture Dylan's complexity. His interviews have been, for the most part, studies in advanced manipulation of journalists. Dylan is the master of the put-on and an expert at turning the enthusiasm of his interviewers into a weapon for his own use.

His self-imposed privacy helped to create the myths that so

upset Dylan that he was eventually prompted to help Scaduto. The myths are various, but it's fair to say that Dylan has been publicly suspected of almost every sin, addiction and political perversion the counterculture could think up. The man recognized this as early as 1964 and addressed a song to those who would cover him with "the dust of rumors." His answer then was to ignore the rumormongers, warning them that "If the arrow is straight, and the point it is slick/It will cut through the dust no matter how thick."

But the myths have at the core concepts that are basically accurate. Dylan is seen as a prophet for his generation, gifted with the power to scan the future and report back the possibilities. Dylan is not, of course, a seer. But what he is is a man of almost frightening sensitivity to the events affecting his life. Time and time again, in his work, he has detected feelings in himself that only later emerged among his listeners.

When Dylan opted out of the political struggle in 1964 and chose instead to examine the politics of his own soul, he prophesied, in effect, an event that would not occur among his peers for three years. But those who had criticized Dylan back then could only stand in wonder as the summer of love lured thousands of once politically active youngsters into a world of flowers, acid and self-contemplation.

In 1965, when Dylan chose rock-and-roll, howls of protest were heard from those still entangled in street politics. Three years later, rock had emerged as the primary medium for the young, and long political essays were written attempting to link it to the political struggles.

When, 1966, Dylan settle down in Woodstock, ninety miles north of New York, it was generally assumed that in leaving the urban battlefield he had abandoned his generation. Now the movement of young people out of the cities has taken on epic proportions, with thousands of communes functioning in the backwoods of the nation.

There are many examples of this kind of seeming prophecy, some involving the course of musical trends, but Dylan would be the first to deny that he has ever sought the role of leader. Instead, he has followed his own instincts with great sensitivity, and these instincts have more often than not later manifested themselves among his peers.

Dylan is a humanist. At first he was satisfied to relate the truth about the injustices of our social system. But for the great part of his career, he has been seeking whatever truths he finds inside himself. He is a caustic self-critic, uncompromising and harsh in analyzing his own actions, dreams and nightmares. At the same time he is a passionate man, and his work is full of an eagerness to experience everything, from the pain of insanity to the joys of child-raising.

Because he has chosen to function mainly in a medium that has for decades been satisfied with surface views, Dylan seems all the more adventurous than if he wrote straight poetry or fiction. And because he presents his material through an electronic medium he has had the chance to reach millions of his peers.

What must never be forgotten in a discussion of Dylan is the man's charismatic stage presence, his ability to hold, even mesmerize, an audience. This ability transfers itself to his recorded work, and his albums are almost as compelling as his infrequent concert appearances. It is rare that a person gifted with such insight into the workings of his own soul and the ability to report those insights in a creative way is also a genius at the art of performance.

When Bob Dylan first performed in New York, just after he arrived in the winter of 1960–61, he was greeted unenthusiastically. Dylan's was a rough and unique talent, and there was no ready-made audience for him. Almost everyone who heard him then will tell you that he was unimpressed with Dylan's style and material. And there were good reasons.

Dylan's earliest New York music was a mixed bag of derivation, imitation and humor. When he wasn't attempting to imitate Woody Guthrie, he could be heard imitating Jack Elliot or any one of a dozen obscure black blues singers. He relied heavily upon humor to supplement his musical presentations and quickly developed a repertoire of "talking blues," a half-sung, half-spoken form that had been developed by Woody Guthrie.

There was little in those performances at parties and at the Folklore Center, a music store that was the focus of the folk movement in New York, that would have led to the suspicion that Dylan was to become the most important songwriter of his time. But hindsight is a wonderful thing, and looking back now one can see in his early work many of the things that later made him so important.

There was his stance. Dylan would come on stage and perform with humor and a mixture of false humility and put-on arrogance. A good part of his humor was self-deprecatory then, and many of the talking blues would use their creator as a butt for their jokes. "Talking Bear Mountain" is one of these—a never-recorded song that involved a disastrous boat trip up the Hudson. Dylan had read in the papers about a crook who had printed thousands of forged tickets for a Puerto Rican boat ride to Bear Mountain. The result was a boat twice as loaded as it should have been. It sank at the mooring, and thousands of Puerto Ricans poured off it onto the pier.

In his version, Dylan is an innocent victim of such a disaster, and he ends up on the pier vowing that his next boat ride will be in his bathtub. The character he creates as himself is a Chaplinesque little man, pushed around by circumstances.

This talking blues might be followed by a sudden, raging version of "See That My Grave Is Kept Clean" which could change the mood of any crowd with verses full of death—a subject as far from the minds of its middle-class, folkie listeners as any could be. Dramatic transitions like this made Dylan an out-of-the-ordinary artist on the tiny stages of Village clubs like the Gaslight and Gerde's Folk City.

The first real indication that Dylan could be something more than another Village folk singer came with his own compositions. One of the earliest of these, "Song to Woody," is a tribute to Guthrie. It is one of the earliest indicators of Dylan's style. It hinted that he was capable of writing about himself in a way that was universal enough to hold his then-tiny audiences firmly.

By the time Dylan's first album appeared, he had already attracted the attention of many reviewers and folk aficionados. He

had joined the small folk circle in the Village that included Jack
Elliot, Dave Van Ronk and Cisco Houston, and he had been out
to the hospital to meet his idol, Woody Guthrie.

Robert Shelton, the perceptive critic of *The New York Times*,
had stumbled upon Dylan playing second bill behind John Lee
Hooker at Gerde's Folk City and had written a review that
promised Dylan would become a major artist in a short time.
Shelton's review ranks now as foresight of the highest order, for
somehow he perceived that the rough-voiced, funny, unfinished
singer would become a major influence. John Hammond, director
of talent acquisition for Columbia Records, had first heard Dylan
at a recording session of Carolyn Hester, another folk-oriented
artist. Together Hammond and Dylan made the first album, titled
simply *Bob Dylan*, for about $400 in recording costs. There was
open hostility toward Dylan's music among the executives at Columbia, and he was quickly dubbed "Hammond's Folly." But
Hammond was the man who had first brought Billie Holiday,
Benny Goodman, Aretha Franklin and many others to the attention of the world.

This first album is not a very good indication of where Dylan
was when it was released. It features very little of his own
material, relying instead upon interpretations of classic blues
songs like "Baby Let Me Follow You Down" and "See That My
Grave Is Kept Clean." It is a rough and uncertain record and
does not give an indication of either Dylan's ability to relate to
an audience or his own writing abilities. But it offers examples
of Dylan's remarkable interpretive powers. The songs that show
this best are an old folk song, "Man of Constant Sorrow," and
one of the best-known blues ever written, "House of the Rising
Sun."

On both of these tracks Dylan makes something completely
new of his material, molding it until it seems perfect for the
twenty-year-old Minnesotan. "Man of Constant Sorrow" becomes
the first of many Dylan songs to capture the pain of growing
away from home and childhood, and "House of the Rising Sun"
becomes a song of pure strain and pain.

This first album was greeted with universal ennui. The folk
audience found it hard to relate to Dylan's ugly, visceral vocals,

and not much could be said for the technical dexterity of his guitar work. Some saw the album as the debut of a great harmonica player, and I can remember a friend's saying then that he thought Dylan was going to become the world's greatest harmonica accompanist and stop writing and singing.

What now seems most important about this early release is its intensity. Through all the material comes the force that Dylan would later learn to turn inward in the composition of his own songs. The album is full of rage and full of questions. But it is also filled with material that was beyond the emotional capacity of both its performer and his audience.

It is a dark little disk, a record that is most of all an indication of the depth of Dylan's range of inquiry. Even though he does not achieve any answers with the record, he does indicate that he will be trying to cope with the questions the songs pose—problems of survival, betrayal and death. The questions will appear over again, with modifications, in all of Dylan's work.

Still another aspect of this first album that later emerges in Dylan's more mature work is its obvious resource of anger. Beneath all the ugliness of the voice and the roughness of the musical technique one can sense real rage. Here it is diverted into passionate blues imitations; later it will form the core of much of Dylan's work as he learns to direct his wrath at those who he believes deserve it. In his political songs, which follow closely on his first album, Dylan begins the long process of learning who is deserving of his anger, and it is not until *Blonde on Blonde* that his question reaches any kind of resolution. But it is important to note that one of the reasons for his success as a songwriter of other than political tracts is his ability to properly distribute the blame. A number of other, self-righteous political folk singers, like Phil Ochs, could not perceive this, and they lost their audiences. Their audiences had learned to deal with the world in a more sophisticated, less dogmatic way than they had, and it is the kiss of death to a songwriter when his audience has slipped past him.

Dylan's next album and the stage performances that followed its release in early 1963 are both political events. With "Blowin' in the Wind," Dylan fulfilled his promise as a political folk singer, and the hordes of young people who were then just beginning to join the ranks of both the civil rights and peace movements recognized this immediately. Where the first album had sold poorly, *Freewheelin' Bob Dylan* sold well in both urban markets and college towns.

Although much of the material on this second album was political and powerful, the most important of the songs were personal statements and love songs. "Don't Think Twice, It's All Right" was the best love song to have emerged from the folk movement, and it stands now as one of the most rerecorded of Dylan's songs. "Bob Dylan's Dreams," in which Dylan reminisces about friends and ideals, both lost and gone forever, is one of the first indications of the range of emotions he could handle in his songs. The tune is nostalgic and forceful at the same time.

But it was the political songs on the album that attracted the most attention, and it was "Blowin' in the Wind" that later produced the hit record that would bring Dylan's name and work to the notice of the larger musical community. The other frankly political number, "Oxford Town," is a trite, empty little song that is almost a throwaway.

The period during which *Freewheelin'* was released was one in which countless young people were developing a new awareness of political inequities. Although the peace movement had struggled through the '50s, it was never a very large group of people, and had proved ineffective as a political force. By 1963, many of those who had once given their time to the movement to end nuclear testing had turned their attention to the more apparent and pressing problem of civil rights.

It was before marijuana had become the national intoxicant of the young, and before assassination had become a regular form of American political interaction.

"Blowin' in the Wind" became, with "We Shall Overcome," one of the few songs universally accepted as the anthems of the civil rights movement.

As a song it does not compare in imagery or intensity with Dylan's later work, but it is the first of a series of ambiguous and political songs that mark the songpoet's career. A more biting song, "A Hard Rain's Gonna Fall," is on the same album with

"Blowin' in the Wind," but is too ambiguous for a proper political anthem and was never adopted by the peace movement in the way in which "BITW" was taken up by the civil rights movement. When you're marching into the teeth of American political reality, it doesn't pay to have an anthem that's more than a dozen verses long and open to endless varieties of interpretation.

So it was "BITW" that brought Dylan into both the political folk movement and the commercial market. The record was marked as an instant hit when it was picked up by Peter, Paul and Mary and given the full treatment, with high, creamy harmonies and forceful guitar parts.

I had been listening to Dylan's work since 1961, having heard him at numerous gigs and having eagerly bought the first album, to be somewhat disappointed that there were none of his own compositions. But I had never considered Dylan a commercial artist in the usual sense. He was a folkie and a political folk singer, and that was fine for the Village and Cambridge and perhaps a few other college towns, but not for general consumption.

When I first heard Peter, Paul and Mary's version of "Blowin' in the Wind" come wafting out of a radio in the back of a building-supply store in Rutland, Vermont, where I was sweating out the summer of '63, I realized for the first time that Dylan would soon be a national figure. I stood there amazed at how different a feeling it was to hear Dylan's complex and beautiful images come out of a radio that had been playing pap. I also was aware that if the Rutland station (there was only one) had picked up the record, it had to be an immense best seller. That moment felt like a beginning of something grand, and if my instincts have failed me many times since, that day in Rutland they were working.

Later that summer, "Blowin' in the Wind" was sung at the great Washington Civil Rights March, again by Peter, Paul and Mary and then by Dylan himself, and it was clear that this was *the* new voice of youth politics in America.

There is some need to account for Dylan, to trace him back to his roots, out there in the great, vacant Midwest.

Dylan is the product of a Midwestern middle-class Jewish

environment. Born Robert Zimmerman, May 24, 1941, Dylan got interested in rock-and-roll in high school. His attempts to organize a group there met with a mix of enthusiasm and derision, and this experience is reported in both Scaduto's biography and Toby Thompson's gossipy book on Dylan, *Positively Main Street*.

After graduating from high school, Dylan went off to the University of Minnesota in Minneapolis. Although far from the centers of the music industry, the St. Paul–Minneapolis area had a well-developed folk scene, and Dylan soon appeared in it as a folk singer and storyteller. Dylan discovered Woody Guthrie while at college and was soon off on the road to New York, hoping for a chance to meet his newfound idol.

Dylan did, as noted, meet Guthrie, and he later told interviewers that although this meeting was exciting, it cured him of his belief in idols. Dylan soon found a niche in the well-developed New York folk community, performing by himself in many of the basket houses (where artists are unpaid and a basket is passed for contributions) and picking with other musicians. He developed a repertoire of Guthrie songs, talking blues and comic songs. As he mastered these, he began to revive blues songs of long-forgotten black singers, interpreting each as if it were a newly written song.

By the time he recorded for Columbia, he had begun to write prolifically, and his own material was a dominant part of his stage act.

Dylan's youth in Minnesota was probably an advantage. Where many of the other urban folk singers had been immersed in folk music throughout their childhoods, Dylan came to the music in his late adolescence. This and the man's obvious genius combined to give him a fresh view of the possibilities of the form. His background also provided him with a chance to create a mythical history of his own to tell other people, and possibly to believe a bit himself. Using his imagination, Dylan came up with a character, and by acting out this role he made it a part of his experience. Perhaps he had not really spent years on the road, but the character he created surely had, and could prove it on stage.

Dylan's third album, *The Times They Are A-Changing*, is

dominated by political material and is best known for its title song. Here we find a leaner, angrier Dylan portrayed on the cover, and a more polished set of tunes inside. In retrospect, the album can be seen as transitional, put together just before Dylan began to shift the focus of his songwriting from the political to the more personal.

Although there are those who would have us believe that the most important shift in Bob Dylan's career came with his adaptation of rock music in 1965, there was an earlier shift that has proved, with time, to have been more important. This came with the release, in late 1964, of Dylan's fourth album, titled *Another Side of Bob Dylan*. This record is exactly what the title suggests: a new and different side of Dylan, one that had been over-shadowed by his more political works. It is a simply produced album filled with poetry that is both powerful and complex. From the first cut, a mock-serious proposition of a friend called "All I Really Want to Do," it is clear that Dylan has moved on from the simplistic, dogmatic poetry of his early political songs.

If Dylan's albums have colors, as some believe, this album is best represented by the color of smoke, constantly shifting from blue to gray.

Where once the statements Dylan made with his songs were clarion-clear calls to battle, this album features only songs of reflection, songs that are no longer directive. Dylan is no longer instructing his audience on how to deal with the madness or fight the politicians. He is now hinting to them that they must turn inward and confront the true sources of their distress. But only hinting, not directing.

There is so much passion in this record, and real passion was the one ingredient that had been missing from popular music for decades. Dylan attempted with this album to present his own version of the blues he once sang so imitatively. These are the blues of a white, middle-class, Middle Western manchild. He touches upon problems of love and survival in the city and takes up, for the first time, his own rejection of politics.

This album also establishes Dylan's debt to rock-and-roll. He had managed, up to this point, to totally avoid his own rock-and-roll roots, probably assuming that they would not be appropriate to the folk material he was writing and interpreting. But here is "Bobby Dylan the Piano Man"—the same Bob Zimmerman who once filled his high school auditorium with raucous, screeching rock-and-roll. Two songs take up the rock banner, "Spanish Harlem Incident" and "Black Crow Blues."

"Spanish Harlem Incident," in which Dylan relates his sudden and overwhelming reaction to a "Gypsy girl," could have been swiped right off the top forty. It is marked by a repetitious rhythm and by simple lyrics and even features a hook—a musical strap for the younger audience to hang on to and remember. The song also features a subtle use of the sexual entendre, something that is in the best tradition of AM rock-and-roll. But alas, it was too subtle a statement for the disk-jockey mentality of 1964, with its poetic imagery and its lonely guitar.

Dylan takes up many new subjects here and treats them in a new manner. "All I Really Want to Do" is the antithesis of the typical love song. Rather than expounding seething passions, he writes with conscious limits to his commitment. He wants to be friends with someone, and he does not want to be misinterpreted. Earlier songwriters were not so careful in their pronouncements on this subject, but Dylan is treating here of real emotions, emotions capable of dealing with someone more than an acquaintance and less than a lover. And there is humor here, humor in the outlandish rhymes. The song is like a tickle under the chin. A friendly tickle.

Three other songs stand out as innovative statements for Dylan. "To Ramona" is a song of spiritual counsel, a lilting poem that pleads for an understanding of the pressures the city can place upon a sensitive country child. But this is not the kind of spiritual counsel one could expect from a psychiatrist. It is emphathetic counsel, which ends with the poet reassuring Ramona that one day soon he may be as confused and hurt as she is, and come to her for help. Dylan's humanism is a primary factor in this album, and he emerges for the first time as a perceptive, emotionally mature and poetically skilled writer. Where there had been the bluster of the demonstrator there is now the whisper of the personal poet, and it is only when these two characters are reconciled, in Dylan's later work, that he comes into his own as a poet of his generation.

"Ballad in Plain D" is a long and difficult confession concerning a smashed love affair. Where one might lash out at someone who has left him, Dylan instead tears at the facts of the experience until some sort of lasting lesson appears. This peeling away of pretense is what makes "Ballad in Plain D" such a difficult and emotionally scathing experience. Dylan applies the same harsh rules of analysis to his relationship with a girl that he once did to the masters of war. The song is free of self-pity and full of self-reproach. This ability to look beyond the surface of an event is one of Dylan's great attributes. By his public self-criticism he forces his listeners, those who respect and wish to emulate him, to do the same.

It seems that I am forgetting the musical aspects of this album. The music is simple and repetitious, but it always complements the lyrics, and since this is the last of Dylan's purely acoustic albums, it shows him at the height of his powers with just his guitar and his harmonica. Dylan could easily have made it as a great mouth-harp player, for he is capable of applying this ancient blues instrument to the most modern of his songs. His harmonica sweeps and wails and supplies the lead instrumental voice of these songs.

This whole album makes me think of winter in New York, when the cold gray weather forces one inside for self-evaluation. Where once Dylan found it easy to lash outward, it has become increasingly difficult for him to place the blame for his anxiety on either the society or his acquaintances. He must face up to his own emotional confusion and conquer it, and this album is a step in that direction that will be followed religiously with his later work.

On the back of *Another Side* there are a series of poems that take up this same task of self-evaluation, and they are even harsher in their self-criticism. The poems fit Dylan's description of his poetry, "too long for songs." One poem is a consideration of a deep and pervasive pessimism. He tells of seeing a man about to jump off the Brooklyn Bridge and discovering with horror that he wants to encourage him. Through a long and complex series of questions, Dylan traces his own feelings on who should be able to judge others and, therefore, to judge him. He decides for freedom from judgment on both counts. He will not be so self-righteous as to take it upon himself to judge the actions of others, and he expects the same from those who would attempt to judge him. The ending is not really a conclusion, for Dylan begs off to "go to the woods" for a while, apparently to further consider this crucial question.

"My Back Pages" is a song about college and about politics, and it is in effect a renunciation of dogma. Dylan tears at himself for once having believed that he had all the answers to all the questions. He attacks those who educated him for having filled him with this arrogance and renounces it. This is amazing statement from the author of a song as baldly dogmatic as "With God on Our Side."

So Dylan abandons the old politics with this album; but he does not turn completely away from the social ideas that have formed the basis for his earlier work. With "Chimes of Freedom," a long and beautiful political song, he attempts for the last time to relate his own view of the political world, and what emerges is a broad and underdog-oriented humanism. The song runs through a list of those who need sympathy and seems almost to say to the listener, "Go ahead, if you want to fight for someone, here they are, those who need your help." But the rest of the album makes it clear that Dylan can no longer fight those battles, that he must move on to a deeper and more austere set of struggles. He states this simply and beautifully at the end of his poem on the back of the album sleeve.

"So go Joshua/ Fit your battle/ I have to go to the woods/ For awhile/ I hope you understand/ But if you don't/ It doesn't matter/ I will be with you/ Next time around."

And with this final farewell to the political-folk-song movement, Dylan moves on to new, more complex battles: battles of the soul. *Another Side* would be the last nonabstract statement from Dylan for years to come.

CHANGES—DYLAN

As Bob Dylan's singular use of lyrics was turning on John Lennon and Paul McCartney, the Beatles' fantastic success was influencing him. According to Scaduto, when the Beatles broke out in early 1964, Dylan was on a national tour, traveling in a station wagon loaded with pot, good friends and guitars. As this merry carload moved around the country, Beatle tunes began to slip in among the AM-radio selections. By the time Dylan had reached Colorado, eight out of the ten top numbers were by Lennon-McCartney.

"They were doing things nobody was doing," Dylan later told Anthony Scaduto. "Their chords were outrageous, just outrageous, and their harmonies made it all valid. You could only do that with other musicians. Even if you're laying your own chords you had to have other people playing with you. That was obvious. And it started me thinking about other people.

"But I just kept it to myself that I really dug them. Everybody else thought they were just for teenyboppers, that they were gonna pass right away. But it was obvious to me that they had staying power. I knew they were pointing the direction of where the music had to go. I was not about to put up with other musi-

51

cians, but in my head the Beatles were it. In Colorado I started thinking it was so far out that I couldn't deal with it—eight in the top ten. It seemed to me a definite line was being drawn. This was something that had never happened before. It was outrageous and I kept it in my mind. You see, there was a lot of hypocrisy all around, people saying it had to be either folk or rock. But I knew it didn't have to be like that. I dug what the Beatles were doing, and I always kept it in mind from back then."

With these words Dylan quietly demolishes the myth of his early work as the product of some sort of pure folk consciousness. From his earliest days as a performer Dylan showed an interest in becoming a rock-and-roller, and I believe he moved into folk music because it was, at that time, the only medium in which he could express himself satisfactorily. Although rock-and-roll was possessed of intense energies, it was not designed to convey ideas. While folk music was built on imagination and did not require a big band and equipment, it did not reach great masses of the population, as rock did.

From the first hurried chords of "Subterranean Homesick Blues," which opens the rock side of his fifth album, *Bringing It All Back Home,* it was clear that the quixotic Dylan had finally committed himself to rock. And it was no halfway commitment. He was out to be the best. When one considers the options open to him at the time, the extent of his commitment is even more impressive. He could have chosen to play it low-key, utilizing essentially folk musicians like guitarist Bruce Langhorne or bassist Bill Lee. Instead he sought the best of the new electric blues artists, including Michael Bloomfield, the lead guitarist for the then fledgling Butterfield Blues Band. He could have introduced rock gradually into his work and made the transition easier for his most rabid folk fans, but Dylan was never one to spend too much time contemplating the needs of his audience, and so the transition was sudden, loud and shocking. Another compromise would have been to work out rock arrangements for the best-known of his earlier tunes, which would have allowed his audience to recognize and respect the lyrics even if they couldn't hear them very well above all the electricity. But Dylan did this very little, and when he did, as with "Baby, Let Me Follow You Down," the tune was nearly unrecognizable.

One of the revelations of Scaduto's biography is that Dylan was more than slightly interested in becoming a rock star on the level of Elvis Presley, and that he feels he blew it, somewhere around 1966.

With this insight in hand, we can examine his first rock work with new understanding. The pure-rock songs on *Bringing It All Back Home* are, for the most part, simple numbers. At the time, many thought this was simply Dylan testing the rock waters with hesitancy. Now the motivation for the simplicity of tunes like "She Belongs to Me" and "Maggie's Farm" is clear: Dylan wanted to break into the top forty, and he was trying the best way he knew how: by making music easier for the mass audience to understand and like. But he failed, and the reasons for the failure are inherent in his particular genius.

Even if "Maggie's Farm," with its repetitions, is a simple rock number, the intensity of both the message and the performance lift it above the usual. Again, Dylan's rage surfaces, and it was too much for both the radio stations and the rock listeners. "Subterranean Homesick Blues" has the same quality. With its humorous rhymes and driving rhythms, it would seem a natural for success with the AM crowd. But its message is revolutionary, and it is full of references to paranoia, drugs and politics. Although the revolution demanded is one of the *soul*, there was no way at the time to expect the AM disk jockeys and their program directors to get this.

"Subterranean Homesick Blues" is Dylan as father figure. Father figure is the wrong term; brother figure captures him better. With this song, as with a number of others on this album, he attacks the basic structure of American society, especially child-raising. He tells his audience, "Don't follow leaders/ Watch your parking meters" at the same time that he points out the insane banality of the choices open to a young person in America. The song is full of good advice on how to survive in this world while maintaining your humanity. The guidance he offers is really not directive; Dylan is beyond that here. Instead, he tries to talk to his audience about methods for survival on the streets they must know in order to escape a system that would narrow their lives.

This brotherly relationship is important to understand. It is the key to the fanatical devotion of Dylan's audience. At a time when leadership was scarce and many young people saw themselves facing a void, Dylan was *there* with his hints on survival. The lessons were never in the heavy-handed language of academe, but ironic, impressionistic, imaginative, and they were sympathetic to his brothers and sisters. He is saying: the situation we're all in is a mess, and we may not be able to fix it, but we can learn to exist without being crushed by it. Literally no one else had either the balls or the insight to tell it this way, and Dylan is to much of his audience still their only leader, even if the man is reluctant to take on the responsibility.

If Dylan failed to make the top forty with this album, he became the voice for his generation, and guaranteed himself an audience for as long as he wants it.

The basically acoustic first side of this album, its cover and the weird piece of prose on the back are all part of Dylan's new surrealism. With *Bringing It All Back Home,* he leaves logic and begins to skirt the edge of madness. The songs become longer, more abstract and infinitely more powerful.

Dylan is an admirer of Rimbaud, and the first signs of the French poet's influence appear in this album. No longer satisfied with literalness, Dylan leaps into the void. A lesser man might have been overwhelmed by what he perceived once his blinders were off, but Dylan had the intelligence and the courage to confront his nightmares. This kind of courage is a rare and dangerous gift, and Dylan nearly destroyed himself on the journey to his own soul.

Not only did he survive, but he sent back messages—perceptions unmatched by any of his contemporaries for their intensity, insight and grandeur.

The beginnings of this flight from surface reality are on this album in two songs, "It's All Right, Ma, I'm Only Bleeding" and "The Gates of Eden."

The first song is Dylan's final declaration of independence from the expectations of others. "I have no one to live up to," he sings. It is also an indictment of the alternatives available to Dylan, the paths more traveled by those around him. The song is bitter, yet sad. Dylan seems almost sorry that he must pursue this new path, and he reassures his listeners that he is not mad, only tired of the paths they would have him follow.

"Gates of Eden" is one of Dylan's most philosophical songs. Here the poet rejects men's utopias, comparing each with his own vision and finding them wanting. "There are no kings inside the Gates of Eden," he sings, and rejects both the religions and the philosophies that envision a heaven burdened with men's pettiness.

Another song on this album relates to the journey. "It's All Over Now, Baby Blue" is filled with the sentiments Dylan will later express in "Like a Rolling Stone."

He could be singing to himself as he outlines how and why "Baby Blue" must take "What [she has] gathered from coincidence" and hit the road. What Dylan is saying here is that one cannot change by simply hoping. The potential for change can be made real only when one totally rejects the old life patterns and steps courageously into the unknown.

Yet the song is full of reassurance and comforting phrases. "Light another match, go start anew," Dylan sings—telling his listeners, and reassuring himself, that even if the light you carry is tiny, like a match, you're bound to see more of what is real than you would by sitting in the darkness.

A good part of Dylan's audience freaked badly when *Bringing It All Back Home* hit the record stores. The opposition was led by Irwin Silber and *Sing Out!* magazine and aided by Pete Seeger and Izzy Young, proprietor of the Folklore Center in Greenwich Village and one of Dylan's earliest boosters.

The objections ranged from expressions of distaste for rock-and-roll and the top forty to accusations that Dylan had "strayed from the path" of political folk music and was now entering into the dangerous realms of show business where he might easily lose his political soul. Silber proved to be the worst kind of dogmatist of Dylan's changes and proved once more that the political-folk-song establishment thought little of artistic needs and was concerned exclusively with what it judged to be an artist's political commitment. None of this criticism directed at Dylan at this point is worth going into. *Bringing It All Back Home* is probably the most politically potent record of the '60s, and it was only the shortsightedness of the folk ideologues that prevented them from seeing it.

Dylan had moved to pragmatism, and in this he differed considerably from most of the writers for *Broadside* and *Sing Out!* With his abstract, piercing and highly emotional songpoems, he was launching an assault on the problems of the soul that lay beneath the political struggles of the '60s.

Where Pete Seeger might scratch the surface of the struggle with a song like "Where Have All the Flowers Gone?," Dylan got beneath appearances and came up with a song like "Subterranean Homesick Blues," which, in three or four minutes, demolishes the American middle-class concept of happiness and freedom. Where Phil Ochs might create a journalistic tirade, Dylan chose instead to focus on the essence of utopian ideals in a song like "Gates of Eden." And who could doubt Dylan's rejection of American values when stated so clearly in a song like "Maggie's Farm"? Thus, *Bringing It All Back Home* marked Dylan's final break with the political-folk-song movement. He had surpassed it and moved into realms more complex and dangerous.

When Dylan first performed the electric music publicly, at Newport in 1965, he was either overridden by the noise of the Butterfield Blues Band or soundly rejected, depending on which version you believe. Either way, it was clear that he would have some struggling to do before he could settle in comfortably with both his old and his newfound audiences.

At Forest Hills in August, 1965, Dylan had run into clear opposition to his rock-and-roll, and there had been a scene. If ever Dylan had had a chance to back down, this was it, but he did not waver. By October, at a concert in Carnegie Hall, the problem seemed to have resolved itself. The audience did not boo at all, and it appeared that the folkies had either given up or split. Either way, Dylan had found an audience which greeted him enthusiastically in his new role as rock-and-roll star.

But let us not forget the quality of the music he was providing.

At Carnegie Hall he played with Levon and the Hawks, later to become The Band, and the music was more intense than ever before in rock-and-roll. The organ would surge and the drummer would pound, but the true power came from the interplay of Dylan's new screaming voice and the pulsations of the band. In Robbie Robertson he found a genius on the electric guitar who could match the intensity of Dylan's vocals with a piercing accompaniment.

Dylan in concert, in the late months of 1965 and the early part of 1966, provided some of the best rock-and-roll we are likely to hear. He put together lyrics of distinction with a rock professionalism that had not been heard before on the concert stages of America or the world.

Dylan's concerts had always been emotionally charged affairs, but the addition of rock made the earlier ones seem subdued. The new format demanded that Dylan do half the show acoustically, while the electric equipment lurked behind him, threateningly. After intermission the band would appear with him, and the crowd, depending on how it felt about rock-and-roll, would either begin to object loudly or act restless. With the first blasting notes it came clear that a new music was being born.

Dylan rocked and swayed and slapped at his rhythm guitar, shouting the lyrics and then turning away from the mike to face Robbie Robertson and trade graceful, screaming guitar licks. The two musicians would stand, separate but joined, and sway together until the duet had peaked and Dylan could get back to his mike and his words.

There is a bootleg recording made during this period, in early 1966, at the Albert Hall in London. It is without a doubt the best concert recording of Dylan ever made, and most likely the greatest "live rock" recording extant. Although recorded crudely, this album is the only testimony to the intensity of the rock that Dylan in concert offered. The album has cuts nowhere else recorded and features The Band as backup musicians. The crowd, not fully prepared for Dylan's new rock image, shouted obscenities and reprimands at its idol, but Dylan responded by plowing ahead with his music and only once, with a bit of nonsense talk, attempted to quiet them down.

Once Dylan had committed himself to the rock format, he went out on a grueling tour of one- and two-night stands. Scaduto's portrait of Dylan during this period is of a man shot out of the cannon of success, speeding along above the heads of the crowd. He comes across as a frantic, almost psychotic personage, torn from the safety of the folk idiom and thrust into the fluorescent world of rock-and-roll stardom. And the music written and recorded during this period reflects that kind of intensity.

Highway 61 Revisited, released at the beginning of Dylan's entrance into rock, reflects the first hints of madness that Dylan must have felt in his new situation. "Like a Rolling Stone," Dylan's anthemlike bit of advice to his fellows, was recorded earlier as a single but leads off the album.

"Like a Rolling Stone" is the classic Dylan rock-and-roll number. The writing is inconsistent with Dylan's using the old rock technique of two or three dull lines to preface one or two lines of dynamite. But it is sufficient to get the message across. Dylan is telling his audience, in the person of a young friend, that the safe, middle-class ride is over and the time for heading out alone is at hand. This is also the theme of "It's All Over Now, Baby Blue," but "Like a Rolling Stone," with its mountainous crescendos and piercing climaxes, is the more effective. "How does it feel/ To be on your own," Dylan sings to a whole generation.

Somewhere on this album, Dylan plays a device that sounds like a police siren. That sound characterizes the music on this sixth album. It is a painful album, full of angry words and angry music, and for this reason many critics feel that it is Dylan's greatest work. I disagree, if only because *Blonde on Blonde,* Dylan's next album, is a double set and has twice as much room for Dylan to bring off the same effects he attempts here with one record. You almost feel rushed on *Highway 61,* as if Dylan had so much to say and such a need to say it that he jammed it together unmercifully.

This record has got to be one of the most critical comments on the '60s in America: Dylan's unrelenting assault on the corruption he finds rampant even in the very world to which his new stardom gives him access.

Every song on this album can stand analysis. I take those that most clearly reflect Dylan's attitudes at the time. "Desolation Row" and "Just Like Tom Thumb's Blues" are both comments on a sort of nether world of injustice that Dylan perceives as making up a good part of the society he lives in. "Desolation Row" is a place where all those who have been ravaged by society must emigrate and await death's salvation. There is no hope on this street; even the poets quarrel, and the lovers are perverse. Only "calypso singers and fishermen with flowers" can be even mildly happy—and it is a place where everyone else is either shredded like cabbage or forced to be a shredder. "Desolation Row" is a critical and horrific view of America. Its surrealism creates an almost unearthly glare around the work; the viewer has seen too much too fast. Psychotics often report this phenomenon—the feeling that the world's light is too intense for their eyes. The world that Dylan creates has a similar quality of garish fluorescence.

"Just Like Tom Thumb's Blues" is a gentler song, but it is also obsessed with oppression and injustice, as is "Desolation Row." "Juarez," the setting of the song, seems to be a place of escape for those with no hope left. It is a town of sickness and drug addiction and of crazy police. The women are either bloodsuckers or whores, and the town doctor cannot diagnose the singer's problems. In 1965 this world seemed impossibly harsh, like the sullen streets of "Desolation Row," but sitting here in 1973, the vision seems close. The urban nightmare that has emerged in the last six years is not very different from the crazed image Dylan presented in his early rock albums. Lines like "The cops don't need you/ And man, they expect the same" reinforce Dylan's mythic image as a seer. But Dylan had merely perceived the strain of confusion in our culture before it became a topic of everyday conversation.

There is one song of extreme gentleness and beauty on this album. "It Takes a Lot To Laugh, It Takes a Train To Cry" is a slow blues in which Dylan again assumes the role of brother to his suffering comrades. He gently chides a lover for having expected too much from him and then delivers a warning that more broadly applies. "The wintertime is coming/ And the windows are filled with frost/ I tried to warn everybody/ But I could not get across."

In the context of the album, this is Dylan commenting on his own role as shit detector. He has tried in his songs to describe the problems that must be solved, but no one has seriously attempted to come up with solutions, and now the wintertime is on its relentless way.

Two other songs reflect Dylan's attitudes toward two bastions of the Establishment, the press and the business world. He wipes out the press in "Ballad of a Thin Man," which seems to be a song about the misapprehensions and terror of a journalistic observer of the real world. Dylan has been worked over by a hostile and uncomprehending press, and here he pays back the debt of bitterness, complete with homosexual implications. "Highway 61 Revisited" is about businessmen who see a profit in anything, including the world's destruction.

In retrospect, *Highway 61 Revisited* seems to be Dylan's angriest album, the record on which he unleashed his rage with the most precise aim and effectiveness. The later albums progressively show less anger and more compassion, yet at the same time they are not as musically intense as *Highway 61*. This album represents the peak of Dylan's frenzy and of his vision.

One major effect of Dylan's songpoems on his listeners has been to put a new value on the simple quality of honesty. Exposed to his assaults on dirty politics, dishonesty in personal interactions and business and the mendacity and banality of the educational system, it is more difficult to retreat into rationalization and self-deception. During the campus movements of the late '60s, in meeting after meeting Dylan would be quoted as an antidote to dogmatism and deception.

It is ironic, then, that the Weathermen, the most dogmatic and violent of the political groups that arose in the late '60s, took its name from Dylan's "Subterranean Homesick Blues." The line goes, "You don't need a weatherman to know which way the wind blows." Dylan would surely have rejected both the closed-mindedness and the violence of this faction had it not been for the fact that at the time of its rise he was making no public statements. But the name is indicative of how deeply Dylan had penetrated the consciousness of the young radicals of the world.

By the time Dylan's seventh album, *Blonde on Blonde*, appeared, in the spring of 1966, it was clear that he was not going to be a rock-and-roll star. "Like a Rolling Stone" had achieved number one status, but the follow-ups, songs like the raucous "Rainy Day Women #12 and #35," were not selling very well, and deservedly so. Dylan was simply not served by commercialization; his music was too subtle for much of the broadcasting world of 1966.

One senses that Dylan realized his own failure as a rock-and-roller just before cutting *Blonde on Blonde*. The choice of songs and the choice of musicians indicate that he was directing himself back to his more intellectual audience, those who could follow him into the forests of ambiguity.

Blonde on Blonde was cut over a long period of time, mainly because of Dylan's concert commitments. The most important change in the recording process was that Dylan had taken the advice of his new producer, Bob Johnston, and started recording in Nashville. It is important to understand the influence of the Nashville musicians—all skilled, professional stylists—on Dylan's work.

Blonde on Blonde, although it features much solid rock music, is a much mellower album than *Highway 61 Revisited*. Much of this can be attributed to Dylan's new accompanists and to the general atmosphere of the recording industry in Nashville, which is much more relaxed than it is in either New York or Los Angeles, the other two great recording centers. Dylan was able to do much of his writing at the CBS studios, and in one instance he spent twelve hours alone in the studio writing one song, "Sad-Eyed Lady of the Lowlands." Bob Johnston reports that the musicians were kept on standby while Dylan was writing and that they returned to record only moments after the last verse was completed.

Apparently the musicians sensed that what they were doing was of more than usual import, and Johnston says that they were frankly excited about Dylan and his work. This respect shows through on the tracks, as musician after musician reaches for the best possible solo he can produce. *Blonde on Blonde* is Dylan's most precise and professional piece of work.

This album was also Dylan's first double set—the result of a burst of writing during late 1965 and early 1966. But one must remember that one side of the album is devoted to "Sad-Eyed Lady," which is not one of Dylan's strongest efforts. The remaining three sides also have a number of weak spots, including Dylan's "Leopard Skin Pill Box Hat" and "Rainy Day Women"—throwaway numbers. But most of it is superb, and is a fine illustration of Dylan's expanding range of abilities as both a songwriter and a musician.

The most popular song on the album is also one of the best: "Just Like a Woman." This song rivals "Blowin' in the Wind" and "Don't Think Twice, It's All Right" in the number of cover versions released by other artists. Like so much else in this album, "Just Like a Woman" is about a personal relationship. This is a process that continues throughout the rest of Dylan's work and is most noticeable in his last two albums.

Although numerous recordings of "Just Like a Woman" have been done by other artists, including Richie Havens, Joe Cocker and Nina Simone, the best version I have ever heard is by Dylan himself, at the Bangladesh concert at Madison Square Garden in August of 1971. The recording of this concert contains a number of Dylan songs, and "Just Like a Woman" is clearly the best of these, with Dylan singing with great range and even greater confidence.

"Visions of Johanna" is one of the strongest songpoems on *Blonde on Blonde,* and although Scaduto seems pretty sure that this is about Joan Baez, this song could apply to any lonely lover, consoling himself in the arms of somebody unimportant in his life. Dylan plays at least three parts in this song: that of the narrator, that of the lover on the floor and that of the derisive boy in the hall who tells him about his lover. This role-taking is common in Dylan's work and accounts for much of the difficulty his interpreters have had.

Here we find Dylan as the scorned lover remembering his love at the very moment he is having sex with someone new. The song is extremely sexual in both its phrasing and its music, with a climax and a letdown written into the text. To me this is the most beautiful song Dylan has ever written, for with it he captures an experience poets have always written about. He does this in a completely modern way, in the language of his peers and with an impressive understanding of his own shortcomings as a person and a lover.

The music of this album is quite varied, ranging from the raunchy rock-and-roll of "Leopard Skin Pill Box Hat" to the folk sounds of "Just Like a Woman," to the Nashville smoothness of "4th Time Around," which is a parody of the Beatles' "Norwegian Wood," to the Muzak of "I Want You." The solos are brilliant, and the general level of musical competence is high.

Blonde on Blonde is a work of irrefutable genius, but it is also one of the most inconsistent and diffuse of Dylan's albums. Even with its great range and high points, *Blonde on Blonde* does not have the rough intensity of *Highway 61 Revisited,* where Dylan's enthusiastic discovery of rock-and-roll shines through on every cut. Here we have an artist relaxing in his medium, assured of success, and this album reflects that relaxation. Dylan is at his best when he is struggling against the tide of public opinion, and that struggle is lacking on *Blonde on Blonde.*

Perhaps the most important event of Dylan's short career occurred shortly after the release of *Blonde on Blonde,* but it was not a recording session or a songwriting binge. In the early evening of an August night in Woodstock, New York, a wheel on the motorcycle he was riding jammed, and Dylan was thrown to the ground. As news of the accident and of his badly broken neck spread through the world, there were those who said they'd been expecting it and many who wondered if Bob Dylan would ever be heard from again.

MORE CHANGES—DYLAN

DYLAN's injuries forced him to stop the touring which had become increasingly frantic during 1965 and 1966. He was bed-ridden in his big house in Woodstock. This period of exile and contemplation influenced his musical outlook profoundly.

Looking back, the accident might be seen as a sign from Dylan's muse, for if it had not happened, he could well have burned himself out with drugs and touring. Instead, he turned inward and apparently found much that he wanted to change about both the direction of his life and that of his music. The one interview he gave during this period to a persistent *Daily News* reporter, Michael Iachetta, reveals a subdued and humbled Dylan.

"What I've been doin' mostly is seein' only a few close friends," Dylan told Iachetta, "readin' little about the outside world, porin' over books by people you never heard of, thinkin' about where I'm goin', and why am I runnin', and am I mixed up too much, and what am I knowin', and what am I givin', and what am I takin'. And mainly what I've been doin' is workin' on gettin' better and makin' better music, which is what my life is all about."

The result of all this self-analysis appears on Dylan's next album, *John Wesley Harding*, which was released in January, 1968. The album does not represent all of Dylan's songwriting during this period, for he had been writing songs and releasing them to other artists. "Too Much of Nothin'," one of Dylan's best songs, a treatise on the effects of boredom, was released by Peter, Paul and Mary as a single and sold quite well. "You Ain't Goin' Nowhere" was released by the Byrds, a band that had helped Dylan break into the rock world with its renditions of songs like "Mr. Tambourine Man" and "All I Really Want to Do." Dylan apparently liked the band, and his blessing, represented by a photo of him on the back of the group's first album, helped the Byrds to find acceptance with both a rock and a folk audience.

John Wesley Harding is, as Scaduto points out in his biography, Dylan's resurrection record, his return from the near-death of his accident and recovery period. The singer is humbled on the album; he has abandoned loud rock and relies upon a small, laid-back bunch of Nashville musicians. If you play *John Wesley Harding* and *Highway 61 Revisited* one right after the other, it is hard to believe that the same man is responsible for both pieces of work.

Where all of Dylan's previous albums had been blessed with a certain amount of self-deprecatory humor, *JWH* is a serious, almost morose, record up until the last two cuts, which are joyous, funky country numbers close in feeling to Dylan's later work on *Nashville Skyline*.

Much has been written about these sparse, poetic little songs, and of that criticism, only Scaduto's seems to me to capture the essence of what Dylan was attempting with *JWH*. Somehow, during the long months of contemplation after his accident, Dylan had developed a religious sense of himself, something that is almost totally absent from his earlier albums. Because so many in the counterculture in 1968 had not resolved the questions of religious belief for themselves, they found it hard to see Dylan, their prophet, as a follower of any religion. He was just too iconoclastic a figure for that, they thought, and when the reviews of Dylan's album came out, almost every reviewer ignored the religious parallels and focused on the folky, Americana qualities of the album. Only Scaduto, years later and with Dylan's assistance, has been able to express the deep religious qualities of songs like "The Drifter's Escape" and "I Dreamed I Saw St. Augustine."

"*John Wesley Harding* is infused with a belief in God, with self-discovery and compassion," writes Scaduto. "It is Dylan's version of the Bible, songs written as parables describing the fall and rebirth of one man—Bob Dylan.

"The album is Dylan's avowal of faith."

Dylan's comment on all this is one of the most important he has ever made on his own work. Dylan explained to Scaduto that he had discovered that his earlier songs were all autobiographical.

"I discovered that when I used words like 'he' or 'it' and 'they' and talking about other people, I was really talking about nobody but me. I went into JWH with that knowledge in my head. You see, I hadn't really known before, that I was writing about myself in all those songs."

With these two comments on *JWH* one has the essence of the album. It is a series of parables reflecting Dylan's renewed interest in religion, but it is also a series of tales about the frantic life that Dylan, "the drifter," had so recently been lifted from by his accident and self-exile.

Dylan's interest in religion at this point seems to provide another example of prophetic qualities. Two years later, every major magazine in the country would be headlining the religious revival among the young, and people would be listening to *JWH* with changed ears; but in 1968, the idea of a youthful religious revival would have been considered outlandish by most observers.

Each of the songs on *JWH* is important. There are no clunkers here, and there is none of the sprawling quality of *Blonde on Blonde*. The songs are short and tight, the music is simple and played by a small, closely knit group of veterans and even the cover is subdued. Dylan is expressing something through the very form of this album—expressing his own retrenchment and self-analysis.

JWH is one of Dylan's most difficult albums if one attempts to translate the lyrics into literal allusions. But this has never really worked with Dylan, and if *JWH* is seen as one long religious statement, it is much easier to comprehend.

The album consists of a series of short tales in which Dylan tells what he has learned from his experiences as a rock-and-roll star and part-time prophet. The entire work is an admission of vanity and of failure. Dylan rejects that which he admits he once owned. He also recognizes that he failed as a leader to his generation and indicates that he will not attempt to resume that role now that he has emerged from hiding.

Two of the songs on *JWH* seem to capture the essence of the new, reflective Dylan and are also among the best he ever wrote.

"All Along the Watchtower" is a spare songpoem about the loss of faith in contemporary America. Dylan takes all the roles in this song; he is the joker and the thief, and he is the believer in the watchtower. Paul Williams has pointed out in his book *Outlaw Blues* that this song is one of the most oddly constructed of Dylan's writings. Williams suggests the song would seem more logical if the last verse were first, and indeed, it would seem that he is correct. If this is true, the only explanation for Dylan's having shifted around the verses is that he intended a disjointed feeling that would enforce the statement of the song.

"Watchtower" works well as an eery presentiment of doom, and it is reminiscent of Yeats's poem, written between the First and Second World Wars, that describes the world as out of control and churning toward either a rebirth or a sorry end. Here Dylan has a joker and a thief discuss their lives, and their conclusion, that the insanity of a society is trivial to their true, spiritual lives, sums up Dylan's reflections during his long exile. "Let us not talk falsely now," he writes, "for the hour is getting late." He is asking his listeners to examine their spiritual assumptions and beliefs. In a way this is one of the most optimistic of Dylan songs, for it rests on the belief that there is a solution to the troubles of the world, and this solution lies in good men accepting their own faith.

Another song of great significance on this album is "The Drifter's Escape," in which Dylan envisions his own judgment before his peers and his rescue by a sympathetic deity. The song is either a pure religious parable or a simple autobiographical statement. I opt for the latter, for the account so clearly parallels the events of Dylan's life. He has been led before great audiences and been judged; still he has been unable to fulfill their expectations of him as prophet and savior and leader. Yet he has escaped from all this by an accident that can be seen as a saving act of grace. Dylan's accident allowed him the time and the peace to seek out and sort out his own beliefs.

The album ends with two delightful and simple tunes put there, Scaduto suggests, to show the result of Dylan's philosophical thinking. "Down Along the Cove" is a happy song, full of the uncomplicated rhythms of early rock-and-roll and topped with a lyric that might have emerged from Tin Pan Alley, or from Nashville. "I'll Be Your Baby Tonight" is another simple song, but is filled with such a sense of relief that it stands as more than just another country number. Dylan has freed himself of so many of the shackles that bound him before his accident, and here he is chortling over that fact and reveling in the role of protective lover, strong enough now to take care of his own.

JWH was well received, if not well understood. One could sense the relief that the reviewers felt at having Dylan back on the scene. Rock had not been the same without him, even though his old backup band had appeared as a brilliant new musical entity called simply The Band.

It was rumored that Dylan would resume touring, but each rumor was denied by his management, and the denials proved accurate. Dylan did make one appearance, though, at a concert in memory of Woody Guthrie, his old idol and influence. The concert, at Carnegie Hall, featured a host of folk performers, including Pete Seeger, Judy Collins, Richie Havens and Woody's son, Arlo. Each performed a few Guthrie tunes, and the atmosphere was like that of the hootenannies of the late '50s and

early '60s. Each performer accompanied himself, and there was
no reason to expect that Dylan would not follow suit, but when
the time came for his contribution, The Band suddenly appeared, the electricity was turned up and the hall went wild.
Dylan ripped his way through three little-known Guthrie numbers, "Mrs. Roosevelt," "Grand Coulee Dam" and "Roll On,
Columbia," with The Band howling along. Dylan was back, and
just as in the days preceding his accident, he was full of surprises.

But this isolated concert appearance was one of the least of
the surprises Dylan had in store for his audience. With the
Guthrie concert he left his fans wondering about the next step,
and he did not answer for more than a year. During this period
Dylan was not seen or heard from publicly, but was frequently
seen around his home in Woodstock, functioning as the reserved
country gentleman—patrolling his land and attending church
services each Sunday morning, accompanied by his wife and
children. Woodstock became a mecca for wandering teen-agers
who appeared in town looking for him. This impulse was later
channeled by a pair of hungry promoters into the Woodstock
Music and Art Festival, which implied with its very title that
Dylan was somehow involved.

Meanwhile, across the country, the students' mood was growing more and more rebellious as the Vietnam War ground on
and the colleges failed to respond to a need for responsibility.
In the midst of this growing rage, in April, 1969, Dylan released
a new album titled *Nashville Skyline*. If the rock Dylan had
been a shock to his audience, the country Dylan was an even
greater jolt.

Nashville Skyline is the most laid-back of all Dylan albums.
It is a tribute to the simple joys of country living and country
music, and it is the least intense work Dylan has ever produced.
There is nothing in either the music or the lyrics to suggest the
earlier Dylan, and no matter how pleasing these country tunes
are, they do not compare with his earlier work. The critics had
a field day with *Nashville Skyline*—especially the underground
press, which could not believe that Dylan had gone over to the

other side in a deeply polarized country. Nashville represented redneck America, the killers in *Easy Rider* and the racist South. Dylan had always represented independence and cynicism, and it was hard to reconcile these two scenes.

Not that *Nashville Skyline* isn't a pleasant album or a popular Dylan product. In fact, it is the most popular Dylan album ever made, having sold more than a million copies, a figure none of his other albums have come close to. But from the standpoint of songpoetry, *Skyline* is not in the same league with any of Dylan's earlier work. It has none of the insight, the sensitivity or the intensity of, say, *Highway 61 Revisited*. It does not attempt, as does *JWH*, a major statement on faith—or on anything else, for that matter. It is simply a collection of pleasant, Muzak-y country tunes, written and performed with great professionalism.

Although my immediate reaction is to say, "Dylan is an artist and let him be," I must admit that *Nashville Skyline* was an incredible disappointment to me when it was released, and in the long run it has proved to be even less substantial. Dylan did not again begin to turn out meaningful songs until he abandoned his romance with country music and musicians. Both *Nashville Skyline* and the later *Self Portrait* seem now like mere placeholders in Dylan's career. They show little or no value as songpoetry, and merely fill time between the moving and poetic songs of *John Wesley Harding* and *New Morning*.

Dylan was forgiven *Nashville Skyline* by many of the critics, but his next release, *Self Portrait*, which appeared in the summer of 1970, was the greatest critical disaster of his career. A two-record set, *Self Portrait* is even more vacuous than *Skyline*, and it was attacked by *Rolling Stone, The Village Voice* and even *The New York Times*. Oddly enough, Dylan's influence and prestige did not diminish during this country period. His influence had been too great to be forgotten so quickly, and his integrity as an artist was beyond question for those who had first learned of the possibilities in their own music from the Dylan of the early and mid-'60s. But if there was ever a time when it seemed that Dylan might lose his hold on his audience it was immediately following the release of *Self Portrait*.

Dylan apparently sensed this, and he rushed out his next album, *New Morning*, in October, 1970. Previously, he had issued an album a year, with a two-year gap between *Blonde on Blonde* and *John Wesley Harding*, so this three-month gap between *Self Portrait* and *New Morning* is a good indication of exactly how much he was affected by the critical lambasting.

New Morning, if not one of the best Dylan albums, is far superior to the country records, and it reestablished him quickly as the most important influence on the more intellectual portion of the rock community—a position he might have lost had he rested with *Self Portrait*. Everything that Dylan has done since the release of *New Morning* indicates that he wishes once again to become a functioning part of the music community. He has assisted in the preparation of his biography, has appeared at a number of concerts with other musicians and has generally made himself more accessible to both the public and the press. In the light of all this activity, *New Morning* is rather a statement of reentry into the real world, and it is his most important record in a long time.

Unlike the country albums, *New Morning* is full of the kind of worldly observations that have made Dylan such an influence. There are love songs, but they avoid the corn of *Nashville Skyline* and display the kind of anticliché writing at which he excels. Someday, someone will surely make a study of Dylan's use of clichés as stepping-stones in his work. As critic Greil Marcus has pointed out, Dylan has a way of slipping up to a cliché and then twisting it to make a new statement. Marcus cites a line from the title song of *New Morning*, "Automobile coming into style," as an example of Dylan's twisting a cliché into a new and ambiguous statement.

New Morning is full of moments when one fully expects Dylan to come out with some piece of corn and then is surprised.

The album begins with a declaration of a new beginning and ends with a hymn, and in between, Dylan provides songs that touch upon experiences common to his generation. In "Day of the Locusts," he takes the listener along to his acceptance of an honorary degree at Princeton University in June, 1970, and relates his discomfort.

His attitude was ambivalent. He tells us that he almost split, frightened by the same authorities who sought to honor him, but that the humming of locusts, an expression of nature, helped him to stick it through, even though he had to flee once he had his degree safely in hand. The last lines of the song, with Dylan fleeing the school, could be expressive of the experiences of a vast number of American students who have rejected academe for the world of the locusts.

In "Went to See the Gypsy," Dylan describes an early experience with rock-and-roll in which he seeks out a Gypsy whom he never meets. The feeling of the song is one of nostalgia—an artist contemplating the moment when he chose to pursue his art. In my eyes, rock-and-roll is the Gypsy of the song, and when Dylan cannot find him he is forced to make his own music.

"Time Passes Slowly" could be seen as one more in the current series of escape songs, tunes that carry lyrics expressive of the exodus of many young people from the cities to country farms and communes. But if you listen carefully to this song, you cannot help wondering if the vision of country life that Dylan paints is enough to satisfy anyone, let alone an artist. "Time Passes Slowly"—too slowly, it seems—and Dylan is left to wonder whether country living is really all it's made out to be.

Two songs on the album are similarly deceptive. "Three Angels" and "If Dogs Run Free" both seem at first to be typical Dylan throwaway numbers, along the lines of "Leopard Skin Pill Box Hat." But Dylan has too much to say in too little space to let that happen here. In "Three Angels," done in a style reminiscent of early rock-and-roll and late Johnny Cash, Dylan bemoans the lack of awareness people have of the world around them. "If Dogs Run Free" is a philosophical treatise set to cocktail-lounge piano, and Dylan uses this odd situation to ramble on about his own genius and freedom as an artist. It is typical of Dylan humor that this serious set of philosophical sentiments is backed by the bebop wailings of a soul singer scatting her brains out.

New Morning was received by the rock critics as an indication that Dylan was far from through as an artist. Ralph Gleason of Rolling Stone clichéd enthusiastically his relief and joy at seeing Dylan come alive again musically. If Dylan had intended this album to make up for the dismal failure of Self Portrait, he was right, and he achieved his purpose with an ease that must have surprised even him.

Bob Dylan can be seen in many ways: as a political leader; as a supersensitive observer of the current scene, able to foresee new developments before anyone else has the slightest idea they are occurring; as a frustrated rock-and-roll star who never became the new Elvis. But I see him foremost as the man who helped American songwriters move beyond the traditional boundaries of their medium.

Before Dylan, the best of our songwriters stuck to their commercial material, and if they had impulses to attempt more serious songs, they did them at home and saved them for their friends. But Dylan changed all that by challenging his contemporaries to cross over the same boundaries he had ignored. At the same time that he was shattering those bonds forever, he managed to create a body of work that has had tremendous influence upon the thinking and actions of his contemporaries.

He is the only philosopher of any importance to a vast portion of this society, and has wielded tremendous influence. A lesser man might have chosen to capitalize upon this power, but Dylan is above all a poet of integrity, and he has always refused to allow his music to be used for more than songpoetry and entertainment.

He knows that if those he is addressing receive his message, they will have little to do with politics or organizations. Instead, they will become stronger and better people at everything they do, people less likely to be fooled into living their lives by someone else's arbitrary rules and inhibitions.

His music is intense, and that in itself has been a message to his listeners. Like many of the poets before him, he has let on through his work that there is great happiness to be found in experimentation with life, and those who have listened have been reassured in their struggle to break away from the paths society has set for them. His images are often blessed with great beauty, but it is never a detached, idealistic beauty. Instead, it is a vision that demands to be tied to reality, to the hard ground on which we all must stand.

Dylan was the first songpoet. The phenomenon this book tries to talk about could not have existed without his work. The greatest testimonial to his songpoetry has been the number of talented musicians who have taken Dylan's lead and ventured into their own minds and hearts to produce a new musical form. Each of the songwriters whom I interviewed for this book expressed his gratitude to Dylan for showing the way, and the work of each clearly manifests Dylan's influence and indirect guidance.

There was a time when it was fashionable to call all young folk singers "Woody's Children"—after Woody Guthrie. Now it is appropriate to call the host of fine young writers who have appeared in the late '60s and and early '70s "Dylan's Children."

ROBERT HUNTER—
AN INVISIBLE SONGPOET

T HE Felt Forum at Madison Square Garden is far from felt, being mostly cold cement, and the Grateful Dead, being mostly hot music, are far from dead. There they sway, five of the best in rock, sweeping their way through another frenzy, making a music as unique as their name. There's Bob Weir, the voice of the group, pumping away on his rhythm guitar and warbling like a schizoid combination of Marty Robbins and Tony Vale. And there's Bill Kreutzman, the drummer, drumming; Phil Lesh playing on his bass as if he were some grand classical guitarist gone thick-fingered. Can't forget Pigpen, isolated behind his organ, pumping along. Finally, all beard and guitar, is Jerry Garcia, mother of the group, specialist in the long swooping solo, mixing fire with water every time he takes a break on lead. The music is cruising, and they're all singing—"Playing, playing in the band/Daybreak, daybreak cross the land."

Off in a corner somewhere is America's greatest invisible rock-and-roll star, Robert Hunter, the man who writes the words the Grateful Dead sing. Hunter is invisible by choice: no photographs, no publicity, rare interviews granted reluctantly. He is

our most inaudible songpoet as well, for the words he weaves
are some of the most important, but only lately has one been
able to hear some of them. There was a time when Hunter's
words took a back seat to the musical fantasies of the Grateful
Dead—back when acid was king and people came to Dead
concerts to get their swinging and swaying and screaming done.
Even the records buried the words, with track after track of
good rock-and-roll covering the vocal sounds.

Somewhere along the way, probably in 1969, a decision was
made to quiet down the music and let the words come through.
If the intent was to let the audience hear what the Dead had
to say and further involve them more deeply with the band, it
worked, for with the first album of this kind, *Workingman's
Dead*, the band expanded its sales and its audience tremendously.

If it seems that I am ignoring much of the Grateful Dead's
recorded work here, that's right. There are only isolated instances in their first three albums when you can actually hear
Hunter's words. It was only with *Workingman's Dead* that he
became a songpoet, at the moment when his words could be
heard and understood and sink into the collective head of the
community.

Proof of Hunter's sudden rise in influence can be found in
the last supplement to *The Whole Earth Catalog*, edited by mad
novelist Ken Kesey and mad realist Paul Krassner. References to
Hunter's lyrics began to pop up all over the place, and there is
even a feature article devoted to the analysis of one song. A
writer named Ed McLanahan takes on "The New Speedway
Boogie" and finds in it reams of insight into the bedlam of Altamont, in which the Grateful Dead played an important part and
after which they were proportionately burned for their participation in an event that ended with mayhem and murder.

My own awareness of Bob Hunter did not come until I sat
down and listened to *Workingman's Dead*, though I'd always
loved the Dead and have danced with them till dawn on many
occasions. But only with *Workingman's Dead* did I realize that

there was someone out there in California trying to tell me something, and only then did I start to seek out Hunter.

When I first went looking for him, through his record company, the general response was "Who?" No one seemed to know exactly who Hunter was, and people were sure of only one thing—that they didn't know where he was or whether or not he was up for interviews. Eventually I was able to extract a phone number which was guaranteed to be the number of the office of the Grateful Dead in San Rafael, California.

When I finally did go West to Berkeley, I picked up the phone and dialed the number, expecting to be answered by some tripped-out hippie chick whose job was to be the telephone personality of the Grateful Dead. Instead a male answered the phone. "Is Bob Hunter available for interviews?" I asked. "Speaking," Hunter answered. I swear, Bob Hunter is the easiest-to-find invisible rock star we have.

Later on I visited Hunter at his home, a little house hung on a cliff overlooking San Francisco Bay. There, as we sat in a comfortable room with a thick carpet, surrounded by his collection of old war medals, Hunter explained his invisibility to me.

"I'd rather own my own face," he told me. "I have a lot of friends who don't own theirs, and it gets them in all kinds of trouble."

The face that Hunter hides so well is that of a man in his early thirties who has obviously chosen to live his life as a "freak." He is not a physically large man, but he gives the impression of being possessed of an almost childlike energy. Ideas bubble up as he speaks, one on top of another. A veteran of the frantic San Francisco musical surge of the late '60s, Hunter now seems to have calmed down and accepted his role as part of one of the best bands in the land. And he is considered a part of the band. When he speaks of the Dead he speaks of "we," and when Jerry Garcia speaks of the Dead you know he is including Hunter, the wordsmith. Garcia had joined us for the interview. After a while listening to these musicians, it was clear that they are close friends and alike in their approach to the world and to their music.

Workingman's Dead, the first album in which Hunter's influence is strongly felt, is the most subdued record the Dead have ever come up with. It features a great deal of acoustic guitar, and on the few occasions when it bursts back into rock, it is a kind of subdued, bastardized country rock, with a lower level of sound and the occasional use of a pedal steel guitar. The songs are quite separate offerings, but they do seem to form a net of consciousness in which Hunter and the Dead are trying very hard to present a new sort of cultural history.

Recently we've had a burst of this kind of writing, with Hunter and Robbie Robertson leading the way. In their songs one can detect a new set of purposes; both songwriters seem to have made a conscious decision to create their own view of America and its history. Where Robertson is more interested in analyzing specific events, as in "The Night They Drove Old Dixie Down," Hunter is preoccupied with creating a series of personalities uniquely American and deeply involved in the cultural experience of the last century or so. The title of the album is a clue to the kind of persons Hunter is out to create. They are indeed workingmen, men who see the country from the bottom looking up.

Hunter's relationship with the Grateful Dead dates back more than a decade, to a time when, fresh out of the service, he met Jerry Garcia and formed a folk duo to perform at local clubs.

"We were both living in old cars outside of Palo Alto," Hunter said, as Garcia chuckled along at the retelling of their first meeting. "Jerry happened to have a huge tin of pineapple chunks, and I had a glove compartment full of spoons. We became a sort of symbiotic unit."

Later on, when the Dead was formed, Hunter was assigned the role of songwriter after it had become clear that he could not add much musically to the band.

"I'm just not good enough on anything to play with band," Hunter told me.

He has been writing much of their material since their first album, yet only recently has he been listed in the album credits.

On *American Beauty,* where there is a small box devoted to listing the members of the Dead, Hunter is listed at the bottom, as songwriter. He does travel with the band most of the time, and the song "Truckin' " was written one verse at a time, from city to city, on a tour.

One of the most refreshing things about the Grateful Dead is that they have avoided isolating themselves from the rest of the community. They too are workingmen, and of a very special and generous nature. Since the band's inception, the Dead have made a point of playing as many gigs as possible, even if there has been little or no money involved. Elsewhere in this book we will meet one of the executives of their recording company, Warner Brothers Records, and hear him speak of the financial problems of the Dead. Many of these problems could have been easily resolved if the Dead had stopped playing for little or free. They chose to continue, and the rock community should be grateful.

When they do perform, the Dead make a point of giving the audience a full show, not just a short sequence of favorite songs. They have been known to play for as long as six hours before packing up and stumbling home. For this reason any Dead concert is a unique rock experience, with a relationship between crowd and band that is singular and exciting.

Hunter likes to speak of a Dead character who can be found in many of the songs on *Workingman's Dead* and *American Beauty,* their next album. This character is indeed a workingman and an underdog, and he is expressive of the group personality. Any other group would have problems of credibility if they sang about the concerns and feelings of this kind of character, for he is a crusty fellow, without pretense or slickness, and there just aren't many unpretentious and crusty rock bands around.

You can find this character in a song like "Dire Wolf." The narrator of the song, who tells a tale of confronting danger in a snowy waste, is obviously a man of human fears, as un-superman as you could find. But his fear of the unknown is one of the most common of emotions, and must have been even more common in the period in which the song is set, which seems to be the late nineteenth century. His plaintive plea of "don't murder me" is one of the most basic requests a man can make of the world around him.

"The situation that's basically happening in 'Dire Wolf,'" Hunter told me, "is it's the middle of winter, and there's nothing to eat for anybody, and this guy's got a little place. Suddenly, there's this monster, the dire wolf, and the guy is saying, well, obviously you're going to come in, and why don't you pull up a chair and play some cards? But the cards are cut to the queen of spades, which is the card of death, and all the cards are death at this point. The situation is the same as when a street dude, an 'up against the Establishment' guy, approaches the Establishment and says, 'We can coexist.'

"Also, 'Dire Wolf' is Behemoth; that monster, the Id; the sub-conscious—it's that too. Out there in a barren setting, stripped; there's no setting really, just blank white, and these characters in the middle of it."

"That song may seem absurd," Jerry Garcia added, "but it's truly real. I mean, I've been hung out on acid and pretty sure that there were a lot of people out to murder me. That fear is as real as anything else I've felt, and when I sing that song and say, 'Don't murder me and I won't murder you,' that's about as far as you can go. After you can state that positively, you can be friends or whatever."

Others of the entries on *Workingman's Dead* and on *American Beauty* are message songs. Among these is "The New Speedway Boogie," in which Hunter and the Dead give out their "official statement" on the disastrous rock festival at Altamont, filmed as *Gimme Shelter.*

Bob Hunter: "In 'Speedway,' the character isn't there. I was just translating what everybody was saying after Altamont. At that point I was just being a reporter, almost, in trying to get explicitly what everyone was trying to drive at. Why Altamont was so terrible, and in another way, why it was to be expected. I wasn't actually there, and I don't know if I could have gotten that kind of third-person perspective if I had.

"Everyone was upset, and we were getting attacked from all

fields on it, and we felt we needed a statement. But we didn't need to say, 'We are guilty' or 'We're not guilty,' or anything like that. We just wanted to say, 'The wheel turns, and this is what comes of it.' "

Jerry Garcia: "In the song, and at Altamont, the whole thing of what freedom is comes into play, which is a thing I think has needed light shed on it for some time. Murdering somebody is an expression of freedom. I mean, you're free to murder somebody. You take the basic human situation and everybody's free on that level. The thing is that obviously some restriction is called for along the line, for freedom is misleading. There's freedom and then there's license."

"Character" and "message" make up most of both *Working-man's Dead* and *American Beauty*. I'm not going to get into listing how they break down, but for those who wish to go back and listen, I'd advise they put on "Uncle John's Band," which is a good example of a song without the Dead character, and then give a listen to "Cumberland Blues," in which this character emerges as a poor miner.

Much of what the Grateful Dead sing is political. Not that they are involved in conventional politics in any way. Even in San Francisco, Jerry Garcia would have a problem functioning in the regular political establishment. But many of these songs are political in that they deal with the basic problems to which politicians must address themselves.

In these songs we meet common people burdened with many problems, from the oppression of poverty to the brutality of addiction. We meet our own contemporaries—oppressed, repressed, confused and deluded. Hunter is involved in the immediate events of the world around him, but rather than deliver pronouncements, he chooses to tell about individuals who come up against it in the world. During our discussions, Hunter mentioned repression a number of times. To my surprise, he expressed a sort of perverted gratitude to the forces of oppression for having provided him with an opponent and a stimulus to his writing. Both he and Garcia spoke of 1971 as a perfect year in which to be a writer, with just enough oppression to keep you angry and involved and just enough freedom to allow you to express this anger.

"We've been listening and taping off the radio lately," Hunter told me. " 'Goodnight, Irene' type of stuff and things like 'Why Do Fools Fall in Love?' and 1957 rock-and-roll. That was peacetime music, Eisenhower time, and there's not much vitality to it. It's well put together, but they weren't really pushing against anything and you can feel it. There was really nothing happening then, and we all look back with beautiful memories of it."

"When there's no oppression," Garcia added, "when the oppression goes away, then it's time to go off to the desert island, or hit the streets in Bombay or go to a Tibetan monastery, or do those things that you're holding in reserve, because this is a time that requires that active, going-forward trip. It's the right time to be doing that type of stuff. Peacetime's the time to be going off and, you know—"

"—making orchestrated music," Hunter interrupted, "or having stuff orchestrated. You don't need the messages then. You could say, 'Watch it, eternal vigilance is the price of liberty,' or something like that, every once in a while, but there's not much you can say in peacetime. I'm not what you'd call highly political, but at least sixty percent of what I do is stuff that I'm called upon to do because it's happening. It's reaction to one thing or another. Even though the repression really never comes down to us. You notice that the place isn't surrounded by the National Guard or anything like that; but it has to do with the squeeze on society that we're feeling down here at the shallow end. We always know it's there. I mean, we have friends in jail . . ."

Much of Hunter's concern with workingmen and with those at the "shallow end of the pool," as he puts it, can be traced to his own childhood in northern California. His father was an itinerant electrician and owned a motorcycle and a great affection for freedom.

"My dad was sort of a soldier-of-fortune-type dude," Hunter told me. "He was a good hustler. He could go into a grocery store without any money and talk his way into two bags of groceries. I remember, we'd be driving along in the old panel truck and we'd drive by a bar—he was an electrician too—and the neon sign would be out. So we'd park in the parking lot and he'd go up there and do a few things with the wires and the sign would go on, and then he'd go in and drink up his pay. And we'd sit out there in the car.

"What would happen was, my dad would meet somebody in a bar and get to be pals, like that, and the next thing we knew, me and my mother and my brother would be up and moved into this fellow's house and then my dad would split. He'd kind of park us there, and then we'd have to make do with the family he'd parked us with. I guess my mother got tired of that after a while. Anyway, they were divorced."

Hunter's mother remarried, and her second choice was a man who prided himself on his intellectuality. Without engaging in amateur psychoanalysis, it is still possible to perceive the influence of these two men on Hunter's songpoems. The character who inhabits many of the best of his songs might well be patterned after his father, while the poetic and philosophical approach of the songs could well be attributed to the influence of his stepfather. Either way, Hunter is one of the most effective writers we have in terms of relating the feelings and philosophies of a portion of America that is increasingly ignored in poetry, literature and art: the little man. Through his work we can perceive that he is truly not so little, and that this country was put together by men who had to have strong philosophies and a strong sense of themselves in order to survive.

Hunter's lyrics are full of tips on survival, as are the lyrics of many of the songpoets. In a time when young people are without leaders, the songpoets have often taken the role of guide. One can assume that the songs that do attempt this gentle guidance are expressive of Hunter's own philosophy of life.

American Beauty, which is the follow-up album to *Workingman's Dead* and shares many of its attributes, including the basically acoustic sound, is much more concerned with songs of survival than with representing characters from our history.

In *American Beauty,* the songs express Hunter's view of different aspects of survival in troubled times, and the album is topped by "Truckin'," a song that catalogues the experience of the Grateful Dead on the road. The chorus of that song sums up the dilemma of many of Hunter's contemporaries.

"Sometimes the light's all shining on me/Other times I can barely see/Lately it occurs to me/What a long, strange trip it's been." At another point in the same song, Hunter uses one of his frequent poker metaphors to express his most basic attitude toward living: "If you don't lay down your hand/It ain't worth a dime."

In other songs on this album Hunter takes up religion, music, love and a variety of other subjects. In "Ripple," he affirms his belief in God with the lines of the chorus: "Let it be known, there is a fountain/That was not made by the hands of men."

During our interview Hunter referred to a song that had virtually written itself. This phenomenon is reported by almost all songpoets and all creative artists I have encountered.

"Some of my songs are written during what I call 'peak' experiences," he explained. "For some reason conditions are just right for me, and everything falls away and I see for a bit. You just see, and the stuff comes in, and if you've learned how to use a pencil—which is a real skill, to just sit there and to write and say, 'Here it is, here it is' . . . There's this presence sometimes, and I get a feeling that someone is looking over my shoulder, that what I'm writing is not going to be put into a book and shoved away and eventually lost somewhere."

Hunter told me that he thought that the character who populates so many of his songs will soon be laid to rest.

"I think I might've mined that particular vein clean," Hunter said. "It seems that this character is well taken care of, and I can be free of him. Right now I'm trying to find out what's next. It's sort of like finding out who you are in terms of what you've done, and then being free to *be* who you are—who I am, uniquely, after I've gotten rid of all my influences. The question is, is *me* my experience? I don't think so. It's like pouring ice into a mold: it melts and then it's water again. There are those people who tell me that the way to find a new direction is to stand back from experience and take a sane perspective on life.

But I think that may well be insanity. I really don't have it worked out yet, but that may not be the way to live life: maybe you should get into it up to your ears and wallow in it. Whatever happens, I'm looking forward to it."

In other of his lyrics Hunter seems preoccupied with the problems of memory. He also has developed a skill at writing some of the most surprising and funky love songs around. His love songs are, like Dylan's before him, completely outside the previous boundaries of pop music. In a song like "Till the Morning Comes," Hunter addresses a young woman and promises her not riches, or everlasting passion, but a sort of congenial protection. "You're my woman now/Make yourself easy," he writes, and in the midst of these relaxed sentiments one can recognize a realistic attitude toward the relations between men and women that is typical of his generation. Hunter's love songs are sung to equals, to women whom he obviously considers intelligent and to whom he offers but on whom he does not impose advice. There is not that vulgar condescension toward women here that one finds in the work of the hard-rockers.

It is apparent in much of Hunter's work that he has been influenced by Dylan, in the use of colloquial language to make sophisticated statements and in a number of articulated attitudes toward the world. Hunter is much closer to the later Dylan, because he is concerned with survival rather than revolution, and his songs are appropriately subdued. Yet Hunter is also very directive in his work, a tendency that Dylan eventually discarded. Still, it's easier for Hunter to be directive, since he does not perform his own material on stage or on records. When Bob Dylan sings out his advice to his audience, he almost always treads the thin line between helpfulness and arrogance; but when the Grateful Dead sing Hunter's songs, the effect is greatly diffused, and there is correspondingly less arrogance as it is offered.

Much can be said for group presentation of a writer's material. Hunter surely benefits from having the varied vocal and musical talents of the Dead to work with in his writing, and many of the songpoets have similarly benefited from their work with groups. Dylan found a whole new audience through the cover versions of his songs done by the Byrds and The Band and others.

Neil Young has benefited from his involvement with both the Buffalo Springfield and Crosby, Stills, Nash and Young. Laura Nyro might never have found a mass audience without the many cover versions of her songs, and Joni Mitchell first came to prominence in this country because she wrote for Judy Collins, who had already found an audience for her interpretations. But perhaps the best example of a songpoet working within the group context is that of Robbie Robertson, lead guitarist and songwriter for one of the best of the current American pop conglomerates, The Band.

VAN MORRISON—BELFAST COWBOY

V̧an Morrison is one of the most promising practitioners of the art of songpoetry. His songs, public performances and recordings provide good examples of what I find to be of value in these singer/songwriters.

A few years ago, when Morrison's career was on a downswing, I caught his act in a tiny New York rock club. He had been booked on the basis of one nearly forgotten hit record, "Brown-Eyed Girl." But here he was performing with only a bass player and his own guitar, and singing long, intricate and mystical songpoems. The audience was not very respectful, and it's true the songs did seem out of place in this rock cellar. The sweetness and sadness of these long songs did dent the audience's resistance, but there was too much to overcome. He had been typed as a singles artist, relegated to the AM bands, and he was not to be allowed to attempt anything else.

Only now, five years later, has Morrison overcome the limitations laid on his work by his listeners. He reemerged as an artist comfortable with both FM and AM audiences, capable of bridging a gap that few even attempt. In the process, he has accumulated a repertory that covers the whole range of young emotions

—songs that are unlike anything else being written, both rhythmically and lyrically.

Back at that club date Morrison was an uptight performer, straining to keep his composure and reach an unwilling audience.

I recently caught a Morrison concert at Carnegie Hall, and it was one of the best concert experiences of my listening life. Morrison strode out onto the big Carnegie stage and proceeded to destroy all the myths about his lack of ability to communicate in live settings.

He had a band of eight skillful musicians, but it was his own personality that dominated. Simply dressed, wearing dark glasses, he worked the audience in much the way in which an evangelist preacher works his flock. The music surged and diminished and surged as he played out mood after mood. Morrison has established himself as a master of dynamics. He worked the audience to a peak of excitement and then, swiftly and confidently, he would slow the pace or lower the sound. He had the audience totally involved, something increasingly rare in these declining days of rock-and-roll.

He played it all that night, taking us back to the early days, when simple rock songs like "Gloria" and "Brown-Eyed Girl" established him as the Irish answer, however muted, to the English invasion of 1964 to 1970. Morrison was born in Belfast, and his music has always seemed tinged with a bit of the Irish poetry that we have come to associate with Yeats and Joyce. He gave us songs from *Astral Weeks,* his long concept album, in which his poetry first soared.

Then he romped through his later songs, which are nothing less than an amalgamation of the best elements of his earlier work. In his latest songs, the ingredients are poetry, simplicity and rhythm, all balanced with a skill unrivaled among the current crop of performing writers.

What was most encouraging about this magical evening at Carnegie Hall was Morrison's obvious relaxation, his triumph over the stage demons that have plagued him for so long. Here he was in total control, and by the end of the evening, with the audience as exhausted as he was, he had established himself finally as one of the best we have.

So Morrison's roots are in Belfast, that great, gray city under perpetual siege. He was born there in 1945, child of working-class parents. He left school at sixteen to join a rock band and toured with it across the Continent. He returned to Belfast in 1964 and formed his own band, Them, and the group soon began a regular stand as the house band at the Maritime Hotel ballroom. Them, like many other bar bands, was rough and raw, and its recordings, even though made long after it had split the Maritime ballroom, retain some of the flavor of that kind of gig, where the musicians must compete with booze, seduction, bar fights and a general lack of decorum for the attention of the audience.

When Morrison and his band first emerged from the local bar scene in 1964, they were touted as Ireland's answer to the Rolling Stones and the Animals. The comparisons were accurate, for all these bands specialized in the kind of fierce, blues-based rock-and-roll that was suited to the locations in which it was played. The working-class bars and dances required volume, strong voices and simple statements.

Listening to the few recordings of Them that we have, one can almost hear the sounds of drunks and smashing bottles and bar fights in the music. Out of this period came "Gloria," Morrison's first real American hit and one of the raunchiest rock-and-roll songs of all time. It is explicit, coarse, insidious, gross —obviously, the makings of a rock-and-roll classic.

But listening again to the recorded output of Them can be a disappointing process for many of those who have since discovered Morrison. Even though many rock critics, lost in nostalgia for the simplicity of early rock, write of these records as if they were recorded on tablets of stone instead of plastic, they are nowhere near as emotionally effective as Morrison's later, less *macho* writing and performing. No matter what these critics would have the listener believe, one good listen to the Them records is enough to convince one just how special the Rolling Stones really were in 1964. The music is simplistic, harsh and repetitious, and even Morrison's rich rock-and-roll voice cannot rescue it from mediocrity. The musicians just didn't have the individuality or the will to experiment with the old blues forms that the Stones had.

The production of the two Them albums, released on Parrot in this country and rereleased in 1972 by that same label in a two-record package, could be a showpiece of early-'6os rock-and-roll mistakes. The sound is cold, with a hard edge on every instrument and, most regrettably, on Morrison's vocals. On only two of the cuts, "It's All Over Now, Baby Blue" and "Mystic Eyes," is there any warmth at all. It is apparent that the producer was calculating his mix on the basis of the tinny speakers of AM radios, hoping for one more "Gloria" or "Here Comes the Night." Because of this, I believe, the sophisticated American audience soon passed Them by. You just couldn't listen to these records on a real system without wincing, and that did them in.

Yet one cut on the Them albums does give an idea of what Morrison was later to produce in his work for the Bang label and Warner Brothers. This is "It's All Over Now, Baby Blue," Dylan's harsh bit of advice to a jilted lover, which Morrison quickly reduces to a less surreal, more direct love song. His vocal is not experimental in the least, and his treatment is routine, but there is a power here, a sense of dynamics, that will later emerge with even greater intensity.

Morrison moved in 1967 from Belfast and London to Boston, and signed a solo contract with Bert Berns, the head of Bang Records, a label that had distinguished itself in the singles field. Both the music that Van produced under the aegis of Berns and the hype that surrounded it indicate a constant confusion in concept. Apparently, both Berns and Morrison were seeking a way to cover both bases—singles and albums. Certain of the cuts on Morrison's one Bang album, *Blowin' Your Mind*, are clearly singles and nothing more. They are short, catchy bits of commercial sound intended to hook into the brains of the young purchasers of 45's. This is true of "Brown-Eyed Girl," one of the best singles of 1967, which features a folksy and rhythmic background fronted by a strong Morrison rock vocal. But the same album that led off with "Brown-Eyed Girl" also features "TB Sheets," Morrison's rambling, bluesy and often befuddling comments on a woman, her TB, her sheets and other things. Definitely not a singles cut, no matter how you cut it.

The album cover to *Blowin' Your Mind* is another indication of this confusion of purposes. It is a ripe, superpsychedelic jobbie, with Morrison's face popping out of a multicolored bit of bad Peter Max–ian artwork. On the other side, the liner notes, written by Berns himself, add to the confusion by taking off on what seems a slightly stoned reverie concerning Morrison.

"Van Morrison . . . turbulent . . . today . . . inside . . . a multicolored window through which one views at times himself and his counterself. Van Morrison . . . erratic and painful . . . whose music expresses the real now! ! the right now of his own road his ancient highway."

Now, I wouldn't ordinarily quote an effusion like that, but in this situation it's important. It's important to understand that Morrison was, at this juncture, a musician working at cross-purposes with himself. At the same time that his music was obviously leading him toward an accepting FM audience, his commercial instincts were leading him to "Brown-Eyed Girl" and that audience. For the most part, Morrison's crisis was unremarked in the rock press, which consisted of a tiny number of publications and columnists, because they couldn't figure him out either. If Morrison had continued in the vein of *Blowin' Your Mind*, he might well have vanished from the American musical scene in a self-created cloud of confusion.

After the commercial failure of *Blowin' Your Mind*, Morrison left Bang Records. He faded almost totally from both the rock press and the listening public. Those who were waiting for him at all were waiting for another "Brown-Eyed Girl" or "Gloria"— another lively hit single, perfect for the summer day and the car radio. But Morrison apparently had no intention of satisfying that desire on the part of his already diverse and confused audience.

He signed a contract with Warner Brothers Records, a company that had just recently begun to have a real impact on the rock scene. Warners has been noted for its creative approach to artist relations and advertising—especially its series of revealing, self-deprecating ads depicting the company and its executives. More important, Warners had made a strong commitment to a number of songwriters, including Joni Mitchell and Tom Paxton, and therefore could be expected to invest time and promotional energies in an artist like Morrison.

The first hints of what Morrison was to release on Warner Brothers came in a short tour of rock clubs and colleges he undertook in 1969. I heard Morrison for the first time during this tour, when he was performing songs mostly from his forthcoming album. The tunes were loose, long songpoems, sung with wistfulness and strength over a constant and lovely rhythmic background. Morrison would set up a riff on his guitar and the bass player would join in, and then—a few lines, a chorus and—magic, the kind of musical magic that happens so rarely that you close your eyes, open your ears and savor it when it comes. Each line and each chorus revealed a new and totally unique Van Morrison, a man singing love songs to his childhood and his lovers, singing with grace and lilting Irish force.

During that spring of 1969, *Astral Weeks*, Morrison's first album under his Warner contract, was released, to universal confusion. Many reviewers simply could not accept the idea that the man behind these long, lyrical songpoems was the same Van Morrison of "Gloria" and "Here Comes the Night" fame. One major reviewer did recognize what had happened, though, and that was Greil Marcus, writing for the supreme journal of the rock culture, *Rolling Stone*. Marcus played an important role in the return of Morrison to an audience that would understand what he was attempting. His review, printed in the March 1, 1969, issue of *Rolling Stone*, looked back over the Them albums and the disastrous *Blowin' Your Mind* experience and then raved joyously about the new Morrison of *Astral Weeks*.

"The music is not rock-and-roll in any ordinary or hyphenated sense," wrote Marcus. "Rather it is music that is intelligible to us because of rock-and-roll, intelligible given the complexities which hide behind the simplicity of intent."

Marcus recognized the album as a work of art, an extension of the work of Bob Dylan and the few others who had begun to work seriously as songpoets. He carefully prepared his readers for an album that was, essentially, one song, from beginning to end, intended to create a long, sustained mood.

But even Marcus' perceptive review and his attempt to revive interest in Morrison's drooping career failed to help the sales of *Astral Weeks*. It was too complex for most radio programmers, even on FM stations, and therefore reached the ears of few—too few—listeners. But what the album did do was prepare a new audience for Morrison, even though small. This audience proved to be loyal and lavish in its praise of Morrison's new work, and as they say, the "word of mouth" was good.

Even though not a great commercial success, *Astral Weeks* stands as one of the paramount achievements of songpoetry. It is an amazing effort, especially when one considers the limitations of Morrison's earlier work.

From the first notes of the album, it is clear that something new is happening. The rhythm pulsates as if it were a part of some great aural bloodstream, and the first lines promise renewal. "To be born again/ In another world," sings Morrison; and compared with *Blowin' Your Mind* and his earlier work, this album is a rebirth. What is immediately striking about the music is its subdued nature, with emphasis on acoustic instruments, whether guitars or cellos or violins or flutes—instruments that rely upon human contact for their major thrust. Yet there is none of the limpness or reticence of much folk music here. All the instruments are strong, moving along with force and grace.

The first side of the album is entitled "Beginning," and it includes four long tunes which, as Greil Marcus astutely pointed out in his review, can really be considered as one song. The song is about childhood and rebirth. The childhood is of the mind and memory, and is therefore made more beautiful and more sensual than it would have been if transcribed literally. The statement the first part of the album makes involves a yearning for a return to the sweet experiences of childhood, in this case a childhood in Belfast during the 1950s. Interwoven is the theme of a return to the kind of consciousness that characterizes the child: the ability to accept, a sense of wonder and an intensity of feeling.

Morrison's vocal work in this album surpasses anything else released in this country in the last ten years. He uses his voice in ways that most rock singers seem incapable of conceiving, let alone realizing. Although much of the lyric is sung at full intensity, there is never a sense of a singer's pushing himself too hard, or a quality of loudness. The vocal is the only sign of melody here, with all the other instruments serving as a sort of chamber-orchestra rhythm section. Each cut has its own special solo instrument, with "Astral Weeks," the opening cut, dependent upon the flute; "Beside You" featuring a high, limpid and lovely guitar. "Cypress Avenue" uses a harpsichord, which complements the vocal and often breaks into a countermelody. I can't find a single instrumental lapse on this album, and in this it is reminiscent of the albums of Bob Dylan, who is known for being able to summon up magic from the studio musicians who have recorded with him.

Out of context and analyzed separately, the songs seem much more standardized than they do if one listens to them together. The reason for this is Morrison's vocalizing: the way in which he makes a verse into a small epic of vocal dynamics, and makes a chorus a new experience each time it rolls around. I do not think it would be possible for another singer to properly or creatively reproduce these songs. They're extremely rare and personal creations performed in a unique manner.

The last song in the beginning section is entitled "Cypress Avenue," apparently a street of Morrison's adolescence. Here it becomes, as Morrison sings, "the avenue of dreams." It tells of an adolescence of shyness, of lonely strolls with a bottle of wine the only company. A woman enters into the song and the vocal goes wonderfully crazy, with Morrison taking off on the line "Rainbow ribbons in her hair" and making it something rich and bold and joy-filled. With that line, the song turns back to "Astral Weeks," and Morrison's meaning is clear. "To be born again" is to be brought to life, drawn from one's own shyness by experience.

The second side of *Astral Weeks* carries the subtitle "Afterwards," and these four songs deal with a later period of Morrison's young life. Here we have songs of late adolescence, songs of lust and the discovery of sexuality, songs about the paths open to almost-adult human beings. The first cut is the record's only bad song: a short, jazzy number called "Young Lovers Do" that in quality is nowhere near the other tunes on the album. It is such a lapse in taste that it would be futile to try to explain just why it occurred. Perhaps it was due to Morrison and Warner Brothers' attempting to "get a single" onto the album. Either way, it is a song easy to forget. In the past few years I've found myself consciously skipping it when I put the record on my stereo, and I'm thankful that it's the first cut on the side, for it saves me a lot of needle pushing and futile searching. But as soon as the raucousness of "YLD" fades, we are right back up on Cypress Avenue with one of Morrison's best-known numbers, "Madame George."

"Madame George," who appears to be a transvestite but may well be simply a local madam, is the central character of this reminiscence. "Madame George" is full of the images of the discovery of the sly joys of sin. Dope and sex and all those good things float through the song, all seen in a fresh light. Only at the end of the tune, with the narrator on his way out of Belfast and out of childhood, do we get a sense of perspective on all these things.

This is a tune of gratitude, with Madame George as its object. Morrison is thanking the Madame for all the joys she brought him, during a short time when he could appreciate them fully. But that time passes, he seems to say, and we must move on to adulthood and a different, harsher reality. Like all the other strong songs on this album, this is a song which creates a sustained mood, a mood of longing and of fond memory.

From the discoveries and farewells of "Madame George," Morrison moves on to the sweet reassurances of "Ballerina." The music is piercing, but the vocal is loud and sweet and confident. The lyric exhorts a lady to come on out and shine, to be the ballerina she is capable of being. It is a gentle and most moving reassurance, and the image of the ballerina is well placed and appropriate. The music suggests the spinning and graceful movements of a ballet, and the effect is very emotional. One of Morrison's backup musicians told me that he's seen fellow musicians so moved by their boss that they cried as they played. This tune is the kind that can draw tears, even from a hardened road musician or a staid rock critic. It is a testament to love and to strength, and that's a rare event in songpoetry—or anything else, for that matter.

The last cut on the album strikes a harsher note. Listening to it many times, I have come to the conclusion that "Slim Slo Slider" may be about drug addiction. The lady who rides the white horse may well be a heroin addict. If this is the case, it completes the passage from childhood to the harshness of adult reality. The song includes the lines "I know you're dying, baby/ And I know you know it too," and does end quite abruptly. The music, again, is sweet and fine, and one can only stand back in wonder as Morrison completes the journey through experience that *Astral Weeks* represents.

If there is one album that I would use to support the thesis that the songpoets have moved into new realms of emotional experience with their songs, it would be this one, with its depth of feeling and moving music and precisely tooled arrangements.

From *Astral Weeks,* Morrison, apparently disappointed with its commercial failure, moves on to shorter, AM-oriented songs, but the lyrical sophistication he displays in this album will be present, more or less, in all his later work. However, it will be a long time, I am sure, before we hear another *Astral Weeks* from Morrison, who has found more than a little success with his latest sides. Or from anyone else.

With the rise of FM radio in influence and importance, there has been a change in the way in which single records are marketed in this country. At one time, not so long ago, an artist would be signed by a record company and put to work creating a single. If the first, or perhaps the second or third, of his efforts proved successful on the all-important charts, the artist would be allowed to put out an album, with the single prominently featured, probably mentioned on the cover with one of those pithy little statements like "Includes 'Dropsy,' Milt Flugel's Latest Smash Single." As FM radio rose in stature, record executives and producers slowly came to the realization that they could work things in reverse.

Where it used to be that a single release would be decided by a small group of people, it was now to be decided by hundreds of disk jockeys, who were considered to be more apt to know what the public wanted. So many companies will now release an album and let the FM airplay determine which cut should be pushed as a single release. It is a strange and circular business, with still what seems to be too much emphasis on the single market, but it has improved. Artists are now allowed the luxury of an album release, a chance to expose more fully their range and ideas. And if there is a single on the album, the theory goes, some FM jock somewhere will find it and sales in his broadcast area will confirm the find.

The handling of Van Morrison's follow-up to *Astral Weeks, Moondance,* is a classic example of this new form of marketing. Morrison had set out to return to the singles charts as swiftly as possible. He put together a new band, took over the production from Lewis Merenstein and recorded an album almost opposite in concept to *Astral Weeks.*

The songs are all short, catchy tunes, each offering a release clear and strong enough to force its way into the consciousness of the larger singles audience. Morrison's strategy was to break back into the singles field and so expand his album audience. It worked. *Moondance* marked the beginning of a new career expansion for him, even though it was a major setback creatively. Gone are the intensity and experimentation of *Astral Weeks,* and he offers us some quite lively rock-and-rolling. But if one considers Morrison's intentions, it is an unqualified success.

Not that Morrison splits entirely from songpoetry with this more commercial venture. There are tunes here, songs like "And

It Stoned Me," which pick up the saga of reminiscence of *Astral Weeks*. But most do not attempt the kind of statements of the earlier Morrison epics, and therefore have not the same emotional impact. What they do have, though, is some of the most polished and understated rock-and-roll sounds to be found anywhere. Morrison proves himself to be a genius of modern rock production and instrumentation. His band here, and the bands he organizes on his later albums, are precisely chosen and well-drilled units. Especially exceptional is Morrison's longtime horn man, Jack Schorer. During the early Belfast days, Morrison played a bit of saxophone himself, and in playing with Schorer he seems to have found a way to bring that experience to bear.

The range of sounds and styles on *Moondance* is broader than on any previous Morrison album, with everything from the balladlike "And It Stoned Me," with its fresh images of children playing in the rain, to the jazz-tinged and lightly laid-back "Moondance." Each of the tunes has a strong release, easy to hum, and each song is short, sweet and to the musical point. My favorite cut on the album is the last, "Glad Tidings," in which Morrison sends his audience regards from the studio while the band rocks out a joyous and ingratiating bit of rock-and-roll magic.

Yet for all the rock-and-roll delights of *Moondance*, one has to come away from the album with a sense of loss in the lyrics, a sacrifice made on the slippery altar of hit-recorddom.

If *Moondance* was the first real hint that Morrison had chosen to abandon the goals of *Astral Weeks* for more commercial intentions, *Van Morrison: His Band and the Street Choir* confirmed it. Apparently encouraged by the increased sales of *Moondance*, Morrison pressed on in the tight modern rock-and-roll mold he had created.

Street Choir features few examples of songpoetry, but it is an album frothing over with rock-and-roll energy, and in this it served as a sort of directional sign for rock-and-roll. While many critics, especially the aging and unenthusiastic Albert Goldman of *Life* magazine and Columbia University, were bemoaning the death of rock, Morrison was off in Woodstock making a serious attempt at expanding and revitalizing the form. He succeeded with *Street Choir*, and all indications are that he is continuing to succeed.

From the first bouncing guitar strains of "Domino" to the last sweet exhalations of "Street Choir," Morrison manages the impossible: he is both precise and funky, tight and loose. There is no excess on *Street Choir*—not lyrically, and surely not musically. The music is involving, the kind of sound rock-and-roll was always meant to have. It combines many moods, is both ebullient and reflective. Through it all, the band shows great energy and skill, and the music rolls along, constantly new and constantly changing. And above all it rides Morrison's incredible rock-and-roll voice, the perfect vehicle for this emotional form. There is simply no other voice in the current world of popular rock-and-roll that combines intensity, warmth and emotion as well as Morrison's.

And the lyrics perfectly match the sound. They rarely call upon myth, philosophy or the history of Western ideas. They are involved with the images and moments of love, and work and characters seen and dreamed in the brief and onomatopoeic way the music demands. In "Domino," for example, Morrison reviews his own instability, musical and otherwise. "I don't want to discuss it/ I think it's time for a change/ You may get disgusted/ And think I'm strange/ In that case I'll go underground/ Get some heavy rest/ Never have to worry about/ What is worst and what is best."

There are a couple of other songs here about rock-and-roll and its world. "I've Been Working" chronicles Morrison's work life, "up the Thruway, down the Thruway," and his dependence on his woman to help him survive the whole business. "Call Me Up in Dreamland" is a testament to the man's love of his music: "Radio to me man/ Never to grow old/ On the saxophone." That would be the first time I've ever heard a songpoet claim that rock-and-roll has rejuvenative powers, though its audience has known it for years.

There are a couple of Morrison love songs—one a falsetto exercise called "Gypsy Queen" that is reminiscent of the beautiful

"Ballerina." The album is rounded out by two songs that can't really be categorized.

"Blue Money," also released as a single, seems to be about a young man watching his girlfriend model for pornography and chortling over the money they're making and the way they'll spend it. The beat of the song and the laid-back vocal contribute to a general feeling of nonchalance about the whole business that could only be the feeling of the very young. The song works in capturing an experience and a mood.

"Street Choir" is about America, rock-and-roll, audiences, political change. Choose any of the above. What is sure about this little number is that it caps the album well and further illustrates Morrison's mastery of the backup vocal group—something that few white singers have managed. In recent years, backup groups have been the province of black singers and a few white groups like the Rolling Stones and Joe Cocker's Mad Dogs and Englishmen ensemble. But Morrison seems to make the best use of the type of musical show put on by the likes of James Brown. At a number of Morrison performances I've been able to detect references to James Brown acts of the past, and at one show Morrison even parodied Brown's famous cape routine.

Morrison shares a basic humanism with most of the other important songpoets around today. This is not a soppy exaggeration of false affection for the human race, but instead, a well-developed interest and concern for situations humans can stumble into and how they deal with them. In *Astral Weeks* he indicates this concern in clear fashion on every track, as he ventures back through his own childhood and late adolescence. Just as Dylan seems preoccupied with driving his listeners to a more honest view of themselves, and Randy Newman is interested in examining man's foibles himself, Morrison seems fascinated with memory: the misty images that remain even after years of not looking back.

Morrison's follow-up albums to *Street Choir—Tupelo Honey*, released in the fall of 1971, and *St. Dominick's Preview*, released during the late summer of 1972—are further illustrations of Morrison's commitment to short, sweet rock-and-roll ditties.

But on *St. Dominick's Preview,* Morrison began to hint at a return to some of the lyrical and musical experimentation of *Astral Weeks.* The album features two long cuts, "Listen to the Lion," in which repeated vocal treatments of the same phrase create an effect not unlike the rhythms of *Astral Weeks,* and "Almost Independence Day," a long, dense and rhythmically similar number.

Yet on the same album, the lead cut is a short, stomping piece of almost perfect rock-and-roll entitled "Jackie Wilson Said." In it, Morrison indicates again that he is on his way to becoming one of the great white rock artists. His mastery of the single form seems so complete that it is hard to conceive of his faltering. If he desires, he can probably continue to churn out singles like this forever, each one with a perfect little hook of its own, ready to snag into the American imagination for a short, very profitable period of time.

But if my feelings are correct, we have not yet heard the last from the more reflective, looser Morrison of *Astral Weeks.* There are strong indications that he will yet return to that form, buoyed by the success of his singles and encouraged by grateful record executives and fans. If that happens, and his stage performances continue to improve, Morrison is on his way to becoming one of the major figures of songpoetry and rock-and-roll.

JONI MITCHELL—A TRIUMPH IN BLUE

Okay, rock-and-roll is an integral part of songpoetry. But there's more to rock-and-roll than one might think. It's not just a rhythm-and-blues beat, or a sound filled with electricity and extended with simplicity. It is more a feeling and a sense of strength. Even the most inane rock-and-roll actors of the early '50s stood center stage and belted their numbers. This is part of the charm of the music, for it originated in a time when few American teen-agers were capable of speaking strongly about anything. There was a self-confidence to much of early rock that was catching, and even the silliest lyrics can sometimes seem important and pressing when presented with authority and an obvious feeling of self-esteem.

The best songpoets learned this lesson from rock, and they gained strength from it. It does something to music when this confidence permeates your work, your writing and your performance. I, for one, believe that a singer doesn't stand a chance of getting an audience to listen if he does not assert himself on stage. Not just in his performance, but in his material as well.

Joni Mitchell, a Canadian songpoet, has learned the lesson well, and in recent years the feeling of strength that exudes from her work has been startling and wonderful. In a few years, she has moved from an introverted writer and performer who turned out weak songs to a songpoet whose work is rich and strong and full of that special confidence I've been discussing here.

Not that Mitchell's early work was ineffective. Her songs even then had imagery and humor and wisdom, and they were recognized and recorded by a number of the best interpreters we have. Judy Collins finally found her way to a hit record with a Joni Mitchell tune, "Both Sides Now," and Tom Rush was provided one of his best performances with "Circle Game."

With all this prerelease publicity, Mitchell's first album had a great deal to live up to, and in many ways it justified the expectations of this writer and many others. But I remember the moment when I realized that there were deeper possibilities in a Joni Mitchell song than I had realized. It was at a club where Dave Van Ronk, the legendary white blues singer, was appearing. In the midst of a bunch of dirty blues, Van Ronk attempted an interpretation of "Both Sides Now." He pushed his low, growling voice to a falsetto, and the lyrics were lent a new weight, a new importance. Van Ronk's is far and away the most moving interpretation of that song I've ever heard, and the reason is clear: He had injected strong emotions into what others had treated as a slightly precious poem. Instead of emphasizing the poetic qualities, he went for the guts, and it worked. He added a new power to the song, and I realized then that if Mitchell could find a way to do the same (without severing her vocal chords trying to imitate Van Ronk's raspy voice), she would have found her groove as an artist.

Blue is one of the best albums of songpoetry we have—Mitchell's masterpiece, and a triumph of rock-and-roll. With this album she managed to reconcile her poetry, with its strong imagery and strong emotional outlook, to the assertiveness and power of rock. In the process she has moved from folk singer to songpoet.

I can almost hear the rock purists groaning out there as they contemplate Joni Mitchell as rock-and-roller. But rock-and-roll is more than a screaming electric guitar; it is more than minimal lyrics and sequined capes; it is a feeling, a looseness and a self-confidence. I contend that Joni Mitchell has all these qualities and intelligence as well—and further, that this combination is the future of rock.

The primary change between *Blue* and Mitchell's earlier albums involves relaxation. She has learned to ease up on her vocals, to employ intricate and varied timing, instead of relying on the high folky sound that Joan Baez popularized more than a decade ago. Baez herself has apparently changed her mind, for her most recent releases do not have the hair-raising high notes that sent chills up the spines of folk listeners in the early '6os. In abandoning folk classicism, Mitchell has achieved an immediate effect: her lyrics are much more accessible to the casual listener. Before, her vocalizations often interfered with a simple understanding of her lines. This can be fatal. It is self-defeating to sweat out a lyric of merit and then bury it under a vocal style.

Not that on *Blue* Joni Mitchell does not fully use her wonderful voice. It's in full power—a tool of many emotions. It is one of the most expressive voices I have ever heard, capable of sudden flights of sound that seem impossible. But now she is delivering up these sounds within an easier context, and they are sudden surprises instead of required pyrotechnics.

Blue starts off with a song titled "All I Want" that sets the tone for the entire album. It is a rhythmic delight, with guitars setting a calypso beat and Mitchell's voice soaring above it all with a declaration of desire for freedom from greed and jealousy. "Alive, alive, I want to get up and jive/ I want to wreck my stockings in some jukebox dive," she sings with strength and warmth, the two characteristics of *Blue*.

The use of rhythm on this cut is unusual, as if Mitchell had reached out into the world of rhythm and found for herself something unique and new. James Taylor supplies the second guitar on "All I Want" with great subtlety, never intruding on the strong lyrics. Taylor plays on three of the best cuts on this album, all up-tempo numbers, and he never once hits a bad note or interferes with the presence of the star. Stephen Stills provides the bass and guitar tracks on "Carey," perhaps the best and most jubilant of the songs on *Blue,* with equal politeness and taste. One of the qualities that Mitchell clearly shows is the ability to choose the right people to do the right musical jobs on her records. Unlike many of today's artists, she has been in a progression toward simplicity of arrangement and instrumentation. This takes a special kind of courage, for it indicates a real and justified confidence in her own presence.

Another singular aspect of her talent is Mitchell's ability to vary the length of her lyric lines without ruining the flow. Her phrasing is so loose, and she is in such clear control, that she makes it seem effortless to squeeze an extra phrase or two into any line. Only a few vocalists—for instance, Dylan and Van Morrison—can pull this off. The effect is of great ease and fluidity, but the performer is flirting with disaster, for a skipped phrase could ruin the meter.

"All I Want" is played on the dulcimer, an instrument that has had little real impact on the recent musical scene. Only the late Richard Fariña seemed able to adapt the special sound of this ancient traditional instrument to the new music. Fariña died before he could make his dulcimer work known to the greater public. Now Joni Mitchell has revived the instrument, this time as a purely rhythmic tool, and it is this ancient sound that weaves throughout this album. On stage, she seems able to create an entire rhythm section, a little band, with it.

The next tune on *Blue* features Mitchell on piano and is a love song titled "My Old Man." The song focuses in on the tiniest elements of a relationship in order to capture the feeling of loneliness: "The bed's too big/ The frying pan's too wide," Mitchell sings. Her voice slides around the lyric, bursting into sunspots of sound, exploding with warmth and love and capturing, for one moment, an essence of feeling about another person.

Mitchell has the ability to put a lot of her own experience into short statements in both her lyrics and her music. Although nearly all of her songs focus upon relationships and the interactions between a woman and her lovers, they manage to dramatize aspects of these relationships that seem fresh. There are few clichés and no cop-outs. In "My Old Man" Mitchell writes of the sad discovery of the many little facts that remind one of a lover's absence and convey the rediscovery of the joy of a lover's returning.

"Little Green," the next cut on *Blue,* is the weakest here. Not that it is a weak song, but it is a weak Joni Mitchell song—which would make it exceptional on the albums of any one of a hundred other artists. She fails to keep up the rhythmic intensity, and the lyric about a child is too vague and too short to make an effective statement.

But even here there are style and warmth far beyond the usual.

"Carey," in which Mitchell returns to the rock-calypso beat she introduced on her *Ladies of the Canyon* album, is the best example of how she has reconciled herself with rock-and-roll. This song is dependent on rhythm for its success. The vocal is piquant and rich at the same time, and the lyrics are constructed like an early rock hit, with a repeated chorus that sticks with you. The bass and guitar tracks, again provided by Stephen Stills, are perfect foils for the singer. Mitchell makes it all seem so easy, but "Carey" is full of vocal intricacies and tricks that would stagger and choke most singers. Through it all there is a sense of an intimacy, contributed to by a production that pushes the vocal so far in front that you could believe Mitchell was singing from your lap. The clarity is remarkable, and since no producer is listed, one can only chalk this up to Joni Mitchell and what she has learned about the recording process through four albums.

Here again the lyric focuses on small things to make a more general statement. The music matches the words, and the song is, like the sirocco in the first line, full of the feeling of a hot wind blowing in from Africa. There is vitality here, tremendous energy, and it spills over onto one of the best tracks that Mitchell has ever recorded.

Much of her appeal is a quality of confronting reality from a certain innocence as she stands there with her long hair and pure face. In "Blue," the next cut on the album, she does just that with great effectiveness and charm. In a clear, sweet voice, she lines out a lyric that is quintessential to the dilemma faced by thinking young persons. Rather than condemning drugs, the song goes through the emotion a young person would feel confronted with the devil and his limitless temptations. "Acid, booze and ass/ Needles, guns and grass/ . . . Everybody's saying/ That hell's the hippest way to go/ Well, I don't think so/ But I'm gonna take a look around it, though." Four lines and she's said as much about being young today, the pressures and temptations, as anybody I've heard or read. Her language is vernacular and precise; there is not a wasted word here or anywhere else on this extraordinary album.

"California" continues this idiosyncratic combination of innocence and worldliness. What grabs me most about this song is its pragmatism and realism. When Mitchell sings of California, it is not of rolling hills and spacious skies. She sings of "Sunset pigs"—the overeager cops along the Sunset Strip in Hollywood—and rock-and-roll bands, and the heat. She speaks of homesickness when one reads news from home, even when the news is of the war and its "bloody changes." This song is not fantasy but a piece of honest rock, and it is a vivid little portrait of a moment of loneliness and of homesickness. Again we have the rock-tinged sound, with the addition of one of the creamiest pedal-steel solos. With the pedal steel appearing on the word "lonely," Mitchell approaches the border of sentimentality, but as usual, she manages to avoid it by the facts of reality.

From "California," with its images of returning, we move on to "This Flight Tonight," a song about leaving. This is one more love song presented in a very personal way, and the theme still manages to seem fresh and unused. But then, how can you place a song with lines like "You got the touch so gentle and sweet/ But you've got the look so critical/ I can't talk to you, baby, I get so weak/ Sometimes I think love is just mythical" into a single category with all the mush that has passed as love poetry in pop music for so long?

"River" is an odd Christmas song—another love song, and a plea for forgiveness even if only from oneself. Mitchell takes to the piano here, and the vocal is a bit more expansive than on the earlier cuts, but the effect is much the same. The honesty is forceful—a personal crisis against the commerciality of modern

Christmases. Again this is music without fantasy, music that makes the world a little clearer.

"A Case of You" is perhaps the subtlest offering on *Blue*. It is another example of the integration of rock feeling into Mitchell's work, but more as well. Here is a love song about total devotion, surely a familiar commodity on the pop scene, but it is so rich with imagery and wisdom that it seems criminal to compare it to most of the love songs on the market. The mood is of resignation and of a wonder at the joy that another person can bring into one's life. There is fear here, and regret that love brings such total emotional domination, but there are also acceptance and contentment. The vocal is subdued throughout most of the song, but suddenly takes off at one moment like a soaring bird of color, and the intensity of emotion bursts out in a short sound.

Finally we have one of Mitchell's strangest songs, and one of her most telling. "The Last Time I Saw Richard" is about a failed romantic, and it tells the story with wit. The character is drawn quickly, with few details, and the situation is revealed through conversation. Since the conversational tone is constant throughout Mitchell's recent work, she has no problem adapting it here. The song has humor and intelligence, much in the style of Randy Newman. But behind the humor one can feel the bitterness of the true romantic doomed to continual disappointment. Even the self-deprecation of the humor cannot hide the message. Mitchell seems to be resigning herself here to the description of her given by Richard—a hopeless and aging romantic, whose life is a series of ordeals and disappointments and "dark café days."

And *Blue* is finished. Looking back over Joni Mitchell's earlier albums, with their folk-art quality and their high, unnecessary vocalizations and their overly dramatic lyrics, it is hard to believe that she has come so far. She has developed into something like a national resource, and the Canadians ought to put up a monument in her first English classroom or something like that. Here we have a poetry of honesty and precision, delivered over music that draws on rhythms that reach for the gut. This song-poet has a warm and charming way with the language, yet she uses this to say things that would seem almost too harsh to hear if they were coming from a less beautiful person.

There must be something in the air up in Canada that produces such good musicians. Robbie Robertson, Neil Young, Ronnie Hawkins and Joni Mitchell are among many Canadians who grace the American musical scene. Joni Mitchell is a native of Calgary and a former art student in Alberta. She was born in 1943 and made her performing debut at the Mariposa Folk Festival, a homey affair that annually draws some of the best folk talent to Canada. She was signed by Warner Brothers' Reprise label in 1967, but had developed a reputation in this country long before that on the basis of others' recording her songs. Tom Rush and Judy Collins were two of the first to record Mitchell songs, and many others have followed suit.

Her first album, *Joni Mitchell,* established her as one of the better writers on the folk scene. Yet it also established her in many minds as the epitome of a certain kind of folk preciousness, an almost ultrafemininity, in both her imagery and her vocals. It is true that there was much in the way of coyness and preciousness on this first album, which was produced by David Crosby, but there are also much wit and signs of a poetic sensibility. The imagery in songs like "Michael from Mountains" and "Sisotowbell Lane" is a bit reminiscent of college-literary-magazine poetry, but it often hits home. The album had a loose concept to it, with one side devoted to "city" songs and the other to "country" songs; a couple of the songs supported this idea, but most did not, and the concept fell flat. Perhaps the most important song on this debut album comes in a short, throwaway song titled "Night in the City." Here Mitchell breaks into a sort of semirock boogie beat, behind some bright lyrics about getting out and living in the night city. The song is definitely indicative of better things to come.

Mitchell's second album, *Clouds,* features some of her best early songs, including "Chelsea Morning," "Both Sides Now" and "Tin Angel," but is weighed down with a number of melodramatic attempts at complicated narrative poetry. These include "The Gallery," which almost works as a bittersweet, cold-eyed examination of a dead relationship, but bogs down in words and more words, and "That Song About the Midway," which stumbles into needless ambiguity and is possibly the worst song Mitchell has ever recorded. It should be noted that Mitchell took over the production here, except for Paul Rothchild's work on "Tin Angel," and that this marks the point at which she began to develop her skill as a producer of intimate music.

The third album, *Ladies of the Canyon*, marks a major turning point in Mitchell's recording career. Here she begins to loosen up her vocals, although she still spends too much time trying to send her voice to the moon or beyond with high and most unnecessary howlings. But what is most noticeably an improvement here involves the lyrics, which are much more economical and much less ambiguous. Here we are introduced to a bunch of characters who are succinctly summarized. There are three clear gems on the album. First is "For Free," a tribute to a street clarinetist and a very honest comment on the difficult art of performing for fees. The next is "Big Yellow Taxi," a sweet little throwaway of a tune in which Mitchell cuts loose, finally, into a pure rock-and-roll beat. The chorus goes: "They paved Paradise and put up a parking lot" and provides one of the best slogans for the new ecology movement. It may not be political rhetoric, but it sure makes its point. Last we have "Woodstock," which, although a bit overblown, captures much of the feeling of almost religious unity that bubbled up after the Woodstock Festival of 1969. Crosby, Stills and Nash turned this one into a respectable rocker soon after.

With *For the Roses*, released in early 1973, Jonie Mitchell continues her attempt at further expanding the musical variety of her work. Although this album suffers from the repetition of one theme—the loss of a rock–and–roll-star lover—in a number of songs, it is still musically ahead of much of what is released today. The album's strongest cuts include "You Turn Me On (I'm a Radio)" and the title song.

It has been known for some time that Joni Mitchell is not the most willing of stage performers, and that is easily understandable. It can be a great drain for a writer to go out on the road and to make her most personal statements to crowds of thousands, appreciative or not. Many writers find the road conducive to writing, but the great majority with whom I've discussed this find the atmosphere of the countless Holiday Inns that form the rock-and-roll trail too impersonal and too sterile for anything more than imbibing, sleep and late-night phone calls home.

Knowing Mitchell's feelings about performing and being on the road, it was with great surprise and much delight that I saw her perform at Carnegie Hall, on a bill with Jackson Browne, himself an important figure in the new songwriting. From the first second on stage, it was clear that Mitchell was in command. She came out unaccompanied, a thin, lanky figure in velvet with long blond hair dipping to her shoulders and beyond.

With a minimum of talk, she launched into a stunning presentation of the songs from *Blue*, some newer material and some of her best-known numbers from her earlier albums on Reprise. What is most striking about the woman's stage performance is the way she manages to reproduce the sound of her album cuts on stage with no help from other musicians. She plays a strong rhythm guitar, and although she is no single-string-folk-guitar genius, she holds her audience with every chord. She played "Carey" with just the accompaniment of a dulcimer, and by the response of the audience, which stood and cheered, it was clear that no one felt deprived because of the missing bass and guitar sounds.

When Mitchell performs, feelings of ease seem to flow through the auditorium. In this case, at Carnegie Hall, she was faced with an audience that was surprisingly rowdy—oddly similar to the audiences that usually show up for concerts of much "heavier" music, the Ripple-and-reds crowds. But she confronted even the rowdiest elements of this audience and quieted them with grace and charm. It is, in fact, her secret weapon, this grace with which she surrounds some of the most concrete and strong-minded lyrics around. She catches her audience by surprise, and once captured, it is enraptured. Mitchell is truly a magical performer. Anyone who feels that live music has been somehow cheapened by the recent abundance of "studio" albums should go to hear her in person.

RANDY NEWMAN—A CHILD OF L.A.

Without Los Angeles there could not be Randy Newman. Usually it is risky to assume that much of an environmental influence upon an artist, but in this case it seems acceptable, especially since Newman keeps insisting to interviewers that there's no place like L.A. for him.

Los Angeles is a child of the twentieth century. There is a restaurant on Santa Monica Boulevard that claims to be the oldest in town on the basis of fifty years of continuous operation.

Everything that is twentieth-century America can be found in abundance in L.A. It is a city of automobiles and MacDonald's, and of air pollution so thick and persistent that the residents long ago dropped it as a subject of conversation. There is no way to transport yourself around the city without a car. The confusing and expensive bus system is reserved for the crippled and the elderly.

It is a flat and persistently ugly city, with oil wells out on the streets and neon the basic color. It is a city of motels and of buildings often constructed to last less than ten years. I've seen buildings torn down in L.A. that would look modern in any Midwestern metropolis.

There are signs of sudden wealth throughout the city. Above the semiarid plain that is its core there are hills dotted with expensive homes, precariously perched in areas that are constantly threatened by fire and mudslides. Driving through these hills, down twisting roads lined with big houses, it's impossible not to notice the abundance of FOR RENT and FOR SALE signs. This is directly attributable to the unique flow of cash in Los Angeles. Young people strike it rich, perhaps in records or films, or in less spectacular businesses, and they rent these magnificent houses up in the canyons. When the money begins to go, the house with the huge rent tag is likely to be the first extravagance to follow. Thus the terse signs on the weaving canyon streets.

Down below, on the Sunset Strip, which is really the city's main street, one can walk for hours and be confronted by almost nothing but burned-out cases and the police who avidly watch over them. Speed freaks with eyes so wide they could hold two eyeballs stagger up to you seeking change. Jesus Freaks seek your soul with a pitch so aggressive that they have been known to pin people to the ground while attempting their conversion. Scientology has its own office on Sunset Strip, filled with blank-eyed venders of the latest of L. Ron's dictates.

People don't go out too much in L.A. It's not that the streets aren't safe (for with nobody walking, they are among the safest in the United States); it's just that, well, there's really no place to go, and if there were, it would probably be an hour's drive on the most crowded and deadliest freeways in the world. Besides, driving around L.A. without a specific destination can be dangerous. The city is patrolled by some of the country's most overeager cops—big, bruising characters who wear helmets and specialize in sticking flashlights in the faces of the city's younger citizens. Word has it that there are few lovers' lanes in L.A.

Because of all this and more, people stay home in L.A. And that's where you'll find Randy Newman: at home in Mandeville Canyon, one of the town's upper-middle-class enclaves. He doesn't go out much.

His music is a perfect representation of the lessons of Los Angeles. In his short, wise songpoems he chooses to focus in on often tiny human idiosyncrasies. In a city like L.A., latching on to the smallest possible unit, the individual personality, is the only way to survive. And this is Randy Newman's strength. Focusing on the high school success who turned out to be nothing, the fat boy and his friends, the rapist and his victim, the cowboy without a range, his songs remind us that we are still, in the twentieth century, a nation of individuals trying simply to cope—and often failing.

If things had worked out, Newman would have ended up a writer of "follow-ups"—carefully constructed sequels to hit records. That's all he really wanted to be, he'll tell you. But the follow-ups never seemed to work, and some of the reactions of independent producers were brutal. Newman's voice is an acquired taste, and one can imagine the typical L.A. singles producer wincing upon first hearing one of Randy's black little numbers sung in that nouveau-raunch voice of his.

"When I first started," Randy says, "I think most of what I did was pretty horrible. The first few were definitely different, but a lot of them were just like everything else in those days [1962]. I was trying to write rock-and-roll songs. Still am. Lou Adler was the first person in the business I ever played a song for. To make myself be able to sing it, I was playing the tune right along with it. There was no accompaniment. He just told me I shouldn't do that. He was right, of course, but I had to do it so I could sing. He didn't seem to like the song too much. I was trying my best then to write follow-ups, just like Carole King. She was my hero. I thought she was the greatest because she was so good at follow-ups.

"You know, I never made a conscious decision about writing music professionally. Oh, my uncles had been in the business, writing music for movies, and I would go and watch them record, and I guess I always suspected I was going to be a musician. I just brought some of my songs to a publisher and they signed me up while I was still going to school. There was really no money in it—a hundred and fifty dollars a month—but to me it was terrific to be making money in that.

"I don't really remember how I felt about it then, but I knew it was kind of exciting, to have somebody recording your song.

But then it was always disappointing to me because I hated the records so much. Eventually you harden yourself to that. That's why I finally started recording myself. I figured it wasn't fair to be pissed off at all those faceless people."

What Newman started recording was tiny songs—none over four minutes in length, the great majority around two minutes long. The shortness of the songs is an indication of his original intention to write hit singles, but it is also a comment on his sense of precision. Newman is hardly likely to fall into the trap of excess verbiage. Throughout his recorded repertoire of perhaps fifty songs, there's not one spot where you can fault him for overstatement. Granted there are a few tunes, like "Beehive State," his pithy comment on the middle part of America, where an extra verse might have added to the effectiveness of the song, but better one or two short than thirty or forty too long.

Newman's first album on Warner Brothers was released in 1968, and the reaction of the press and the industry was clearly underwhelming. The record never made it to most record stores, was hardly reviewed at all and suffered from a singular lack of what the industry calls "word of mouth."

Listening to that first album, *Randy Newman*, can help one to understand the initial reluctance of critics and audiences alike to accept Newman's early songs. The problem is mostly in the voice. Newman has a voice that is hard on the ear at first, second and sometimes fourth and fifth listenings. The only artist with a similar delivery I have ever heard was Billie Holiday. But Randy insists he was never exposed to Lady Day's music, and one tends to believe him. What he did was develop a vocal style that utilized his own limited singing power to the utmost and served his material. The songs on this first album rely on spoken lyrics, with Newman adding few vocal embellishments to his speaking voice. The result is a bluesy, slurred effect which almost perfectly complements the low-key, depressed content of the lyrics. This same voice, with its howls and whispers, serves the humorous content of the songs, all of which are wry numbers, intended to tickle the listener while slightly wounding him.

The songs take up the same themes Newman has pursued in

his later work: parents, sad love stories, the banality of contemporary living and plain old perversity. There's even a religious comment here, in the tune "Billy Boy," in which Newman wonders aloud about Judgment Day. "When the Big Boy brings his fiery furnace/Will He like what he sees/Or will He strike the fire and burn us?" These lyrics are delivered in that mock-serious wail of a voice, with a background of rinky-dink piano.

The songs are all tiny by comparison with those of most of the other songpoets, but again, Newman has a way of utilizing the standard single format in ways that no one else can. Even though the songs follow regular patterns of verse and chorus, and the choruses have the same kind of repetitious working one has come to expect from AM singles, the total statement is of invariably more intense impact than singles of the past.

For example, "Love Story," Newman's laconic voyage from youth to age, has a chorus that could fit into anyone's jukebox or car radio. But the verses, where one would expect an equally banal statement on love, are full of those tiny perverse twists that Newman so loves. "We'll have a kid," Newman sings, and there's no reason to expect this vision to be anything but rosy. "Or maybe we'll rent one." Here the listener has to stop and check his ground. Rent one? "He's got to be straight." Ah, that's reassuringly parental. "We don't want a bent one." There's the stinger. Once he's got his listeners wondering and more than a little bit confused about just how much they're being put on, Newman moves in for the satiric kill. "He'll drink his baby brew/ From a big brass cup/Someday he may be President/[all legitimate sentiments for a fantasizing father to come up with] If things loosen up." The result is bemused laughter, the laughter of those caught off-balance by Newman's satirical powers.

One can see Newman's environmental influence clearly here. Just as the city in which he functions is a perversion of a city, his "love story" turns out to be a perverse comment on eager romantics with pragmatic streaks.

On this first album, as in all of Newman's recorded work, one can trace his interests to a solidly middle-class background. The son of a physician, raised in an upper-middle-class district of

L.A., Newman writes mostly of interior problems. He rarely touches on politics, and when he does it is with satiric intent, as in "Beehive State," or in his more recent tribute to the Cuyahoga River in Cleveland: "Burn On, Big River." His concerns are with people like himself, people raised to be students and then sturdy contributors to the society around them.

The use of music on this first album I believe to be less effective than on his later works, but Newman disagrees. He likes strings and woodwinds, marimbas and Moogs, and is disdainful of the smaller musical combo used on his second album. Yet he admits that the material on his second album, some of it of a greater seriousness than that on the first, did not call for such musical elaboration.

It was with the second album that Newman began to come to the attention of the larger music community. His first (and only) hit record, "Mama Told Me Not to Come," was drawn by Three Dog Night from that album. It was a good sign, the single, for it proved that Newman's particular brand of rock-and-roll could be marketed.

The song "Suzanne," which appears prominently in the second album, is a good example of the precision of Newman's writing. Not a phrase is wasted as he details the story of his shy rapist who seeks out lovers on a telephone-booth wall. The song is both chilling and funny, made funnier by Newman's deadpan delivery. The whole technique of utilizing the traditional love song to explore the seamier side of lust is Newman's alone. No one else has ever captured the single-minded and simple-minded attitude of a rapist toward his victim, and surely not in a pop song.

Another example of his would be "Uncle Bob's Midnight Blues," Newman's anthem to drug paranoia, written for a friend deeply entangled in speed.

"I conceived 'Uncle Bob,' Newman says, "in terms of drug paranoia. I thought of calling it 'In Defense of Alcohol.' I think this whole generation's going to be as big a juice-head generation as the last one. I've seen it start already. There's a reason why alcohol came down, as opposed to hemp or something else.

Alcohol's a real blotto, if you can take it. I can't take it. And grass, or anything else, can be rough. I've seen groups of people just go horribly paranoid—faintly paranoid at least. They get along well and then all of a sudden they start to worry about how they're moving, fingers touching and all that shit."

Newman is a writer without a tradition to support him. There just has never been anyone quite like him before. We've had wry songwriters, of course, but none blessed with Newman's precision or depth. In recent years Tom Lehrer, with his manic and often devastating satires; The Fugs, with their sex and drug adventures, and Bob Dylan, with his wise brand of humor, have been able to create good music and tickle their listeners at the same time. But none of these can match Newman's cynicism and sense of compactness.

Another Newman phenomenon is the seriousness of a good part of his audience. He is not an easy artist to listen to, with his slurred words and strangely constructed sentences, and there are those who strain so hard to hear his philosophical stances that they almost completely miss the humor. Kris Kristofferson tells a story about walking into a party where a group of Newman cultists were hunched up near the stereo, savoring each word with great seriousness. "It was my first exposure to Randy," Kris says, "and as I started to hear what he was saying I began to laugh, then to howl, and the people sitting around the stereo began to give me dirty stares. They couldn't see what so funny, and that made me laugh even harder still."

Newman does not perform much. When he does, it is to reverent, standing-room-only crowds. He is not a polished performer by any standard for that term. At his recent New York Town Hall concert, he spent as much time trying to tuck in his shirt as he did addressing the eager audience.

On stage he moves quickly through his material, accompanied only by his own funky piano displays. He does not yet have a carefully programmed set of songs to deliver to the audiences, and this works to his advantage. His rare appearances are full of little surprises: old songs, new numbers and wry stage patter.

Randy's latest "live" album is the funniest and probably the best of his recordings to date. With only a piano accompaniment to cover the words, his finely turned lines are revealed in their entirety. The songs are short, one only slightly over a minute in length. But that tune, "Maybe I'm Doing It Wrong," could probably be restricted to the single title line and still be a comic masterpiece.

Visiting Newman at his home in Mandeville Canyon can be a little unsettling, if one goes expecting to find a struggling artist in his humble garret. Newman, like many other singer/song-writers, is living pretty well, with sizable royalties arriving regularly. He lives with his German-born wife, Rosvita, and their two children in a rambling house filled with stylish furniture and fine contemporary art.

Newman is a tall man with decidedly indistinct features. There are no hard lines to either his face or his body. He wears special glasses to compensate for a lifelong vision problem. A good part of his time is consumed watching daytime television, and one of the rooms in the house is dominated by a huge color TV. An English nurse tends his youngest child, leaving Randy free to watch the tube, wander around aimlessly, read and, occasionally, sit down at the piano and write.

"It can get pretty fucking low around here when I'm not writing," Newman says. "I don't like to go into that room with the piano. I avoid it whenever I can. But then you get something going and that makes it all worthwhile. Somehow I know I don't really have to do anything. It's like they say, welfare robs you of your incentive. I had a nine-to-five job once and I think I liked it. It was just that I had no responsibility and I was good at the job—fast. I'd be home too tired to do anything. I didn't have to worry about writing because I was too tired to do it. Just watch TV and go to work.

"You know I perform very little—just here, New York and England. I'm going to do more. The reason I decided to perform was that I figured at thirty or forty I might regret that I hadn't at least tried it. There's a whole body of literature about the mystique of it all, and here I had a chance to try it, so I did. I had no expectations about it; I was just scared. But I figured that the thing to do was just not to be bothered by it. At least you don't have to hear yourself or pick things apart. If I had started getting really cerebral about it, it probably would have destroyed me. In reality, applause gets boring after a few days of it. It's like a high, you know, it's pretty good. But then, you know, you'd get to the end and they'd applaud and bring you back and all that bullshit. I never wanted to go back. I just wished they'd stop, because I had made it without doing anything gross.

"Sometimes I really wish I had a discipline or a plan. I've wished that all my life, but I've never had it. I write at home, and I should probably get an office, because it's just too easy to lay around here. I play with the kid, or anything. If there's a way out, I'll take it.

"I wonder if all the people who buy the records really understand the meaning that I've given it. You know, you analyze poetry in school and the nice liberal teachers say 'Well, anything you can get out of it is nice.' But I always like it best when people get what I try to do. Like 'Mama Told Me Not to Come.' I was never crazy about that song. I didn't want to record it. The origin of the song is just about a fool at a party, that's all. I didn't think it would be a hit, but I was pleased when it did. But I can always see the dark side, and I wondered whether it was a hit for the wrong reasons. I never give myself a break. It was so big, you know, that there may have been something else. Again, maybe the audience didn't understand the meaning I had given the song.

"I don't listen to other people's work as much as I should, I guess. And when I do—I mean, I always loved Carole King, but her album . . . I was only able to get through one side of it. I found myself getting madder at that than at anything else, because it's so so bland, and the tracks are so sanitized. There's nothing to get into on those tracks. I remember what a great piano player she was. And 'friend' and all those words, they're just so empty. I always liked her songs, but I never liked the words, Goffin's words. But she had a gift for writing melody.

She still does, but all this 'cryptojazz,' I just can't make it. It's just drifting away from me, or I'm drifting away from it.

"You know what she did. She spent all these years being tremendously adept at following up people, and I think she wrote a follow-up album to James Taylor. It's the album he should have made. I like Taylor personally, and I like his music sometimes . . . but I don't want to get into who I like; you'll find out how bitter and vile I am."

Newman reads much more than he listens to music, and many of his songs are drawn from ideas picked up during reading. "Yellow Man" was the result of reading a Will Durant text entitled *Our Oriental Heritage*. When I visited with him, during the summer of 1971, he was fascinated by a new topic—Albania.

"I always liked Albania. I've been trying to write a song about Albanians for quite a while, because I think they're funny. More goats than people. A great place. They've always been berserk, though. Their music! It's the craziest stuff you've ever heard. It's like Red Chinese music, stuff like 'The East Is Red,' songs with phenomenal lyrics about Mao. I've even thought of recording 'The East Is Red.' Or maybe writing a new Albanian anthem. I've got the first line: 'When the moon comes up over the goatherds . . .' Maybe I'll finish it one of these days."

It is gratifying that Newman is finally being recognized as one of the best of the songpoets. If this continues, Randy will have one problem to face in his work.

Up to now he has been able to rely greatly on humor in displacing the emotions of his listeners. But this can backfire by forcing him to pay less attention to more serious statements. Where it's easy to get a response from songs titled "Why Don't We Drop the Big One?" or "Burn On, Big River," it's increasingly difficult to get an audience to confront death and banality and pain, as in "Old Man."

Newman faces this choice now.

LAURA NYRO—THE CITY SONGPOET

A T the Monterey Pop Festival, June 1967, Jimi Hendrix, recently arrived from England, tore the audience apart with a piercing rendition of Dylan's anthem "Like a Rolling Stone." Also at Monterey, a San Francisco keypunch operator strode onto center stage and became Janis Joplin, a symbol of blues and tragedy for a generation.

And at the same festival, an unknown Bronx-born singer/ songwriter sat down at a piano, wearing a dress with a huge black angel's wing at the shoulder, and backed up by a group of musicians and singers who had not had time to comprehend, let alone do justice to her complex music, promptly became the laughingstock of Monterey. She was booed, insulted and banished by the crowd.

Time has proved the crowd to be a bunch of blind, limited boors, and time has proved Laura Nyro to be one of the best of the songpoets.

Born in 1947 in the Bronx, the daughter of a trumpeter/piano tuner and his wife, Laura Nyro is the one native-born New Yorker among the songpoets, and it shows in her sensual, soul-tinged rock-and-roll music. Of all the songwriters we have, she is the one who has shown herself capable of producing an end-less stream of single hits, while at the same time moving off in musical directions that others have either given up on or failed to notice. She has faved up to the gamble of commerciality and prevailed; her music has consistently gone into modes of rock and songpoetry that no one else has either the ability or the will to explore.

No matter where her music takes her, New York with its dirt and its funk and its people is central to her work. She is like a lover to the city—which seems a miracle at a time when many hold the city a destructive force. But as an artist, Nyro perceives and captures something of the city's humanity and its compli-cated joys and emotions. Her songs say sweet things about it, without romanticizing its ugliness or anger.

Nyro is a graduate of the High School of Music and Art, a very special institution that sits on a hill near the upper tip of Manhattan, close to the main campus of City College. There the city's most musically and artistically gifted teen-agers pursue a course of study that emphasizes their special skills. Nyro was a below-average student, but was recognized by her teachers and schoolmates as an exceptional singer and performer. During her high school years she accompanied a variety of street-corner rock-and-roll groups in what were then classics. Her most re-cent album is a collection of just these kinds of songs, and it is not difficult to imagine Laura Nyro singing them in the same subways stations that Columbia pictures in its publicity for her album. Even her most avant-garde work retains traces of the dramatics and urban intonations of a capella street-corner rock-and-roll.

After high school she worked as a mother's helper and began to make the rounds of publishing houses trying to sell her songs. She had been writing since her early teens, beginning with parody lyrics of then-current rock-and-roll hits. She finally signed with a pair of older publishers who really did not under-stand her personality or music, and their efforts in her behalf reflected that lack of understanding.

"They brought me an image-maker," Nyro told an interviewer.

"His name was Terry Cloth. He had a huge gap between his teeth, and, like, he looked at me like he wanted to devour me."

Terry Cloth was not much of an improvement. He had her involved in such stunts as dressing up in a wedding gown to push her first single for Verve-Folkways, "Wedding Bell Blues." This single, released just before her first album in the fall of 1966, had some sale on the West Coast, but Laura Nyro remained pretty much an unknown in New York. There was little doubt, though, that she would become a star. She herself, apparently, was her own best reassurer.

"People say, 'You're going to be a big star,'" Nyro told Michael Thomas of *Eye*. "Well, I really feel that I always have been a big star. I really believe that."

Her first album was released by Verve in 1966, and although it didn't sell many copies, it contained some of the freshest pop songs and performances to be released since the Beatles crashed the American scene in 1964. Bob Dylan might be out there thrashing his own soul and those of his contemporaries, and the Beatles might be lost in a haze of pot smoke and circus imagery, but Laura Nyro proved herself a popular songwriter in the manner of the early rock follow-up writers. She turned out an album of slick, strong pop singles, one after another. A good number of those songs have since been hits by other artists, and the album has been ransacked by everyone from soul groups to marching bands. Laura is, after Dylan and the Beatles, one of the most covered of performers, with dozens of artists and groups rerecording her material.

Quite a surprise after the response at Monterey by the hip elite of England and the United States.

No matter: Nyro has proved them all fools long since, and her music will outlast their sniping criticism. She has taught her audience to accept her for what she is, which seems to be something between a saint and a streetwalker. She is one of the few writers who can write a religious number that has the sensuality of a sexual overture. She has somehow detected the sensuality in religious fantasy and has been able to translate that perception in musical terms.

Although the first album does not have many of the later, more elaborate, songs, it does give an indication of Nyro's ability as both a performer and a writer. Even though surrounded by inappropriate and often schmaltzy arrangements, and apparently prevented from presenting her music with all its rhythmic eccentricities, Laura shines through with songs like "Wedding Bell Blues" and "And When I Die." Although there is much lyrical sophistication here, these songs do not compare with her subsequent intensity or experimentation.

For me, the two strongest cuts are "Flim Flam Man" and "And When I Die." "Flim Flam Man" is a short, swinging number that is a polished portrait of the perfect con man, with lines like "Oh, Lord, the man's a fraud" or "His mind is up his sleeve" popping up all over the place, and the composer singing with obvious pleasure what she'd written and whom she'd written about.

"And When I Die" is a rather mature statement for a nineteen-year-old, assuring us that for every death "There's one child born/ In the world to carry on." Ostensibly the song is about death, but it's joyous; it's filled with religious excitement, joy at the prospect of life lived well and then a passing on to the next chapter. In its music and in its lyric, "And When I Die" sounds as if it had escaped from an advanced Broadway musical. One can easily imagine a character out in the middle of the big stage summing up his life-style, and when Blood, Sweat and Tears made the tune into a big hit, they gave it just that feeling, though their version sounded a bit too much like "Oklahoma!"

There is not a clunker on *Laura Nyro: More Than a New Discovery*. Yet it must be said that none of the songs cut very deep. They are calculatedly commercial packages, and one can almost hear Terry Cloth chortling in the background. Just as it must have confused the hell out of the businessmen around when Van Morrison came up with *Astral Weeks*, the next set of Nyro songs must have caused consternation among her associates.

The new songs, released on Laura's first effort for her new

label, Columbia, *Eli and the Thirteenth Confession,* were the
ones she had tried to get across at Monterey. Perhaps this would
be a good place to quote what I assume is an eyewitness description of the Monterey fiasco. Either way, Michael Thomas,
writing in the now-defunct *Eye,* gives a good description of the
debacle:

"Laura went on stage at this high-class hootenanny, with all
the glittering pop aristocracy there, all the way from England,
some of them, all psyching her act—who *is* this chick, in her
Vegas drag?—and what she had in mind to do was a show, like
the old spade rock 'n' roll shows at the turn of the decade, the
shows that Motown groups do now with a little more flash, but
nobody at Monterey knew what they were seeing.

". . . But she failed perfectly at Monterey, because she did
something unheard of, and she did it rashly, and nobody there
was ready for it."

And all one has to do is sit down and give a careful listening
to *Eli* to realize how deaf the derisive crowd at Monterey really
was. The album is a monument in songpoetry, along with
Astral Weeks and Dylan's *Highway 61* and Joni Mitchell's *Blue.*

Again, there are no clunkers, but this time there are a new
depth and an entirely original feeling to the whole affair. Forget
the kitsch, the overly dramatic Magdalene cover photo, the per-
fumed lyric sheet blushing with color. Forget the few moments
when the arrangements get out of hand and begin to sound like
the Royal Philharmonic on a cocaine binge. Listen to the songs
and the performances. The album took nearly a year to make,
and cost so much that to this day Columbia executives shudder
at its mention. But in a time of excessive studio meanderings,
this album stands out. From the first notes it is clear that Terry
Cloth and his ilk have been banished from Nyro's life, that she
is her own woman, making music to please first herself, with
all the reels of tape and all the engineering overtime, and then
her public.

What makes Nyro the unique songpoet she is is an ability to
draw upon both her street smarts and her extensive fantasy life,

which is most likely a reaction to her involvement with urban existence.

Another aspect of her work worth noting is a marked spiritual inclination, which fused with her fantasies and her feelings about poetry and the stress of urban life to produce what one critic has called her "religio-erotic" songs. She told the same interviewer that she once considered becoming a nun but gave up the idea, and it is clear that she intends the confusion of religious and sexual imagery that fills her songs, especially those on *Eli*.

Musically, Laura never leaves the sphere of rock-and-roll. There is always something of those days singing with Puerto Rican rock groups in her work. One can detect her rock background in both her use of language and the constantly changing rhythms.

Although there are those who have written and spoken of *Eli* as a "concept" album, comparable in its own way to *Sergeant Pepper* and similar attempts at extended songmaking, I believe that this is an afterthought. The two sides are marked Part I and Part II, but one would have to stretch one's critical imagination quite a way to find the real difference between them. Unlike *Astral Weeks*, the album does not have a consistent theme or even design. The songs, in fact, sound similar though that may be attributable to the work of the arranger and the musicians and to the closeness in time of their writing.

The album opens with "Lucky," with Nyro saying to the world, "I'm ready," and within seconds, as the rock-and-roll begins to rise and the joy of her voice shines through, it is clear that she is right. The music is so alive, the rhythm varied, and Nyro uses her voice to back up these changes with wide-ranging dynamic vocal forays. At first the rhythms seem jumbled, but then one begins to see them as elements in the construction of a scene, like a street scene.

One can almost envision the artist looking out the window and watching the many different ways people walk down a street. Here we have the rhythms of a young teen-ager diddy-bopping along, and the slow walk of an old woman, or the exaggerated sway of a hooker. Some rhythms seem to stroll, other to run flat out and still others to take on the sensual strut of seduction.

"Lu" is an uplifting, highly sophisticated version of that old rock-and-roll staple, the dance song. Like "The Stroll" and "The Monkey," this is a song tied inextricably to movement, only here the dance is the Louis, and the movement is more pronounced and powerful. In a way, the song seems a tribute to groups like Martha and the Vandellas, for the effect here is similar to the effect their records attempted. The rhythm is so ingratiating that it would take either a dead man or someone wearing cement overshoes to resist it. The music here depends upon a backbone of guitar riffs, and again it is dominated by rhythmic gymnastics. One can't help wondering what Nyro's first album would have sounded like if she had been allowed the room to experiment with the rhythm that she so obviously has here.

"Sweet Blindness" is a short, swinging excursion into her fantasy land. Here Nyro takes you into a land of moonshine and sin, somewhere upriver in the country of imagination. It is another dance song as well, but the movement is slow and sensual, a physical representation of the sweet, hazy blindness of a good wine drunk. This is a devoutly silly song, with all the coyness and gushing sincerity of a drunk, and Laura plays it for everything it's worth. The music lurches and floats, and if you listen hard enough, you can come up with a sweet contact high.

One of Nyro's city songs is "Poverty Train." No fantasy here, and no romanticizing. The music and the lyric are both heavy with the desperation of poverty. Financial claustrophobia is everywhere, and emotional poverty, and Nyro lays it out warts and all. As a flute provides the backbone of the orchestration, Laura lines out what poverty can do to you, how one can "become God, become crippled, become funky and split." Finally, an escape is found in "sweet cocaine," and the music and the vocal attempt to duplicate the heady, self-assured and detached high of a cocaine user. There are no solutions to poverty here, only a portrait of someone trapped in the struggle for survival in the ghetto. The song ends with one word—spoken by Laura with appropriate wonder and desperation: "Money," she says.

"Lonely Woman" is a torch song and a dirge for all the lonely women—a standard lyric, but delivered in a unique style. Just at the moment when the depression seems complete, Laura switches rhythms and takes off into a sort of ecstasy of despair —as if, having reached bottom, there is nothing to do but boogie and pray. The use of saxophones contributes to the musical variety of this mongrel of an album. There is no musical style of the last twenty years, from bossa nova to cool jazz, from soul to folk-rock, from screamer rock to blues dirge, that is absent. Yet it rarely seems jumbled, and everything fits.

"Eli," the showpiece of the album, though cursed with a few moments of excess, is a matter of heady bedlam. Nyro describes the arrival of some sort of sexual messiah. Here the choice to avoid backup singers and rely solely on overdubs of her own extraordinary voice is a wise move. The song has at least three separate moods, each presented with great effectiveness and intensity. This tune became a hit, with Three Dog Night clipping it a bit and reducing its variety and intensity for the AM kiddies, and helped move Nyro up into stardom. The final bars, when she repeats the theme in a dreamy, wound-down manner, are among the prettiest on the album. The first side ends, and with it the realization that Nyro has managed to produce that record rarity, an entire side without a clunker, without one cut to be skipped during repeated listenings.

One of my personal favorites is "Timer," a song about time and fantasy and about reconciling oneself to the fact of death. In addition, it swings like hell. Nyro sings, apparently to a lover, "I don't want to put you down/But I could walk through them doors/Onto a pleasure ground." The doors give onto the world of childhood fantasy, and the pleasure ground is the world that that fantasy once afforded and can afford no longer. The lyric rails against time, against death at the end of the allotted time, and then, by word and music, effects a reconciliation with inevitability. All that is given is the explanation: "You're a jigsaw, Timer/God is a jigsaw, Timer." In these lyrics songpoetry approaches linear poetry, though the music adds so much that one wouldn't want to separate them.

Nyro proves up to dealing with sophisticated and detailed concepts within the context of modern rock. She offers a pleasant choice. You can listen to hear her view of the world, or you can kick off your shoes and dance. If you're one of those who can do two things at once, like the few who rub their heads and pat their bellies simultaneously, the Lord knows you can do both.

"Stoned Soul Picnic," which was delivered up as a hit single by the Fifth Dimension, is another dance song—like "Sweet Blindness," a fantasy number set in a happy and fertile land somewhere far from the city. Here people don't just arrive, they "surrey on down," and of all the tunes, this is the closest to a throwaway. Nyro is out for fun, and the result is a picnic in a fuzzy paradise with all good things to eat and drink and good company to boot. Again, there are a lot of rhythm changes, and the roots can be found in the best of the soul groups, especially in the Vandellas and Curtis Mayfield of the Impressions.

A love song to a friend, "Emmie" is one of the loveliest tunes Nyro has ever written. The song opens with a gentle, swaying rhythm, and a harp provides a lightness that matches the lyric. The lyric is perfect, simple and complete, as Emily emerges in angelic form, a veritable symbol of loveliness. The song grows organically from a whisper to a roar and then to a shouted chorus of rock-and-roll and joy. Nyro has a remarkable gift for matching music and lyric to motion, and here, when she breaks into a lovely section that begins "Move me, oh sway me," the music follows along into a slow sweet dance. "I swear you were born a weaver's lover/Born for the loom's desire."

"Woman's Blues" and "Farmer Joe" seem to be almost one continuous torch song, with the writer recounting the classic story of the lover scorned. But it is a new kind of torch number with full rock-and-roll orchestra, multiple rhythms and lyrical fireworks. She explores the lyrics until there is nothing more to be found. In a singer of less talent that would be grating, but Nyro pulls it off. The repetitions and reexaminations add to the effect.

"December's Boudoir" is a song about a flaming affair in the midst of the winter, with December's chill and the warmth of discovery. What I think the song tries to say is that when love appears, time disappears. Optimism pours out of the lyric and ends when a mother and father find love forever, with the implication that this might be possible for the two new lovers. The music is typically eclectic but, as always, immersed in the sound of early street-corner rock-and-roll.

The swinging end to an almost perfect album, a shout of love and another rocking dance tune, is "The Confession." This song is about the miracle of love, about becoming a virgin once again. This miracle completed, the music takes off into the rock-and-roll stratosphere, with Laura shouting and wooing more and more sound out of her orchestra and piano. She leaves us with a message, and Lord knows, Laura is not a message singer. The word is "Love is surely gospel," and the confession is complete.

Not too long after the release of *Eli and the Thirteenth Confession*, I saw Laura Nyro give a concert in a large and unattractive skating rink near New Haven, Connecticut. The room was cold, with bare cement floors and cinder-block walls, but the audience, which was dominated by thirteen- to sixteen-year-old girls, did not seem to mind the drabness. They greeted Laura with screams of enthusiasm as she came out alone, a big girl moving with great grace, dressed in a long white gown. On her piano, a bouquet of roses. The impression was of peace and beauty, and one waited for delicate music to match the preciousness of the setting.

Instead, Nyro sat down at the piano and began to rip through her own songs and old rock songs of her teen-age years. The audience was transfixed as she passed from one rock hit to another, giving each one a special, loving presentation. She has a way of treating even the most banal of rock lyrics with seriousness, and it must prove a problem when she is writing. If you can sing *anything* and make it sound important, the temptation must be great to fill your songs with throwaway lines. But if she has such a problem, one doesn't know it from her albums. The lyrics are usually fresh, and the delivery makes them seem even more impressive than when they are sung by anyone else.

There was a lesson from Monterey in that ice-skating rink.

Nyro has opted for simplicity. She accompanies herself on piano and does not risk playing with musicians who don't understand her work and screw it up. She dresses simply and with grace, and when she performs them her songs are clear and musically complete statements. From the size of the crowd at New Haven, it seemed she had found her audience, and that they loved her in that special way in which only young girls love songpoets. Leonard Cohen, even though his voice is harsh and droning, draws a similarly devoted, and similarly young, crowd. The audiences are respectful, unlike most of the audiences at rock concerts nowadays. Laura seems to draw few of the reds-and-wine freaks and more of the intelligent, intense music fans.

After *Eli*, with its fine combination of strong lyrics, widely varied rhythms and strong orchestrations, Nyro moved into a new and chancy realm. She began to try out ballads and to experiment with simpler, more direct means of performance. Her next album, *New York Tendaberry*, was the result of this experimentation, with all its joys and flaws.

New York Tendaberry, released in late 1969, is, on the surface, a much more subdued offering than its predecessors, but this is really not the case. The lack of orchestration gives the impression, at first, of naiveté, but as one sits and listens, it comes clear that while Nyro has abandoned the symphonic aspects of her work, she has moved into new areas in her writing. The songs are actually more complex, lyrically and musically ambiguous, blessed with fresh ideas but cursed with false starts. The total sound is leaner, but the songs themselves are richer in notion, and the performances are way above the usual level of modern singer/songwriters.

The idea, apparently, was to combine balladry, rock-and-roll and new, loose forms of jazz and come up with an entirely new popular music. The attempt fails, but along the way the writer produces moments of sound and emotion unrivaled by her contemporaries. The music winds down throughout, and the words stretch out into long howls of emotion with few coherent statements. For all the rambling and the overextension, when Nyro begins a well-constructed tune—and there are a few here—there are a new clarity and a new intimacy to her work. "Time and Love," the only tune on the album that remotely resembles a commercial single, is a strong rock-and-roll number, full of fun and movement, but managing to remain relatively intimate.

Previously, as in *Eli,* Nyro seemed capable of this feeling only by creating bedlam, throwing in the air much noise from many instruments along with overdubs. Here we have a cleaner, less cluttered rock, and it works brilliantly. Nyro's experimentation with the slower, more intimate ballads may have suggested to her a better understanding of how to perform and record her rock numbers in a less flashy way.

I could also recommend "Mercy on Broadway," another song of a city populated by reefer-smoking women and landlords, street strollers and streetwalkers. Nobody knows how to paint New York the way Nyro does. She loves it so much she doesn't have to put false romantic moods over it. "Save the Country," one of her few political songs, is also strong.

The final impression one gets from *New York Tendaberry* is of a writer gradually reaching maturity and slowly finding self-discipline, overcoming the problems of too-early success. After all, who's going to be the one to tell Laura Nyro when she is being musically self-indulgent, or that a ten-second fade-out can sometimes be more effective than thirty repetitive seconds? This albumn is a mirror of the problem, self-indulgent and sloppy, but mixed in are moments of imagination and inventiveness.

The critical response to *Tendaberry* was a pretty confused affair, with Nyro fans enthusing all over the pages of numerous publications and others, who take a less glorious view of her work, piously doubting her ability to discipline herself. It is extremely difficult to write steadily about recording artists, who, more often than not, are forced by contractual commitments to record every six months or so. An album, therefore, cannot be considered in the same way one might examine a novel, with its years of preparation, or a play or even a movie, with its months of shooting.

An album is more like a short-story collection or a collection of short poems and is usually the result of a frenzied period of work. One can't expect much change or variety in such a short period, yet one judges an artist's evolution and progress. It's a problem that few critics ever really resolve. The upshot is haphazard criticism with few, if any, consistent standards. Nyro has received much harsh criticism, especially after Monterey, but she can also count some of her most enthusiastic fans among the critics. In the end, I feel certain it has little real effect on her work, which is carried on privately in her own cloistered world.

Although Nyro must have been aware of how many of her fans were confused by *Tendaberry*, with her next album she pressed on with her experimentation. *Christmas and the Beads of Sweat* takes Nyro one step further into the future of songpoetry. Blessed with sparkling production by Arif Mardin and former Rascal Felix Cavaliere, and with strong backup work by Muscle Shoals, Alabama musicians and some of the best of New York's studio musicians, this album could, like Van Morrison's *Astral Weeks*, be considered one extended extraordinary song.

Three songs stand out, each radically different from the others. First comes "When I Was a Freeport and You Were the Main Drag," a song of frustration at the restrictions of love and politics. The title is, I believe, a native New Yorker's pun. Freeport, L.I., is the scene of some of the more spectacular drag races in the New York area, and the local AM radio stations have long been full of ads for these events. But the song takes off from this set of puns, to become an expression of rage at a loss of freedom.

"Up on the Roof," the Gerry Goffin/Carole King urban anthem, which was an early '60s hit, is given a slightly artsy interpretation, but as a tribute to both the joys of rock-and-roll and the city, it fits right in with Nyro's style. This is one of the most telling of all rock hymns, for it tells of beauty and the need for privacy simply for dreaming remaining alive in the center of a slum. "When this ole world starts getting me down/And people are just too much for me to face/I climb right up to the top of the stairs/And all my cares just drift into space/On the roof's the only place I know/Where you just have to wish to make it so."

"Christmas in My Soul," Nyro's Christmas prayer, is one of her most overtly political statements. Written at a time when the trials of radicals were popping up all over the country and when the war showed no sign of subsiding, the song is an attempt by Nyro to wish this all away with the sheer beauty of her work. "I love my country as it dies/In war and pain/Before my eyes," she sings. "Madonnas weep/For wars of hell/They blow out the candles/And haunt Noel."

Although *Christmas and the Beads of Sweat* is the result of a natural evolution in Nyro's work, many of her listeners seemed to feel that this was but one more step in the process of an artist killing her work with self-indulgence. The absence of single possibilities, and the introverted nature of much of the song writing on *Christmas* could, I suppose, support some sort of case for Nyro having withdrawn from the mainstream of pop music, but to me it is simply a case of someone having exhausted a form and moving forward.

Therefore, as tempting as it is to attribute the next step in her recording career to the accusations of artistic self-indulgence that followed *Christmas*, this is probably untrue. What she did as a follow-up to *Christmas and the Beads of Sweat* was to step into the Philadelphia studios of R and B producers Kenny Gamble and Leon Huff and turn out a perfect little album of old rock-and-roll standards.

Gonna Take a Miracle, released by Columbia in 1971, is a tribute to rock from one of its greatest experimenters. It is a return to roots—not to the traditional country or folk roots, but to rock's urban roots, to the subway stations and the street corners. It is also the most conservative album of Laura's career, with short songs, each of which is simply presented.

There is little or none of the experimental Nyro here, so the album seems like a respite. But it is charming withal, funky and filled with the simpler and sharper emotions of earlier rock. If Nyro had chosen, she could easily have been one of the great rock voices; she demonstrates it on this album. Her voice is perfectly attuned to the simple rhythms and simple statements of songs that express a world vision in blacks and whites. Early rock is a crystallization of the teen-ager's view of the world, with much emphasis on love and going steady and all the endlessly complicated hassles of early adolescence.

The best cuts on this tribute album are those that retain the simplicity of the originals, but again, as in *Eli*, there are no clunkers. Yet something was missing for me. After much consideration, it dawned on me that what is missing is not in the music but in the listener. This listener is no longer able to summon up the same enthusiasm for early rock, and there are good reasons.

The joys of early rock-and-roll are much touted nowadays, and there seem to be '50s revivals every other weekend. Yet little is said about the realities of the time that spawned rock-and-roll. The '50s were a time of great censorship and cultural repression. Rock-and-roll, with its slightly crazed performers and obvious sexuality, flew in the face of the period. Any simple, heavy rhythm number was a form of cultural protest. This no longer applies. The times, the audience and the music are more complex, and I can't see turning back when we have all come so far with our music.

Yet I am grateful to Laura Nyro for her loving reminders of this period. With this album she acknowledged her debt to early rock-and-roll and managed, at the same time, to come up with new and strong versions of the old hits.

There has been little in the way of original material from Laura Nyro during the last two years, but word has it that she is indeed writing. I recently met her at the recording session of another artist, where she played some of her newest songs. They were as strong as anything she's ever written, a good indication that we can be expecting a new album from her soon. She has been living in a small town on the Massachusetts coastline and, except for infrequent visits to New York, has kept herself isolated from the world of rock.

If there must be a long wait between Laura Nyro albums, and if these albums are, at first, difficult to comprehend and appreciate, I, for one, will be patient. This young woman has given much to rock, but she is still very young and will be with us for many music-filled years to come.

DON McLEAN—AMERICAN PIE

W HEN I was first starting to write this book I decided it might be a good idea, since almost all the artists I was going to deal with were well known, to include a struggling young song-poet. After all, I reasoned, if I'd been writing this book five years ago all of them would have fitted neatly into this category.

About that time I was listening to the radio and a song called "Magdalene Lane" came on. It was an intricate tune, backed by a rollicking accompaniment, and it was, as far as I could figure out, about Hollywood and the Wizard of Oz and migrant workers and many, many things. One chorus caught me. It went: "Over the rainbow/A Kansas tornado/Can twist up a little girl's head." The singer was Don McLean.

A few weeks later I had this McLean fellow over to my house for an interview. I found him bright, articulate and very intense. We had a good talk, and it seemed the "struggling song-poet" chapter was sewn up. After we talked he played me a piece from a song he was working on. It went, "Bye, bye, Miss American Pie."

So much for struggling young songpoets. In a very short time after that interview, "American Pie" had sold over three million singles. McLean's album of the same name has turned platinum, a record-biz term for sales of a million copies or more, and McLean has been accepted at concert halls across the country and around the world.

Even though he no longer has to struggle, Don McLean fits well into this book. His work is an extension of a tradition that includes Woody Guthrie, Pete Seeger and the Weavers, Sonny Terry and Brownie McGhee, as well as his idol, Buddy Holly. Of all the songpoets here, he is most directly the heir of Guthrie and Seeger, in both his music and his general viewpoint. Not that McLean is primarily political or militant. His first album, and earlier unrecorded songs, do have political and militant strains, but what he has taken from Seeger and the political folk singers is something more subtle, something that involves performance and a special sort of direct honesty in his relationship to his audience.

When he performs the most political of his songs, Pete Seeger is engaged in another, much more political act. He has a way of establishing a rapport with his audience that is unmatched. The Weavers had something of the same ability. Perhaps the best way to describe this is to say that these artists never lord it over their audiences. The patrons in the second balcony sense that they are not very different from those on stage singing to and with them.

This is in direct juxtaposition to the star system of show business, with its style of glamour and of chasms between the star and audience. When Elvis Presley appears in concert, one of the major excitements is his isolation from his audience. No one would want to think of Elvis coming out and leaning over to one of his screaming female fans and confessing that he is not very different from any other male, that he eats, shits, screws and worries about losing his hair. But no one would think twice about a Seeger or a Don McLean stepping out and telling his audience, I am just like you, the same idiocies anger me and the same problems plague me.

The advantage of Elvis' method is that he rarely needs to

expose himself; he can easily hide behind the character created by his managers and the media. But the marvelous gift of Seeger's conception and style is that it allows him to reach and touch his audience in a way in which few people can. He moves our intellects and our guts, and this kind of artist–audience contact gives and takes, and brings with it potential for growth and change.

McLean performs with a banjo and a guitar. He rarely uses backup men, even though they appear on his records. "I am lucky in that I have found who I am," he says, "and who I am plays with just a guitar and a banjo."

During the height of the "American Pie" craze, McLean was repeatedly warned that his audiences would expect him to duplicate the recorded version of the hit. Audience after audience and reviewers all over the country proved this wrong. They were disarmed by the simplicity of the music and the complexity of the lyrics and the man. Perhaps more important, McLean was able to survive a difficult situation by keeping the controls in his own grasp. He was able to vary his program as he wished without consulting other musicians and screwing up prearranged orchestrations. But it is not simply the absence of instrumentation that puts McLean in a category with a performer like Seeger. It is something more.

McLean has a way of involving his audience in the experience of the evening. With the advent of the British rock groups and their loud, harsh performances, a distance was created at rock concerts. Some claim that this can be directly attributed to the increase in the use of downer drugs—reds and wine. It is very hard to involve somebody boxed out on reds in anything. You can reach him with loud sounds, for loud sounds can penetrate the downer mist, but even when you've gotten through, the subject has scant energy to respond.

Many concerts at the Fillmore and other rock concerts started to resemble bashing sessions. Bands like Mountain and Led Zeppelin would bash the audiences over the head with their music, and the audiences would respond with sloppy standing ovations, sometimes two or three a night. Because the sound systems were up so loud, it was impossible for a performer to be understood through the feedback of his own amplifiers, even if he wanted to be.

The songpoets, especially Joni Mitchell, Randy Newman and Don McLean, have overcome this distance. It would be convenient to believe that they have distinctly different audiences from the heavier "downer" bands, but there is much evidence that they are the same and that these artists have insisted upon being carefully listened to. McLean, with his wit and intelligence on stage, makes the audience sit up and listen, and then reinforces the relationship with a set of unique sing-alongs. He is perhaps the only performer we have on the pop scene today, short of Seeger, who can get an audience to sing a hymn.

McLean was born in 1945 in New Rochelle, New York, the son of a salesman. His childhood was marked by attacks of asthma and pneumonia, and because of this he was an isolated kid, unable to participate in athletics. "I never had any question about what I'd be," he says. "It was always music."

McLean discovered "folk music," along with millions of other teen-agers, when the Kingston Trio appeared on the scene. But soon after, he was exposed to a record of the Weavers, and discovered happily that there was much more to folk music than the polished commercial sound of the Trio.

McLean fooled around with a number of local rock bands, but struck out as a solo performer in 1963, working his own college and local folk clubs. He played basket houses and small Village clubs, making his debut at the Bitter End at eighteen. He tells a story of that first Bitter End date, remembering a waitress who asked him his age and, when she found out, turned to a friend and said, "What could an eighteen-year-old kid have to sing about?"

During this period McLean was able to meet, pick with and learn from some of the best that our folk music has to offer. Josh White was a major influence on his guitar style, and McLean claims that he is one of the only ones left who can still duplicate White's clean blues style on the guitar. Brownie McGhee and Sonny Terry provided insights into reaching an audience, and the

Weavers were living testimony that a performer could be both real and polished.

In 1968, McLean was selected by the New York State Council on the Arts to serve as its first Hudson River Troubador, with the aid of Lena Spencer, whose Cafe Lena is a godsend to young folk musicians. The job involved a summer of hitching and driving up and down the long Hudson River Valley, performing to crowds small and large. The gig was a rich experience, but perhaps most important was the arrival of Pete Seeger on the scene. Seeger, a resident of the Valley, heard McLean, was impressed and asked the young singer to join his latest project, a re-creation of a Hudson River sloop to be called the *Clearwater*.

The *Clearwater* was to be a vessel of ecological warning. Within a year, Seeger and the Hudson River Sloop Society had their boat and were sailing up and down the Hudson spreading a message of ecological hope. At each stop, whether at Nyack or Cold Spring or Manhattan, the crew would set up exhibits about pollution and then break out the guitars and banjos for a concert.

McLean's first album, *Tapestry*, was a long time in the making and an even longer time in reaching the public. Thirty-eight times record companies turned down McLean, after many promises. McLean describes this period of his life as "excruciating. There were people who believed I was never going to put out a record. I'd tell them and they'd look at me and go, 'Oh yeah?' "

Record companies, for the most part, are run by businessmen, many of whom pride themselves on the quality of their "ears." There seems to be a general belief that success in the marketing or distribution of those pieces of plastic called record albums somehow qualifies one as a judge of the sounds they produce. McLean's situation is a perfect example of how wrong this theory can be, and how it can pummel a young artist's hopes of ever reaching the public.

Tapestry was recorded in Berkeley, California, and produced by ex-Youngblood Jerry Corbitt. Because the album had been so long in the making, its material falls into two categories. McLean had moved from one sort of songwriting to a more subtle, and eventually more successful, type that involved a more personal song. Even so, *Tapestry* is a strong album, with common threads of anger, imagery and style.

It was in *Tapestry* that McLean first wrestled with one of his most pressing problems as a performer: reconciling the sweetness of his voice with the hard edge of much of his material. It would seem to be too much of a contradiction to have a choirboy voice singing lyrics like "I respect the ones you put to death." But with a small bit of vocal adjustment, McLean brings off lines like these. The most effective songs on this first album are those in which he moves from straight politicking into other, more ephemeral realms, as in "Castles in the Air" and "Magdalene Lane."

"Castles" is a swift tune in which McLean declares his intention to leave the city, with its skyscraper castles in the air, and to head for the country, but there is a woman left behind in the city. As in many of his songs, McLean has a way here of inserting a line or two that forces the song above the run-of-the-mill running-away-from-the-metropolis number. "And I will not be part of your cocktail generation/ Partners waltz, devoid of all romance"—and these few lines dramatize much of his generation's objection to the sterility of a dominant mode of city life.

In "Magdalene Lane," McLean tackles another city, Los Angeles (Hollywood, to be specific), but this time focuses more on an abstraction of that strange town. The narrator arrives in Hollywood and confronts the ghosts of its halycon days. He sings of Judy Garland—abstract, as the little girl of *The Wizard of Oz,* and for real; "she died as she walked down the aisle."

The background event is the now-famous auction at MGM studios, during which someone bought Dorothy's shoes from *The Wizard of Oz.* McLean is talking about the brutality of the men who run and ran Hollywood by focusing on the personal tragedy that existed beneath the fantasy glitter: reality and the world of Oz.

As the song ends, McLean splits, complaining that "only the motel man knows my name." The right remark for a city that has a motel on every block. The music beneath all this is light—it rollicks—and the engagement with the harsh lyrics is effective.

Another noteworthy song on this first album is the title tune, "Tapestry," which is perhaps the best statement on preservation of the physical, livable world yet produced by the songpoets. It is succinct and neither pompous nor pretentious. "If man is allowed to destroy all we need/ He will soon have to pay with his life for his greed."

On the same disk there are three songs that show how easy it is for a writer to slide into the role of dogmatic, screeching politico. These are "Respectable," "Orphans of Wealth" and perhaps the weakest song on the album, "General Store." All three make needed political statements, but then slip into the kind of excess that stops an audience from listening to either the music or the message. "Orphans of Wealth" pours out like pus from a wound. McLean lists the horrors of poverty, but by the time the long song ends, the listener is numbed. If a song wants to move its listener to any form of action, numbing must certainly be undesirable. Better to commit oneself to the listener and trust that he will figure it out for himself.

"General Store" uses one of McLean's favorite techniques, which is a sort of song-theater. He creates a dramatic situation, places focus on a character centrally within and then lets the character do the talking. The song, when it works, becomes a cameo theater piece, compact and with a certain power. The problem with "General Store" is that the song is obscure and the meaning stays bogged in the monologue.

"Respectable," in which McLean is attempting to lash out at those who twist justice to their own purposes, also suffers from obscurity and self-indulgent anger. The rage obscures any clear statement—a situation that Lenny Bruce summarized this way: "In the halls of justice, justice is done in the halls." But none of these songs are total failures. Each marks part of McLean's growth, and each contains lines and phrases and music of high quality. *Tapestry* is fascinating for that reason; the listener can follow the writer's progress over a period of time. One can see a difference from cut to cut: a growth of expression and a careful refining of technique.

The album's most impressive song is "Three Flights Up," and it is one of the most innovative songs of its period. McLean creates a building, a family structure, and then follows the situation up the stairs of the building toward understanding. The music ascends along with the narrative. First McLean introduces a young, emotionally troubled girl and then moves up past a party at which a bored matron contemplates death into an isolated room occupied by a lonely man. At the end the connection between these neighbors comes clear. They are all members of the same family, disconnected from one another's needs and feelings.

Finally McLean lifts us out of the scene, moving the audience onto an elevated train and his song into the universal with the lines: "Step off the platform and onto the train/ Look out your window and into the rain/ Watch all the buildings that pass as you ride/ And count all the stories that go on inside/ And then ask yourself if it must be this way/ Should walls and doors and plaster ceilings/ Separate us from each other's feelings?"

Tapestry is filled with compassion which McLean is capable of making very real and visual in his songs. His images are inventive, and he has a way of coming close to clichés and then bypassing them, much as Dylan did. Comparisons to Dylan come easy with McLean, because of his folk origins and his movement through political songs toward more universal statements. But these comparisons are six years too late. For McLean has gained, almost osmotically, from Dylan, but now he is out there at the head of the field, expanding the form and ensuring that it will survive Dylan and the other earlier songpoets.

American Pie was released in November, 1971, and the title tune of the album, an eight-minute-thirty-seven-second epic, got off to a quick start with FM programmers. It was an instant success on every station that programmed it, and eventually the AM disk jockeys, many of whom follow the FM stations religiously, hoping to find something of use, began to edit the long version of the song down into something that would fit their time needs. A minute is worth much more to an AM station in terms of advertising revenue, and there was a reluctance to program a song that would take up nine minutes. When it became clear that there was AM potential for the song, United Artists released a single version, with half the song on each side of a 45-rpm disk. The record went mad, with hundreds of thousands selling each week, and nearly every AM station in the country playing one version or another.

Because so many of the DJs and the listeners viewed "American Pie" as some sort of obscure message about rock-and-roll, it became fashionable to interpret the lyrics of the song, both in print and on the air. One enterprising jock had interpretations printed up and distributed. At one point, he reported that requests were arriving at his station for three thousand a day.

Tapestry, released on a tiny label, Mediarts, sold under fifty thousand copies, but was received warmly by many FM disk jockeys, who especially liked "Magdalene Lane." Mediarts did not have either the money or the staff to push *Tapestry,* and it is amazing that it sold as well as it did. The competition is ferocious, as countless artists release albums only to find them almost immediately in the discount bins. Only the rare and successful artist receives anything but a cursory push from his record company, especially if it's not among the biggest and richest, such as Columbia or the Kinney Group.

And the cost of promotion, including advertising, is tremendous. But if an artist is exceptional (and lucky), he will find followers in at least some of the writers on rock. One of the few advantages of having such a large rock press corps is that it is hard for anything of real quality to slip by without someone's noticing. And one good review, properly reproduced and distributed, can be exploited. I know of one young singer/songwriter who has been able to work for over six months on the basis of one smash review and one song recorded by a name artist.

McLean's first album got the good reviews, and the FM airplay, and this all set the stage for the release of his second album. Luckily, during the interim between the two albums, Mediarts was bought out by United Artists Records, a big company with strong distribution and promotion facilities.

The press reaction to *American Pie* and to McLean was a mixture of hesitancy, fascination and enthusiasm. Within a two-month period, every major publication in the country had printed something about McLean and his music. He was soon booked onto an extensive tour that included such venerable houses as Carnegie Hall, the Kennedy Cultural Center in Washington, D.C., and Boston's Symphony Hall.

Yet in the midst of all this attention, it seemed that most of the reviewers, interviewers, fans and disk jockeys had missed the point of the song "American Pie" and the album from which it emerged. They bogged down quickly in its references to '60s rock-and-roll (and to be sure, the song is full of comments and hints about the Rolling Stones, Dylan, Buddy Holly and the Beatles). But the basic mood of the song, which is the album's opener, is of unrelenting despair. When questioned by a TV reporter as to how he felt about the song's popularity, McLean once replied, "I'm sorry to see that so many people feel the despair I do."

I don't believe it's McLean's fault, or the fault of the song, that its meaning was so widely misunderstood. When a record becomes a hit and is played incessantly by hundreds and hundreds of radio stations, it is bound to be molded into something other than what it was intended to be. But one of the luxuries of this critic business is that once a record runs its course, it can be reexamined in the cold light of morning.

In "American Pie," McLean reviews a fabulous decade of rock-and-roll, beginning with the passionate early songs of Buddy Holly. Holly, who died in February, 1959, in a plane crash, managed somehow to rise above the swarm of rock-and-rollers of the late '50s. His physical image, that of a tall, not-too-pretty type with ever-present horn-rimmed glasses, simply did not fit the required image of a rock-and-roll star. Yet his musical contribution was deep and lasting. His influence is everywhere in the best of rock of the '60s. It is hard to be precise about that influence, but I think it is clear that Holly favored a simpler, country-oriented rock sound, and that he also relied heavily upon a group effort to produce that sound. This was a time when groups were not in vogue, and when subtlety was not a prized element in rock.

McLean is an old fan of Holly's, and he has spoken of him in terms of great respect.

"Buddy Holly was definitely out of the ordinary, and his death was an extraordinary event for me. He was similar to the Stones in a very down-to-earth way. He had a sense of rhythm which was intrinsically his own, uncopiable, and which happened to mirror the life rhythm of a whole generation of people as well. And that's one of the most beautiful kinds of talent there is, when somebody has a life rhythm about them that is not created, compromised or in any way fabricated. It is merely enlarged by the work of others."

After introducing Holly and his death into "AP," McLean then runs quickly through the rise of rock-and-roll in the '60s, stopping briefly to comment on Dylan, Presley, the Beatles, the Byrds and the Stones. But these references are interwoven with the references to the politics of the '60s.

"A good part of what 'American Pie' is about is the question which came first—culture or history? Which influenced which? Well, we all know, because we studied it, that culture and history grow together. They are mates; they influence one another and from that union comes society. That's the song."

Perhaps the key to the whole song is in the lines "The marching band refused to yield." Here McLean puts it to us that in spite of its enormous power, rock-and-roll, and the energy and coherence it represented, was powerless against the omnipresent Vietnam War. The whole song leads toward the conclusion that if rock had once seemed able to drown out the world around us, it no longer pretended to be able to do so. The music dies; it can no longer pretend to shield us from the realities.

The rest of the album takes up this theme and continues it. It tries to illustrate, using different situations and individuals, how each person tries to come to grips with the pressing realities of his time, and how they each fail. No one escapes: not Sister Fatima, who reads fortunes, or the young lovers, who cannot seem to get it together in the face of the world around them. "Vincent," McLean's tribute to the painter Van Gogh, sums it up beautifully:

Starry, starry night, paint your palette blue and grey,
Look out on a summer's day, with eyes that know the darkness
    in my soul.
Shadows on the hills, sketch the trees and the daffodils,
Catch the breeze and the winter chills,
In colors on the snowy linen land.
And now I understand what you tried to say to me,
How you suffered for your sanity,
How you tried to set them free.
They would not listen, they did not know how,
Perhaps they'll listen now.

Starry, starry night, flaming flow'rs that brightly blaze,
Swirling clouds in violet haze reflect in Vincent's eyes of china
    blue.
Colors changin' hue, morning fields of amber grain,
Weathered faces lined in pain
Are soothed beneath the artist's loving hand.
And now I understand what you tried to say to me,
How you suffered for your sanity,
How you tried to set them free.
They would not listen, they did not know how,
Perhaps they'll listen now.

For they could not love you,
But still your love was true,
And when no hope was left in sight on that starry, starry night,
You took your life, as lovers often do;
But I could have told you, Vincent,
This world was never meant for one as beautiful as you.

Starry, starry night, portraits hung in empty halls,
Frameless heads on nameless walls, with eyes that watch the
    world and can't forget.
Like strangers that you've met, the ragged men in ragged clothes,
The silver thorn of bloody rose,
Lie crushed and broken on the virgin snow.

And now I think I know what you tried to say to me,
How you suffered for your sanity,
How you tried to set them free.
They would not listen, they're not list'ning still;
Perhaps they never will.*

American Pie is an album about outsiders—those who cannot, for one reason or another, control their own destinies, and who are bound to suffer. It is a most effective concept album, with a range and a depth that were not at first perceived by many of the critics fascinated with the single of "American Pie."

But one critic did cut through the persiflage surrounding the single. He is David Salner, a young New Yorker and reviewer for a paper called *The Militant.* He is one of the few writers to capture the delicate relationship between music and politics that forms the fulcrum of this important album.

"Throughout the twentieth century, various artists have produced material on the 'American' dream, tragedy, experience, ethic, or whatever else they've chosen to call it. Small wonder that such a monstrous society should claim the attention of the artists, critics, and other mythmakers working in the great American culture factory. It takes a lot of explaining. And as one might expect, the treatment of this theme has often been full of excuses.

"Don McLean's spectacularly successful hit record 'American Pie' ostensibly takes up the theme of the American . . . ('Pie' is certainly as good a word as any other). But fortunately for us, McLean is an artist with no use for the customary excuses.

"More than two million singles of 'American Pie' have been sold in the approximately three months since its release. 'American Pie' has been number one in every area in the United States, as well as in Canada. The album, which includes 10 other songs, has sold more than one million.

"The most striking thing about 'American Pie' is its cunning elusiveness. It's much easier to identify a mood or attitude than to extract a literal meaning from the song. Consequently, the guessing game as to what McLean 'really means' by 'American Pie' has already extended itself into outer space.

"McLean admits to a heavy influence from Woody Guthrie, Pete Seeger, and the Weavers. This important current in American music is very much alive in the 'American Pie' album.

"Another obvious influence is the popular music and culture of the late 1950s and early 1960s. 'American Pie' creates a sort of compendium of 10 years or so of youth consciousness. Every fantasy and delusion that the youth of this period labored under is at least hinted at in these evocative lyrics. But of course the music is central: 'Do you believe in rock and roll?'

"The stages of youth culture, affectionately parodied in this song are 1) the teen-age hero of the fifties ('with a pink carnation and a pickup truck'); 2) the early sixties, characterized by Bob Dylan ('the Jester'); and 3) the period beginning with the Stones (Mick Jagger is 'Jumping Jack Flash,' of course) and the Beatles (it's Lennon, not Lenin, who 'reads a book on Marx').

What comes through most clearly is McLlean's devotion to music. His satirical reflections on the simpleminded aspects of what has sometimes been called the 'automobile-culture' of the late 1950s are muted by his respect for the incorruptible spirit that emerged, amazingly, from this jungle of commercial values.

"McLean has dedicated his album to Buddy Holly, creator of 'Peggy Sue,' 'Rainin' in My Heart,' and many other hits. Until Holly was killed in 1959 in a plane wreck, he was one of the most influential and respected popular musicians. Holly best captured the pure romantic sentiment that many other rock and roll stars of his period aimed at. His influence on McLean is certainly more spiritual than literal or technical.

"Some have wondered if 'American Pie' can be considered a form of social protest, dealing with the commercialism of American life, its plastic values, etc. Perhaps a better way to characterize this record is to call it simply a glimpse, affectionate as well as critical, into the life of a generation that is struggling to free itself from these values.

"A number of other songs on this album are more explicit in their social criticism. 'Grave' for example is a very direct and effective antiwar song. McLean creates the image of a GI sinking deeper and deeper into the shelter of his trench until he is, in effect, buried and dead. Listening to this cut gives you the feeling of watching a movie in which the camera slowly moves in and hovers over a deeply affecting detail: the death of one soldier on an immense battlefield.

"The most hard-hitting song on the album is 'Everybody Loves Me, Baby.' The subject parodied by McLean is a ruling-class-type figure who has internalized the values of a rapacious system. Since conquest is what keeps the social system going, how can his personal system exist without it also?

> Armies go at my command
> my gold lies in a foreign land
> buried deep beneath the sand . . .
> but all the victories I've led
> haven't brought you to my bed.
> Everybody loves me, baby,
> what's the matter with you?
>
> The purest race I've bred for thee
> to live in my democracy
> and the highest human pedigree
> awaits your first born boy . . .
> Everybody loves me, baby,
> what's the matter with you?*

"The representative of this outlook goes on to excuse himself with the flippant remark 'if war is hell I'm not to blame.'

"Several other songs, like 'Vincent,' show how willing McLean is to experiment with themes not usually taken up in popular music. This song is addressed to Vincent Van Gogh and attempts to create a musical equivalent for the disturbing images of the great impressionist.

"Other songs, like 'Winterwood,'" are also worth discussion. If you aren't one of the million who already have, you should get this album so that you can listen to it for yourself. McLean is an extremely ambitious and talented musician. You won't be sorry."

McLean's follow-up to the *American Pie* album, titled simply *Don McLean*, is a tour de force of another color. Here McLean examines the entire process he has been through because of *American Pie* and the response of both the public and the media to the song.

The album is a bit more varied musically and there is no attempt

*Copyright © 1971 Mayday Music, Inc., and Yahweh Tunes, Inc. All rights administered by Unart Music Corporation, New York, N.Y.

to churn out another nine-minute anthem. Instead, McLean turns inward to examine the effects of the unrelenting spotlight on his life. With songs like "The Pride Parade" and "Bronco Bill's Lament," he almost derides his own vanity. "The Pride Parade" seems to be a vicious description of someone who has little talent and too much ego, until you realize that it is McLean singing about his worst fears for himself. "Bronco Bill's Lament," which seems at first to relate to the career of a bogus cowboy star, is more likely a funny and moving self-critique. Here McLean sees himself as someone being led into a situation not of his own making, exploited by others even to the point of mouthing words to await another's voice. The story of this cowboy star, who looks back in amazement and disappointment at his bogus career, could well be the tale of anyone thrust into the center of media attention.

Musically, the album features a subtle use of horns and a subdued tone that is familiar in McLean's work. He apparently still wishes to rely mainly on his voice and guitar to put across what he has to say, and to this day he will not tour with a band.

A sudden rush to stardom has been known to set many a young artist back on his heels creatively, but McLean seems to have weathered the first onslaught.

"Even with a lot of people around you, you're still alone inside your flesh," he told an interviewer. "I don't think I've been antagonistic about the media as much as I've been frightened. The media in effect is telling me what I am, and they have no idea. I've been treated pretty fairly up to now, but the media people haven't finished with me. I'm prepared to be rejected and sacrificed. Actually, I have very little against interviewers as people. Only when they have preconceptions and try to intellectualize about me, accepting what other people have said about me as barometers instead of relying on their own gut instincts.

"The most important relationship is between you and your audience. If you work on that, and give the audience more than just an eight-by-ten glossy picture of what the media says you're supposed to be, then your audience won't forget you after the media has gone chasing after someone else."

OTHERS

R ANDY Newman, Van Morrison, Bob Dylan, Joni Mitchell, Don McLean, Bob Hunter and Laura Nyro are all writers with special and personal styles and something to say for themselves. But there are others whose work shows frequent moments and whole sections of brilliance.

The list includes many who are commercial giants, with sales in the millions of albums. More often than not it is a romantic or sentimental or simple style that captures the popular imagination, rather than a well-written or more complicated or demanding piece. The audience is vast, and those who manage to capture a large portion of it have to have what we call broad appeal.

Dylan, the best-known of the songpoets, can't match the sales of a James Taylor or a Paul Simon. Obviously, mass appeal is no proof of artistry. Some people believe that commercial success is a sure mark of shallowness, and I would be suspicious of a record or a song that appeals to everyone.

All of the artists I have discussed have had success, some more than others, but all have managed to get past the initial taste without becoming addicted.

Included here are some of the almost-unknowns whom I've heard live and who I feel have enormous potential. This is a very tentative prediction and, in this fast-moving business, might be irrelevant by the time this book is in print. But I recommend that if these singer/songwriters come passing through your town you go and give a listen and see if you agree.

NEIL YOUNG

The Buffalo Springfield, one of the best of the mid-'60s rock bands, has produced several singer/songwriters. Stephen Stills has written for and worked with a number of important groups since the Springfield split. Both Jim Messina and Richie Furay have made their musical marks, Messina teaming with Kenny Loggins and Furay leading a country-rock aggregation, Poco. But of all the talents that came together in Los Angeles to form the Springfield, the young Canadian, Neil Young, is the only one who I believe has come close to artistry in his subsequent writing and performances. He has recorded a series of solo albums for Reprise Records, each one full of strong songs, exciting guitar-based music and distinctive vocal performances.

Young's music is simple, and many of his lyrics share this simplicity. He depends a great deal upon his voice, which has a lonesome sound that adds a note of pathos. But when he gets down to it, the man is capable of turning out songs that are ice-clear reflections of the times we're living in and the way young people see them. Most of the songs are very personal affairs, but when Young does attempt a political song, he is likely to come up strong, with a number like "Ohio," on the killing of four students at Kent State University. "Ohio," with its anger and powerful musical stance, is one of the best of the political songs of recent years. Since "Ohio," Young has attempted two other politically oriented songs, "Alabama" and "Southern Girl," but neither of these has matched its intensity.

Perhaps the best songs Young has ever written can be found

on his first two solo albums for Reprise: *Neil Young with Crazy Horse* and *Neil Young*. Here one can find love songs that bite, and long ambiguous Dylanesque statements, some of which hit the mark. The music is prime rock-and-roll on both albums, and the pounding sound adds to the lyrics.

Neil Young contains a few more complex songs like "The Loner" and "Last Trip to Tulsa." "Tulsa" is a long affair, half surrealism, half a sort of road smarts. Each verse is a little more ambiguous than the last; the effect is starkly bitter and resigned. There are some strong lines: "He's a perfect stranger/ Like a cross of himself/ He's a feeling arranger/ And a changer of the way he talks"—"The Loner." "I've been looking for a woman with the feeling of losing once or twice/ I've been waiting for you." Or "Well, she's a victim of her senses/ Do you know her?/ Can you see her in the distance/ As she tumbles by?/ Veteran of a race that should be over/ Can you hear her sigh?/ I've loved her so long."

Young has a special vocal quality that draws empathy. There is something pathetic and weak in the voice, but also resilient. One is slowly drawn into a sympathetic relationship and then hit over the head with images and ideas. It is deceptively simple and very effective. Along with Van Morrison and Laura Nyro, Young has one of the best of the rock voices. Like Nyro, he seems aware that with his voice, he can get away with a certain amount of laxity in writing. This is most apparent on his most recent release, *Harvest,* which has second-rate material and strong vocal performances. Again like Laura Nyro, Young has a discipline problem, and also seems to have trouble meeting the rigorous recording schedule his contracts call for. He is capable of writing the same song four different ways and producing it on two separate albums. He is also guilty of rehashing the same melody in song after song.

I believe Young has the potential to become a major songpoet if he conquers these temptations and overcomes the tendency toward oversimplification and repetition of ideas and melodies. If he doesn't, he can always count on his voice and his guitar to keep him in the ranks of rock superstars. Maybe that's the core of his problem. It's hard to tell a superstar he's slipping and slopping up.

JAMES TAYLOR

After it became apparent that the Beatles had no intention of performing again as a unit, there was an odd series of events. We seem to crave superstars, and we burn them out faster than fast. In rock, this process seems especially violent. Reputations are made on a single album and dashed with a follow-up.

We have seen this happen to Elton John, who burst onto the American scene and is only now being judged critically by his reviewers and listeners, who have temporarily regained their sense of proportion. Joe Cocker was another. Leon Russell, still another. Crosby, Stills, Nash and Young showed that what happens to one can easily happen to four.

Because there is such a craving for kings of rock-and-roll, the new boys in town are not judged with the same critical strictness as the established writers. James Taylor is a typical example. He has made three albums; all should be taken as reasonable reflections of his writing and performance—but he has yet to be critically considered by the rock-writing fraternity, the disk jockeys or his audience.

Taylor is one of those rare media events, a bad case of form without content. He has an individual vocal and musical style and so gets away with murder with many who write about music and many more who listen. His slight and shallow songs attract more attention than those of, say, Randy Newman because his personality and stance are compelling. Taylor persistently repeats himself—droning out the same guitar licks, working over the same subjects. And his albums sell in the millions; he has been elevated to superstar and accepted as a new songwriting genius.

What James Taylor is, of course, is a personality. Like Neil Young, he has found a very effective stance, full of a kind of feigned weakness and an appeal for sympathy. Disk jockeys ruminate over the intimate events behind the lyrics of his biggest hit, "Fire and Rain." Gossip is very fashionable in rock-and-roll culture. The major rock publication, *Rolling Stone,* devotes a good number of lines to who is sleeping with whom, and who is *on* what, and where.

In concert Taylor is a solid performer, and some of his appeal derives from the gossip. One wonders how many of the little girls are there for the music and how many for the thrills and voyeurism about his well-publicized liaisons with other rock people. Either way, he maintains a reticence about the whole business. The rock press and audience have been enough.

After one removes the halo of superstardom, he is slightly better than average as a musician and a writer. His songs are often tedious and hollow. They sometimes seem to be written about a reality that is almost a childlike fantasy of the world. Much is hinted at, but little is done about it. Taylor is much closer to Tin Pan Alley than to Bob Dylan. His songs are carefully prepared commercial creations.

There are reasons for expectation on the three albums—one for Apple and two for Warner Brothers. He has his moments when he finds a way to say something about being young and alive. One such moment is on his latest album, *Mud Slide Slim and the Blue Horizon.* It is a song fragment that touches on war and talks about a platoon's flight from a battlefield. The song ends as the narrator awakens to a beautiful day and an understanding of how blessed life is untainted by war.

A similar moment comes through on his first album in a tune about a mental hospital titled "At the Zoo." Clever lyrics and a pretty good tune touch on the tragicomedy of a modern mental hospital for middle-class kids. But moments like these are rare in Taylor's work. Most of his songs are vague and fitful love songs that indicate very little experimentation and less insight.

Taylor is touted by the trade press and many of his fans as one of the best of our singer/songwriters. He is a thin shadow. It is not surprising that the middle-of-the-road audience should settle on Taylor or Elton John or any of the other shadows, but it's more disturbing that they get the lion's share of attention while the more serious innovators struggle for sales and survival. An artist who is told often enough that he is the best at what he does may well begin to believe it and stop wanting to grow. Only the next few years will tell.

LEONARD COHEN

This Canadian poet is most popular on the Continent. In England he is one of the top-selling artists, and his public appearances are automatic sellouts. In this country he is best known for renditions of his work by Judy Collins, one of the best of the modern interpreters. Somehow, his weak, monotonic voice and meager musical settings for the songs have caught on in Europe, but they have not made much of a dent on the American audience. Yet nothing is impossible in this field, and many of the things now being written as criticisms of Cohen sound remarkably similar to the comments one used to hear about Randy Newman. Cohen may yet catch on here.

Though a poet and singer, he cannot really be considered a songpoet. His roots are solidly in folk music, and there is little trace of rock in his work. Still, he is unquestionably one of the best lyricists and composers around, and is capable of bringing great wisdom and emotional intensity to his work. His songs are richer, stronger statements than his linear poetry. I don't know if you can hear this by listening to Cohen himself, because at least for me, his vocal limitations get in the way, even if there are clever arrangements and strong productions.

Listening to Judy Collins interpreting a Cohen song, his better qualities come clear. He has a gift for images and for creating portraits of desperation or joy, for emotions in general.

"Suzanne," the song that first brought him to the attention of the American audience, is a wildly romantic vision of a lover. It is so romantic a statement, with its visions of a saint who lives down by the river and the garbage and seeks to touch the poet's "perfect body with her mind," that it left itself open to parody. Randy Newman soon came up with a "Suzanne" of his own, a portrait of a lecherous type who specializes in stalking young women. As Newman likes to say, it is Leonard Cohen on a much lower moral plane. At the same time this all has its humor value (the Newman song is one of the funniest and most perverse he's ever written), it does point up a problem in Cohen's work.

Cohen's romanticism simply does not seem appropriate to the times. At his most vitriolic, the man still sounds as if he is speaking of another world, a world in which characters feel so intensely and in which colors glow and moods are unbroken. Cohen's novels are not as precious, and I've been hoping that he will manage to convey some of that grit and weight in his songs.

If that happens, Cohen could emerge as an important song-writer, and if he adds a bit of good old rock-and-roll, he might find a particular way to talk about things. Cohen's appeal could be broader than young girls and Britain.

JIMMY WEBB

It is extremely rare to emerge whole from commercial success. Jimmy Webb, who is responsible for many of the hit songs of other performers, has recently started on a solo career, recording for Warner Brothers and performing in small clubs.

Although I have not yet watched him perform, I studied his two albums with great pleasure. Both are flawed, but cannot be ignored. The Webb who appears on these two albums seems a far more serious and talented fellow than one would expect on the basis of songs like "Up, Up and Away" and "MacArthur Park," an endless lament with a key image of a city park resembling a great cake with melting icing, repeated countless times. Yet even in the man's most commercial efforts, like "Paper Cup," a frantic and sad little song about a man who feels his life is trapped, or "Galveston," a song of a soldier fantasizing his return home from battle, there are traces of originality and the ability to convey emotion and ideas.

His latest album, *Letters*, released in the summer of 1972, is the most sophisticated thing he's ever done. Webb does not have a good rock voice, but he is learning slowly to make it at least distinctive. One does not have to have a huge voice to sing rock. What is more important is to develop it so that it can rise above or pierce through the thick sound that generates so much of the power of rock-and-roll.

There are lapses here, especially in one number called "When Can Brown Begin?" in which Webb gets lost in a kitchen of metaphors (pepper and salt, water and fire) while trying to handle the issue of race.

The album, with all its flaws, represents one of the best efforts I've heard in a while. Webb is trying seriously to expand his form, to deal with emotions and experiences not traditionally open to the songwriter. And he is succeeding, with bitter numbers like "Campo de Encino" and "Catharsis," with biting comic numbers like "Once in the Morning" and with love songs that are fresh and telling. The one tune that he has not written on this album is a gem, "Love Hurts," a product of a time when rock-and-roll made few statements of true emotion. The cynicism of "Love Hurts" and the pain are strongly and plainly represented, and I think I understand what it is about the song that made it attractive to Webb.

JOHN LENNON, PAUL McCARTNEY AND GEORGE HARRISON

The three names above represent the songwriting talent of the Beatles, the most influential rock band in history. Each is now embarked on a solo career, and one of the pities of modern pop music is that all have failed to achieve anything that comes close to their work together. I could never write enough here about the Beatles and the debt that is owed to them by all songpoets and all rock-and-rollers, let alone the debt that is owed by those whose life-styles have loosened up because of their worldwide impact. When they were Beatles, these three seemed to be almost dream figures in a dream group. Their talents meshed so well that many people cannot pick out a Lennon tune or a McCartney tune from the Beatles' work.

After the Beatles broke up, there was a short period of grace during which very little was heard from any of them. But in the last three years we have heard a great deal indeed. Lennon has released a series of solo albums. McCartney has done the same, and Harrison has presented the world with one mammoth three-record set and the Bangladesh concert recording—one of the most exciting "live recordings" ever released.

Lennon has chosen two radically different approaches for his work. First he released an album that represented his involvement in the primal therapy of Dr. Arthur Janov, a popular West Coast therapist. The therapy may have gone well, but the songs were disasters. Gone were the spirit and the humor of the Beatles, replaced by a kind of public self-pity and self-excoriation.

The old Lennon was in there somewhere, but it was a strain and a pain to find him. We were treated to almost tuneless, egomaniacal observations. The album was dressed up in affected complexity. Actually, it is a simplistic piece of work and, in its vaguely expressed obsession with interior and obscure problems, a very limited one. Lennon is gifted with what must be the great rock voice of our time, and his guitar work has always been exciting and inventive, but neither came through here.

The latest Lennon, "Sometimes in New York City," is a catastrophe, not even up to the worst of the political rock bands that emerged in the late '6os. Employing a second-rate New York backup band and the questionable talents of his wife, Lennon has managed a piece of real triteness. "Woman is the Nigger of the World" is a good example of why it is so tricky to mix politics with rock-and-roll. Many program directors of radio stations found it impossible to put the song on the air because of the language. I find it impossible to put the song on the record player because of its ugliness.

And as for Yoko Ono, the less said the better. There is nothing to recommend this young woman's music at all. Her own albums are sonic nightmares—endurance tests for the listener.

Lennon is lolling in self-indulgence. First he inflicts simplistic and unlovely bits of superfluity on his listeners. Then he showcases his wife, who would have trouble getting a record contract out of the Jazz Composer Orchestra Association. If the man somehow manages to get his wife off his records, and begins again to write songs that have some meaning and relevance to his listeners, he will do a great service to record reviewers and other humans.

McCartney and Harrison are in less troublesome situations. Neither has ever tried to claim the role of songpoet. McCartney is a purely commercial artist and he is good at what he does. He is assured a long career making music for car radios and elevators.

Harrison, with his religious leanings and personal ideas about orchestral rock-and-roll, will find that same audience. His greatest gift has always been his guitar work, and in his album and his Bangladesh recording, that's what dominates. Religious rock-and-roll has proved a huge dud, converting few and not helping the growth of the form at all. What does contribute to the advancement of the form is Harrison's ability to build a wall of guitar sound and still present an audible vocal. I hope some other, more capable songwriter will be able to use this in the future. It is wasted on Harrison.

In retrospect, we must now see the Beatles as a great band, a group of experimenters and artists who had achieved great liberty by their own commercial success. But they were not songpoets. Their work was simplistic, limited, and never really had a chance to develop into something of more than passing interest. As individual artists, they are nothing much to write about and nothing, really nothing, to get excited about.

PAUL SIMON

If Paul Simon had not departed Simon and Garfunkel and released his first solo album, he would surely not be included here. I have always been skeptical about the supersensitive and superslick songs on which S and G built their reputation. Simon seemed trapped in the kind of preciousness and overdramatic poetry that wows high school classes across the nation. The students who listen are capable of perceiving the poetry in Simon's work, if only because he has been writing at their depth for years. But now, with his first album on Columbia, Simon has moved up to confront the world and the emotions of adults. And if he is not a total success, he has made a start.

He has always been a skillful commercial songwriter. Somehow the mantle of "young alienated poet" fell upon his shoulders with his first successes, and he took years to shake it off. I've always enjoyed his songs for what they were—simple pop creations a small notch above the great run of singles. His attempts at becoming the Edgar Lee Masters of the LP, while often embarrassing, had the mark of a performer who knows how to draw an audience into his own world.

Now, with his solo album, Simon uses his talents for intimate communication with a mass audience, and manages songs that probe a bit deeper. The production helps this, because it is less cluttered and more unobtrusive than that on Simon's earlier efforts as part of Simon and Garfunkel. Here the songs take precedence.

Among the tunes that illustrate just how much Simon has grown are "Mother and Child Reunion" and "Run That Body Down." "Mother and Child Reunion," which Simon has told interviewers he wrote after the death of his dog, has a lyric that examines some feelings about death and abandonment, sung over a modified Jamaican reggae musical track. The music is driving, the track is simple enough to allow the lyric to emerge with strength and clarity and the lyric is superior to the preciousness and overdramatization of those in his earlier work. "Run That Body Down," along with another tune, "Everything Put Together Falls Apart," explores the preoccupation of Simon and many of his contemporaries with their health and emotional well-being. The song is very simply stated and captures the obsessive thoughts that a young man in his middle twenties might well think when confronted with the first signs of his body's aging. "Everything Put Together Falls Apart" is a warning, soft and subtle, against dependence on drugs. Simon is intelligent enough to realize that his audience would not listen if he were to turn out an Establishment-oriented attack on drug use. Instead he makes his point briefly, that point being that if you have to hold your life together with drugs, eventually the drugs will fail and you'll be worse off than when you started, possibly even dead.

There Goes Rhymin' Simon, his second solo album, was released in the spring of 1973. With this masterful recording, Simon established himself as a solo artist once and for all. "Kodachrome," the first cut on the album, succeeded as a single.

Compared to the first album, *Rhymin' Simon* is stronger and even more varied. There is no one category into which a recording this eclectic can be dropped, but there is a gospel feeling to many of the cuts, and Simon utilizes the talents of such well-known gospel groups as the Dixie Hummingbirds and the Swan Silvertones. On one delightful cut, "Mardi Gras," Simon mixes the beat of current New Orleans music with the soaring, traditional sounds of the Onward Brass Band.

The lyrics here are Simon's best. He seems to have realized that his solo career demands that he make more of his lyrics than he ever had to with Simon and Garfunkel. In addition, he does not hesitate to double- and triple-track his own voice, to provide a richness that seemed lacking on his first solo effort.

What this album proved Simon to be is the Cole Porter figure among the songpoets, the slick New York sophisticate capable of integrating many influences into his work. As for what he has to say, most of it is still slight, but he is clearly on his way toward making a more effective, coherent emotional statement. Perhaps soon we will have a Paul Simon album that seems more complete. If and when it comes, it will surely be one of the better-produced records of our time.

Simon is a master of pop production. His recordings, especially the later ones, are filled with moments of sound that are the result of careful planning, hard work and inventiveness. Unlike many writers who feel uneasy in the technical labyrinth of the modern studio, Simon apparently thrives on the very complexity of recording, and this has greatly improved his recorded work over the years.

Still another attractive feature of Paul Simon's work is its eclectic quality. He takes his time making his records and spends a lot of money in the process, but he spends it well, traveling all over the world to find the perfect musicians for each of his songs. Thus his first solo album was recorded in Jamaica, Paris, San Francisco and New York, and in each of these cities Simon found the right musicians to add to his record.

CAROLE KING

There was a time, back in the early '60s, when Carole King, with her partner and then-husband, Gerry Goffin, were considered the best follow-up writers in the music business. They would sit in offices and churn out hit after hit for groups like the Drifters and artists like Aretha Franklin. Goffin wrote the lyrics, and Carole contributed the strong, bleached rock-and-roll.

Now, nearly ten years later, Carole King is back in the public eye. Nothing essential has changed, and that is the prime complaint with King's work. There have been some small changes. The music has expanded incredibly, thanks to a few of the artists discussed in this book, and songwriters are allowed much more liberty now than Goffin and King ever conceived as possible. The artist performing his own material has also become a current phenomenon, and so King does just that. But what she performs and the way in which she performs it confirm that she has not been able to absorb the important things that have gone on in music over the last ten years.

Her songs are shallow, and they are performed with a seriousness and intensity inappropriate and unnecessary. Trite ideas are presented as if they were totally new insights about human interaction. Of course, she is attracting a huge following, for if what she does is formula—and one that has always been successful with the vast middle-of-the-road market—her music is warm and easy to take and her voice, although no virtuoso instrument, is capable.

But what we have in King is as good an example as any of the commercial songwriter unable to comprehend the freedom open to her. She could explore and rise above vague generalities, but she is either unable or unwilling. Thus she sells millions and millions of records and goes nowhere creatively.

LOUDON WAINWRIGHT III

As I mentioned when writing about Randy Newman, one of the key problems facing any songwriter capable of both great insight and great humor is to avoid keeling over in one direction or the other. Humorous songs, especially numbers that bite, are easy crowd-pleasers, and it is a real temptation for an artist to fall into the role of comedian. Newman seems to be managing a balance, with songs that are often both humorous and full of ideas. Loudon Wainwright III, a young, New York-based singer/songwriter, is facing the same problem and not doing quite so well.

From his first Atlantic album, Wainwright showed himself capable of witty numbers that sting. But what impressed more about that first album was the numbers like "Schooldays" and "Central Square," in which the humor was another tool in the presentation of strong emotional statements. The funny songs were very funny, and Wainwright had a way of presenting them that was charming and inviting, but they were clearly not of the poetic caliber of his best work.

On stage Wainwright proved to be a wonderfully mad performer, the rare individual capable of exposing almost any emotion with his facial expressions. His sweet voice expressed both mockery and innocence.

But when his second album appeared, it became clear that he had limited himself to the role of comic singer. And there were no "Central Squares" to be found. The songs attempted to combine humor and pathos, with mixed results. Perhaps the best song on the album, "Be Careful, There's a Baby in The House," in which Wainwright pointed out how difficult it is to

fool a child, could be the ultimate comment on generation gaps
and such. But even this song tumbles too often into easy cute-
ness.

Wainwright has recently released a new album on Columbia,
and although there are some improvements in the balance, the
vaudeville side of Wainwright continues to prevail. He brings
a rock-and-roll feeling to everything he does, whether it is with
a backup band or alone, but turns out sparse little songs that
say something, but never enough.

JESSE WINCHESTER

There have been few love songs to America written in the '60s
and early '70s. The reasons for this are obvious: the war, the
draft, dope and the generation gap. But Jesse Winchester, who
has released only one album and whom I have never heard in
person, has written some of the only songs that seem to have any
real feeling for the troubled country we live in. Perhaps this has
something to do with this young singer/songwriter's perspective,
for he is one of those who chose Canada over Vietnam. Unable
to return to this country, he writes and sings music full of longing for people and places on this side of the border.

The two albums Jesse has released, for Bearsville Records, are
mature pieces of work. One was produced by Robbie Robertson
of The Band, who provides some backup guitar. This alone
would be a strong incentive to buy such a record, but there is
much more than Robertson present. Winchester has a way with
his music that few others writing today have, and he is apparently able to express much of what is being felt by a lot of
young people.

JANIS IAN

This young woman first came to public attention at the age of
sixteen, with a wordy, searing comment on interracial dating

titled "Society's Child." She was hailed as a teen-age prodigy, shared a television show with Leonard Bernstein, released another few albums and vanished from sight. Her songs then were highly emotional creations, and her insights were often accurate and a bit frightening coming from one so young.

Now she has chosen to return to songwriting and performing and is in the process of preparing a new album. I have heard only a bit of the new material she is writing, but one song, "Stars," in which she sings frankly of what it is to feel the hot flash of success at such an early age, is the stuff of which classics are made. This seven-and-a-half-minute song should be required listening for those who are struggling to become public figures in this field. It deals brilliantly with the conflicts and the joys.

I'm not much on predictions, but if there are more songs like "Stars" rolling around in the back of Janis Ian's mind, she will be a figure to be reckoned with in the '70s.

ROLF KEMPF

This young Canadian is best known in this country for his composition "Hello Hooray," recorded by Judy Collins and, more recently, by Alice Cooper. That song, a poetic and wonder-filled invitation from a performer to his audience, is but one example of Kempf's capabilities. He has started on a recording career in the United States, and from all indications (and a few guest appearances at New York clubs), he will make a strong impact here as both an artist and a songwriter. Kempf's music is strong, but it is his lyrics that are most interesting to me, and he seems to have the ability to bring to songwriting some of the romantic intelligence of the Irish poets. He is free in his use of language, yet never seems to go overboard with his obvious romantic leanings. I look forward to his album.

DIANA MARCOVITZ

It is surely hard to judge an artist on one short listening, but

Diana Marcovitz' appearance at the Philadelphia Folk Festival of 1972 has tempted me into including her. She is a charming performer, whose music draws on ragtime piano, and her lyrics on the best of the humorous songwriters. This Philadelphian is potentially the female answer to Randy Newman with her lyrics full of wryness and oddball wisdom.

Her image is that of a tarnished cherub, and her songs are subtle combinations of a feigned innocence and an urban Jewish consciousness. She sails through material that bites and is totally, wonderfully original. One line that sticks out in my mind is "Even God has a job/ He saves the Queen." If Marcovitz continues to write lines like that, and continues to put them to her own special form of ragtime, she will attract a large and loving following.

JACKSON BROWNE

One of the best ways, and the most common, for a singer/ songwriter to find his way into the public ear is by having his songs recorded by other, better-known artists. Jackson Browne, who has been a feature on the L.A. music scene for a number of years now but only recently released his own first solo effort, is an example of this. His songs were recorded by Tom Rush and a number of others before he began his own recording career, and they guaranteed that his own material would receive much more than the passing attention usually accorded a new release by a young songwriter.

Browne's first album, on Asylum Records, is an exceptionally successful debut, one of those rare records where nearly everything fits. Granted, there are moments of dullness, and Browne does have the young writer's penchant for repeating himself, but in general, the songs on this album are as good as anything else I've heard recently or better.

Browne is apparently aware of the power of songpoetry, for his music is an almost living definition of the form. He has taken the subtlety and honesty of folk lyrics and combined them with a rock-and-roll feeling. It is not surprising that the album produced a hit single, "Doctor My Eyes," for it very much is a rock-and-roll record, even though it features little in the way of histrionics. What it does have is a special sound, produced by a well-balanced combination of Browne's voice and a small rock group.

Browne's songs are commercial entities, but unlike Carole King and James Taylor, he has managed to maintain a very special sense of reality in his work. At the same time the tunes are fun to hear on the radio, they also manage to display emotions not usually touched upon in commercial releases. The lead song of the album, "Jamaica Say You Will," previously recorded by the Byrds, has all the markings of a commercial rock song: the hook, or repeated chorus that sticks in the mind; the small plot, easy to comprehend and associate with, and the high beauty of Browne's warm voice.

But the song has more: a sort of built-in longing that goes beyond the usual love song. Browne manages to sing a short songpoem about a girl and her departure in such a subtle manner that one understands the power of the call that compells her to go. This is undoubtedly superior writing, and the rest of the album, if not as effective as this lead tune, is of nearly equal complexity and quality. So with James Taylor you've got deceptive complexity and with Jackson Browne, deceptive simplicity. I much prefer Browne's work, and I'm sure his subsequent albums will prove him to be one of the most important young writers we have.

RADIO—THE RISE OF FM

⊺HE rise of the songpoets can be directly traced to the rise of FM radio as a new and freer medium of communication. Bob Dylan, the first and most important of the songpoets, could not find his way onto the airwaves even as late as 1964. Before 1965, rock-and-roll music was relegated to the AM band. But in the wake of an FCC ruling that challenged stations to vary their AM and FM programming, a number of contemporary-rock FM stations were formed. These stations had to find something other than middle-of-the-road Muzak to satisfy the FCC, and they turned to the emerging rock scene. In New York, WOR-FM and WNEW-FM were two of the first stations to adapt to the ruling. Only then did Bob Dylan begin to find his music on the air in New York City on any kind of regular basis.

Very few of the artists discussed in this book would have drawn airplay in the old, pre-1966 days. AM programming was usually limited to a tried-and-true playlist, often supplied to the station by an outside consultant, like Bill Drake. In New York, a record would not come on the air unless it had been proved to be a hit elsewhere in the country. This policy still holds true for one New York AM outlet, WABC. But with the new FM programming, a whole new host of recording artists were able to find an audience. This process was by no means limited to New York. Every major city in the country now has at least one good FM station, playing the music of the songpoets along with a varied and challenging program of other sounds.

Eventually the new FM programming began to affect the AM playlists, and today there are many records that jump from FM to AM. All the AM stations really care about is a record's position on the charts of the three major music-trade magazines: *Billboard, Cash Box* and *Record World.* These chart positions are determined on the basis of radio play and sales, and one can easily understand why it was once extremely hard to break a new artist into this self-sustaining circle. Now a record can be heard on FM, begin to sell and thus find its way onto the charts and be picked up by AM stations.

It would be incorrect to assume that the FM stations that have developed over the last six years are the representatives of some counterculture. On the contrary, they are most often simply extensions of AM establishments, with all the traditional reticence and commercialism of their parent stations. It is true that many of these stations seem to pride themselves on being a part of the radical community, but essentially, they are no more a part of that community than the manufacturers of the clothing, pimple creams and records they tout on the air.

What these stations have done is open up the music business to a host of new artists and ideas. Two of the biggest-selling artists, James Taylor and Carole King, both found airplay on FM long before they became the top AM artists. But even if the FM stations are commercial ventures and essentially separate from the community they serve in many ways, they still have a great influence upon that community.

As in the next chapter, in which Joe Smith describes the business end of the songpoets' lives, I thought it would be best here to seek out a typical representative of the world of FM. I spoke to a number of FM disk jockeys across the country and eventually settled on one, Dave Hermann, who was with WPLJ-FM in New York but has since left that station for a rival, WNEW-FM.

I first met Dave in Philadelphia, where he was the most popular jock on a leading FM station, WMMR-FM. He is a man of about thirty-five, whose long hair and clothing mark him as someone who sides with the young life-style. As you read this interview, however, you will surely notice that Dave, unlike the young people he addresses with the music, has had to radically change his life in a conscious manner. Many of the FM disk jockeys have had to go through the same change from AM to FM, and some have made the transition more gracefully than others.

A constant source of satire in the underground press is older types who attempt to stuff themselves into new life-styles in order to profit from both the money to be made and the new freedoms. It would be easy to parody someone like Dave Hermann, but I believe it would be wrong. His sincerity impressed me, and he struck me as one of the few people I've met who have taken drastic measures to change the essential pattern of their lives. I asked him about his background and how he found his way to rock-and-roll.

"I was always into jazz. Being thirty-five, the rock thing really passed me by. Until I was thirty [that was in 1966]. Then I became interested in what was going on, and I was into . . . well, whatever it was, it happened for me in 'sixty-six. Actually, I was into radio and into music, and I wasn't an absolute straight, but my values were straight. My life-style wasn't straight, but my values were. I was still very heavily into my career, and into national fame. I was doing an early-morning music program in Asbury Park, New Jersey, and directing a small radio station down there. Very into radio and into *things*.

"However, my life-style was what would be considered a sharpie. You know, flashy clothes and things—not a restricted life-style. Because of that, I got into drugs—because of my life-style. It was really acid that blew me apart. I'll tell you, it was acid and *Sergeant Pepper*, by the Beatles, which was the first Beatles album I'd ever gotten into. I'd never even thought about the Beatles before that. I had had *Revolver* and I gave it away to some friends of mine. Now I like *Revolver* better than *Sergeant Pepper*. It was *Sergeant Pepper; Freak Out!*, by the

Mothers of Invention, which came out at the same time, and the Velvet Underground's first album. I had those three albums and a little bit of acid, and over a period of four to six months, and by making some new friends, I really went through a real personal rebirth.

"That was in 'sixty-seven, and that's when I decided I can't continue with the kind of radio I'd been doing, so I started to look for a place, and wound up a year later in Philadelphia on FM radio, and into my whole new life. When people ask me how old I am, I generally tell them that my body is thirty-five, but I'm nine. You know, I'm really nine years old. And I really believe that.

"Of the three albums I mentioned before, the one that affected me most is *Freak Out!*, Zappa's album. Again, it was the combination of the acid, too. I don't like to bring the acid up all the time, because I never like to turn anybody on to it. I mean, it's cool, there's nothing in my life I would hide, but when kids call me up and say, 'Should I take acid?' I never say, 'Yeah, because it'll change your life, man, and set you free.' I know plenty of people it did the opposite to, and it fucked them up badly.

"But with me, it was just a combination of the right things at the right time. When I first heard *Freak Out!*, I had no idea what the fuck it was. The music was something that always turned me on, and as I say, I was into jazz, but I just knew, man, that there was something very, very special in the grooves of that record, and I didn't know what. And I had the album for about five weeks or so before I ever listened to it while I was tripped. I happened to listen to it on a night when I was tripped, very, very hard. Those were the days when we'd get it in liquid and drop it on sugar cubes, and you never knew how much you were taking. It could have been thousands of mikes. It was just weekend after weekend of people just filling themselves—just incredible.

"One night I dropped some acid and there were only four people in my house: my old lady and two friends. My two friends were into each other by the fireplace, and my old lady was into her sculpture and all. I threw on a headset and got on by listening to *Freak Out!*, and for the first time I heard those words. I heard them and projected into them in such an incredible degree. When I heard 'What will you do when the labels wear out/On the chrome and the plastic,' and everything —holy shit. Now I knew what this album is all about. It's really about the fact that everything we're doing is fucked up. Everything. From beginning to end, totally and completely inhuman, and off on some weird, insane trip. It freaked me. I couldn't find one thing.

"First, I went into convulsive laughter. I was just convulsively laughing, hysterical. 'Hungry freaks, daddy!' and the supermarkets, and 'Mr. America.' One after another, they were just tearing me up, and I suddenly realized through all this laughter, this convulsive laughter, cosmic laughter that just kind of erupts out of you, suddenly I realized what I was laughing at was myself, and my life, my whole life and everything I felt was useful in it, I was laughing at it.

"As corny and as weird as it sounds, we had two kids, two small babies, at the time. I couldn't even put that together. I couldn't see any value in being a father, or doing anything I was doing, but I did look around and see my two friends, my brother and sister by the fireplace, and my old lady with her sculpture, and I dug very intensely and very incredibly that all there was, man, was just people. All there was was people. I dug that and how alone I was in the universe, and at the same time, how everybody was equally alone.

"We stood alone and we died alone. But also, we were totally and completely together. But if I was going to make any sense of my life at all, I'd have to get involved on a personal level in participation with people, and nothing else matters. You get off on people, and people get off on you, and from then on, every piece of music all related to that same thing, and every book I read related to that same thing, and every great work of philosophy—all the reading and the studying, and the so-called intellectual wisdom that I had obtained during the first twenty-eight years of my life—I had misunderstood, completely and totally; thought it all meant something else, until this one thing brought it all together. And there is only, but one, truth, daddy.

"David Rubinson, who used to be at the Fillmore Corporation and who is now a record producer and all, said that the most revolutionary lyrics ever written were 'Bopa loobop, a lop sham bam.' I agree with that.

"The factors inherent in rock-and-roll music, and even early-fifties music, and why Rubinson said that these were the most revolutionary lyrics ever written, are inherent in the early rock-and-roll rhythm-and-blues, as opposed to Cole Porter, Rodgers and Hart—uptown music, which was really for the privileged classes with this incredible freedom. What some people regarded as little nonsense songs, it was inherent to people who dug it without even realizing why.

"What it is in rock that expresses that freedom is that it's tribal; it appeals to the very core of your soul. Because when you start moving around and thrashing about, or doing whatever you want to do, intrinsic to that kind of dancing, that kind of music, is a mood of freedom, of unrestraint. Let's call it unrestraint, instead of freedom.

"Jazz, even the furthest-out jazz of the fifties, the most avant-garde jazz, was really rather restrained and controlled. Right? And you couldn't even dance to it. But Chuck Berry and Little Richard—especially Little Richard—there was no restraint on them. So it's this lack of refinement, you know, the thing that a lot of people hated most about it. How guttural it was. Totally devoid of class. It's all of that that goes into what the young thirteen- and fourteen-year-olds saw as this incredible freedom. And the nonsense lyrics—'sham a lam a ding dong'—that was the same thing. Again, it was crude; it was crass; it was meaningless lyrics which meant so much.

"The music was coming from the black people, which was an oppressed class. What nobody seemed to realize—what young, white, affluent, middle-class kids began to first realize through listening to the music of an oppressed people—was that they too were oppressed. And that's part of it also, I think. When they started to realize, especially when they started to listen to Dylan, who sang for the white middle class—Dylan didn't make music for ghetto people—and also when they started to hear the music of the Spaniels and the Cadillacs, and all this, from oppressed people, then the idea started to dawn that we're just as oppressed.

"When Chuck Berry sang 'Too Much Monkey Business,' and talking about working in the filling stations pumping gas and going to war—'too much monkey business'—kids started to realize that these same thoughts and feelings applied to them too: not only to oppressed blacks, but to oppressed white youth. And where Dylan's lyrics appealed to white people mainly because Dylan's an intellectual, and his lyrics were extremely intellectual, and were deep, and you had to get past a lot of things to realize what he was singing about, the 'ram a lam a ding dong' school was the opposite, yet the same. It was the fact that it was so anti-intellectual that it broke down all these things. Again, compared with being an intellectual and being sophisticated and being college-bred, it's a restrained way of life, seeing things on one level."

There seem to be a number of people who think of rock writers as prophets of one kind or another.

"To the extent that when the prophecies were being made, people were digging the songs on whatever level, they weren't even aware of the prophecy until it came true. Of course, the two best examples of that are Dylan's 'Like a Rolling Stone' and 'The Times They Are A-Changing.' The latter was done, I believe, in 1963. Now, in 'sixty-three, that was almost two years before the San Francisco hippie flower movement started, right? Here's this dude singing: Listen, you Congressmen. It's gonna shake your walls and the times they are a-changing, and the first ones now will later be last; and what the fuck is he saying, and what is he talking about? Who's the first now that's gonna be last; what roles are changing?

"Dylan saw a new generation and a new world. He saw the fate of this whole globe changing socially. Or 'It's All Over Now, Baby Blue.' The way I interpret that song is that it's a metaphor for blue-eyed white America, middle class. It's all over now, Baby Blue. But it wasn't all over at that point. So Dylan obviously saw through the milieu that he was in, which was the very early beginning of the whole culture. The beats of the 'fifties, who Dylan idolized and hung out with, and Kerouac and that whole scene, the coffeehouse scene. He saw that that was just the beginning of what would be a mass departure from the norm. It wasn't until years later that the prophecy was revealed.

"And in the other song—'Like a Rolling Stone'—Dylan prophesied the fact that middle-class American teens en masse were going to leave home; just pick themselves up and get into the streets. Because they wouldn't be able to take that home environment anymore, and that too was prophetic. And I guess so many of his songs were.

"Or 'Masters of War.' That was written in 1964, and there was no peace movement in 1964. Well, there was, but nothing that the people who were digging Dylan were into. Because they heard 'Masters of War'; they heard 'It's All Right, Ma, I'm Only Bleeding.' They heard these songs, and started to listen to them over and over. And also, the music of these songs was also so grabbing. I mean, why did Dylan forsake folk and go electric? Because it seems to me that he knew that this was the way to get the message across.

"Well, it's hard to say what motivates a man like Bob Dylan. Or anybody, for that matter. I think his songs were directive, but I think the reason I feel that way was that he didn't remain a folk singer. He didn't remain with his guitar and his harp. When *Bringing It All Back Home* came out and everybody made a big fuss and it turned off a lot of people who were into him, it's because of that that I figure Dylan really wanted to be heard— not from an ego level or that he wanted to be a superstar, but he felt that by doing it that way he could turn people on. And Dylan will never answer that question. Everybody's asked him, but he won't answer it.

"Otherwise, I feel he would have remained a folk singer, which is what he really loves; he's really a folk blues singer; he's not a rock-and-roll star. But he saw rock happening.

"And, popular music is really trying to make up its mind now as to what to do. We're really in a famine time. McLuhan says, this is his theory, that all pop cultures work in thirty-year cycles.

You divide each thirty-year cycle into ten years, which is approximately a generation. So the first ten years of a pop culture are generally regarded by the Establishment and the intelligentsia and the critics as being something that's a passing fad and not worth very much. However, it's being dug intensely by young kids.

"So let's look at the thirty-year cycle from 1950 to 1980. That period between 1950 and 1960, of early rock-and-roll, or when rhythm-and-blues reached the mass audience, the critics didn't take it seriously. It was going to be a fad, but the kids dug it, right? Then it goes through the second period—this would be 1960 to 1970—and during the second period there's usually a second wave. And the second wave of that same pop culture, at the same time that it becomes completely accepted by the intelligentsia and the Establishment and the critics, they generally try to make more of it than it really is, and they try to classify it, categorize it, intellectualize it, which is what happened in 1960 and 1970, and when they do that they kill it.

"It generally then goes into the final ten-year cycle, into the death cycle. And in the last period of the cycle, when there isn't anything happening, when this new thing has been killed off, generally people look to the cycle that preceded it—not to the rock thing, but to what was the pop art in 1920–1950. And then they dig that as camp. The thing that died then suddenly becomes camp, which would be movies of the thirties and the forties—the old 1920s music, the clothing styles, which really borders on flappers now—they start digging on that one because their own thing is in the death stage.

"So if McLuhan is right, and the cycles are right, then we're in for a pretty crummy few years, or decade. It could be likened to the decade of the 1940s, which was a terrible decade for music. Rock is dying out, as we know it—I mean what rock meant to us—and there doesn't seem to be any new really heavies coming along. And if rock is dying out, there's gotta be something coming around to replace it. But we can't expect that thing to come too soon. It will probably come in the latter part of the decade.

"And we'll start the next thirty-year cycle, which will also be the last thirty-year cycle of this century. And this will be the first really full-flowered generation of the electric age, the children of the people who finally broke away from the norms up to that point. So who could possibly predict what that will be? I don't know. Nobody has any use for labels anymore, and that's gonna make everything different. We won't be able to call music 'rock.' We'll only be able to call music 'music,' which is what I already like to call music.

"People say, 'What kind of music do you play on your program?' And I say, 'I play music.' See, what kind of music did the Beatles play? The Beatles were not a rock band. They were at the very start, but there's hardly a rock song on *Sergeant Pepper*. A rock-and-roll song: that means four-four backbeat and the heavy drumbeat with repetitive lyrics. Are the Moody Blues rock? Are they folk? Are they classical? What the hell are they? What's Procol Harum? What is Procol? They're not a rock band. They're like a swing band. Savoy Brown's a blues band. So rock really seems to me just a word, a synonym for popular music.

"Besides, the kids take the position where if you don't embrace rock music you have no status at all. They're pretty definitely in that position. You gotta be into rock music. There's also a tremendous move away from commercialism and from the pop-star thing. The music business—at the very core of the music business is the star syndrome. Without stars there is no music at the mass level, as we've known it. Now, if the kids refuse to accept any new stars, well then, what's going to happen? I don't know. Then it's going to have to be something else. The Grateful Dead are really probably the most gigantic superstars as far as groups are concerned, and yet they refuse that role. If the Dead wanted to be, if they really were into it at that level, they could, I think, evolve into a Beatles. There's this idolatrous worship of them by their fans, because their fans are like that about them. Yet they don't want that role."

Many of the people who follow the music are really interested in the life-styles of the artists.

"It's a way of identifying with them. It's like when I was a kid, I'd go to the movies and see Robert Mitchum and I'd just project myself onto Robert Mitchum. So you go and see the Dead, and some dude is Jerry Garcia, or a chick who's watching is Garcia's old lady, or part of that whole thing, saying, 'Wow, if I could just be as free as that.' So it's part of a whole vicarious identification. Nobody's a pop star who's a rather ordinary dude and just a great musician. There are a lot of people who are superb musicians, but they never really become big. Elton John is an example. People will dig his music, and he'll be a star, and his albums will get to be number one, but he won't be a Dylan; he won't be a John Lennon or a Mick Jagger. He's just not that kind of a flamboyant man. Or a Jimi Hendrix. He just doesn't have that flamboyancy, that style that sets this person apart. That you get the feeling, This guy just does anything he wants to do. He's free.

"But the audience is changing. The kids don't feel as seriously about the music as they were taking it a couple of years ago. They're concerned with other things. Well, they're really concerned with the issues; they're getting involved. They're concerned with the environment. I mean, they're really concerned with whether they're gonna be breathing in fifteen years. They got a lot of time ahead of them.

"Some fifty-five-year-old Congressman—he's already lived most of his life. But these kids in high school are really concerned about the environment to the point, really, of almost obsession, which is good. They see the music as, first of all, a cohesive force, something that keeps them together and is at the nucleus of all the problems. The music reflects environmental issues; it reflects the war; it reflects all the things that are on their consciousness, but they're more concerned with the things themselves than with the music.

"And they are reacting to the music as music and not as this overwhelming thing which took up all their time, you know; all they wanted to hear was music and pop stars, like it was a few years ago. They don't really care all that much about that. And they also see the music as their voice, their collective voice, because there isn't any kind of directional music anymore; now all the music seems to be reflective. There isn't any kind of what

Zappa was doing, or Dylan was doing; there isn't that kind of thing anymore. So the music has became the cohesive voice of the culture, the reflective voice, rather than directing the culture, as it did in San Francisco, where it was the music that got the people off. Now the music reflects the fact that people are getting off on each other."

How effective is the advertising you do?

"Well, I really hate doing commercials. Being a salesman. I get offers every week to do free-lance commercials—voice-over TV spots, shit like that—which I do not do because I hate being a salesman. I do eight minutes of commercials an hour, which I figure leaves me fifty-two minutes an hour to do what I want to do, so I really don't think about them too much. I think that the spots for the Fillmore were effective, but that isn't even a commercial, as far as I'm concerned. That's information. So all the informational spots are effective. We've sold a lot of water-beds for the Aquarius Water Bed corporation, I know that. I don't know how much Phisohex we've sold. As a rule, though, all advertising is effective.

"How about if advertising were to become a whole righteous thing, a whole new way for social change? Not for products. Dig it. Some of the public-service advertising is really good. Some of it is really vile, but some of the stuff is really good—what the religious groups have done, weird little brotherhood spots, really nice and tasty. I think that the advertising of a product is going to turn out not to have the same kind of effect it had on people fifty years ago. People are already immune to it all the time. But nobody likes to go out of business, you see. So if you can't advertise products, and if the culture changes, and if people change enough whereby really important issues and messages and ways that people have to get involved in issues—I mean, I think advertising could get into that direction and be an incredible force for social change. And stay in business and make their money."

Some people say the whole culture is hype. What has happened?

What changes has the music actually brought about? Here's an example: Joe Middle Class, who was thirteen years old in 1967— he's nineteen years old now—his family lives in Scarsdale and his father's an insurance executive at Metropolitan Life. What has the music done to him?

"Well, the kid was thinking about doing the same thing. His father's done well. He has a beautiful house and he can just walk right in there and get this really fine gig with Metropolitan Life. I don't think he's so anxious to be an insurance salesman anymore. I mean, he's looking at what other people are doing. What in the music has told him not to be an insurance salesman? The whole thing, everything we've been talking about, especially the aspect of freedom. The only reason you should be an insurance salesman is that you really get off on selling dudes insurance, and you really believe that insurance is worthwhile, and it's important that when you die your old lady's got some insurance policy on you, or something. Really see it as a righteous task. I don't really believe that anybody can see insurance that way.

"Or take me, take the gig I do. I make a lot of money on this gig, man, but I don't feel any guilt about what I do, because I don't think I'm fucking anybody up. I really think I'm performing a worthwhile service and people are getting off on what I do. Now, granted, I'd be just as happy to do it for no money at all if I could go get my groceries free from some farmer who got off on farming—an ideal kind of Utopian situation.

"So I think that the music has made kids realize that human values are over property values. Okay, well, Earth Opera's American Eagle Tragedy, which talks about the king in the countinghouse, counting all his money. The kingdom is crumbling; the queen's in the countinghouse counting up the money. Or, all of the get-together songs. It's hard to remember specific songs or specific lyrics. You come to the intellectual realization that something's wrong—let's say, not taking off your clothes with a group of people. How do you get over these things?

"First, you come to the intellectual thing: 'That's ridiculous. What the hell is clothes, right? There's no reason in the world why I can't take my clothes off in a group of people.' Then you get uptight, but you do it. And you do it a second time, third time, fourth time after that. And it doesn't mean anything at all anymore. So first comes the intellectual realization that this is wrong and this is right, and I'd rather do it this way. And then you've got to experience it and experience it, and the hangup's diluted and diluted and diluted and then goes away.

"So the culture collectively is going through the same thing. Right now people feel that a lot of longhairs are hypocritical; they're really just pigs, because they really are—the way they react to each other emotionally. After all, they talk about brotherhood and global consciousness, rather than labels that separate us all. Yet first time somebody calls somebody and makes a reference to the fact that he's a Jew, or Wop, or whatever, they get all uptight and fight. Sure. First you've gotta go through these intellectual awarenesses, right? But the longer we live it, and the longer we go on, we get our heads together, and work it out. It's gotta take a lot of time for a culture to revamp. Especially an electric culture that isn't really confined to this country; it's really a global thing. It's happening in Japan; it's happening in Russia, man. They've got long-haired hippies in Russia now. So you gotta remember that this thing is just a few years old. And the political people who call it hypocritical and piggish—sure, we're all pigs, man; we've been raised in America. We're consumers.

"It's just gonna take time for these things to work out. But our kids will be a little more together, and their kids will be more together. I mean, can you remember the differences between your parents and your grandparents and their life-styles? It's just a matter of having faith in the human condition, that it's gonna evolve that way, and this culture is gonna evolve into an electric global culture. But that doesn't mean that next year we're gonna have it all worked out. And of course, we're all products of what we come from. That's what 'Rolling Stone' is all about: what that's all about. 'How does it feel?,' what are you gonna do now, now you're out on your own, but your direction's unkown. You're gonna have to pay your dues.

"My feeling, on the other hand, is that the people who're involved in traditional politics are the real counterrevolutionaries. SDS, the Panthers and the women's groups, the gay groups— all the self-interest groups, all of the groups that remind us of the things that separate us all—I think they have a point, and a place, and they're very valid, but I believe that the whole culture will swallow them all up. Besides, I don't think they would have even come about without the music. If the music hadn't happened, nothing would be happening. Plato said, 'When the mode of the music changes, the walls of the city shake.' And that's what happened. The mode of the music changed; it changed in the 1950s, and the walls of the city are shaking. And there would be no women's lib; there would be no Panthers, no Lords, no civil rights movement—no nothing— if we were still listening to Patti Page records."

BUSINESS—THE RISE OF THE ARTIST

How does a songpoet make his living? If the answer seems obvious, you should spend a few minutes with a rock-and-roll accountant and let him fill you in on the intricacies an artist faces in trying to sort out his sources of income and hold on to his money.

The major source of income for all of the songpoets we've been talking about is recordings. Each is signed to a long-term contract with a recording company, and each record company is different, but one fact remains clear: without them, it would be nearly impossible to survive.

First, there is the actual money from the sale of records and tapes, but this is filtered through the record company, often in ways that shuttle portions off to places where no man goes. Allen Klein, who became the Beatles' business manager, began his career in the music business as an auditor—examining record companies' accounts with the privilege of keeping a certain percentage of anything he found that belonged to the artist who employed him. Klein got rich this way—which is a comment on the difficulties an artist faces in dealing with the companies.

Other money is made from what is called publishing. The term is a relic of the days when sheet music was the rage and a musician needed a publisher to put out that sheet music. What "publisher" has now come to mean is someone who serves as a collection agency for the royalties due a writer for the broadcasting of his songs over the radio and for the use of those songs by other recording artists. Each time a song is played on the radio, a few pennies are paid to one of two even larger collection agencies, the American Society of Composers, Authors and Publishers and Broadcast Music, Inc. They distribute the money to the legal publishers, who in turn are to pass it on to the writer. Songwriters refer to ASCAP and BMI royalties as "old age money"—because of the size of the payments, which can be enormous, and because of the rate at which these two giants pay, which is very slow indeed.

Most of the writers in this book have made the greater portion of their money from their publishing. If you'd like to attempt to estimate how wealthy Bob Dylan is, all you have to do is remember the number of times you've heard a song performed or written by Dylan on the radio. It's a good bet that Dylan is making more than a nickel on each of these times.

A third way to make bread is to take your show on the road and perform for the public. But this is the least lucrative and most grueling way. There are too many hidden costs in going on the road. Even if a promoter is paying a high fee, an artist must cough up the travel costs, equipment costs and other expenses. These costs have a way of mounting beyond the fee paid for the gig, and there are many artists, and more groups, who lose money while touring. Add to this the emotional hassles of performing live and you can begin to understand why Bob Dylan, Joni Mitchell, Randy Newman and so many others have retired from the stage or studiously avoided it.

Yet both publishing and performing revolve around success at recording, directly or indirectly. If an artist does not record with a major company, he has little chance of getting his music on the radio; and if his music doesn't make it to the radio, the possibility of his being able to draw a live audience is slim. If his records are not widely distributed, other artists will not record his songs and royalties from those sources disappear.

It used to be axiomatic that the relationship between the company and the artist was an adversary one. Record companies saw artists as spoiled, pampered and overpaid, and they tried in many ways to exploit their artists and, in some cases, to simply steal their money.

In those days, the record companies completely controlled the artistic output of their contracted artists, right down to pre-scribing which songs they would cut and how the albums would be designed. On the whole, those days are gone forever; with the emergence of the big rock stars, the companies had to con-cede that those decisions were no longer theirs to make. There are still some companies who attempt it, but they are few in number and still smaller in influence.

Two great conglomerates now dominate the rock field. One is the Kinney Group, which has little or nothing to do with shoes and parking lots anymore and which includes Atlantic Records, Warner Brothers–Reprise Records and Elektra Records. Columbia, wholly owned by the CBS broadcasting empire, is the other important entrepreneur in the field. Nearly all the songpoets I have discussed belong to one of these companies, either directly or indirectly through distribution arrangements. Bob Dylan and Laura Nyro record for Columbia. Neil Young and Randy Newman record for Reprise; the Grateful Dead and Van Morrison, for Warner Brothers. Joni Mitchell recorded for Reprise for years and now records for Asylum Records, which are distributed by Atlantic Records. Don McLean records for United Artists Records, which is owned by the TransAmerica Industries conglomerate.

One of the reasons for the success of Columbia and Warner-Reprise has been a marked change in their attitudes toward their artists. Both companies are proud of their images as artist-oriented labels, and for the most part, that pride is deserved. Joe Smith, president at Warner-Reprise, is an executive who has conspicuously abandoned the record industry's old ways in an at-tempt to build a better relationship with his artists and keep them happy—and on his label.

Another development has been the hiring of young people in the A-and-R, promotional and production ends of the industry. A few years ago, the phrase "company freak" was commonly used to describe the long-haired sergeants of the industry. Now there are so many that the appellation is inappropriate. For the most part, they are simply company men who happen to be younger and even, possibly, more astute than the old guard.

Other changes are not so obvious. One is the rise of the lawyer-adviser who, for a high fee, will see to it that the recording artist does not end up with the short end of the contractual stick. The result is two-edged. Some lawyers have protected their clients; others have proved to be a new breed of thief. There seem to be proportionately more lawsuits in the recording industry than in any other business.

Another change is that it is now common practice for an artist to have written into his contract a clause granting him near-total control of the artistic aspects of his work. Today, a recording contract will likely call for a performer to have final say on the production of his record, the design of its album cover and, in some cases, the text of the advertising. Some artists have set up their own independent production companies and call on the record companies for financial backing and distribution.

In search of answers to my questions about the relationship between songpoets and their recording companies, I sought out Joe Smith, then executive vice-president at Warner Brothers–Reprise Records. Warner Brothers–Reprise, as the name might indicate, started out as a subsidiary of a movie company. Reprise began as the brainchild of Frank Sinatra and was intended mainly to distribute his own recordings. Through a series of shrewd business decisions and lucky events involving its artists, Warner Brothers–Reprise has found its way to the top of its industry; it was recently purchased by the Kinney Corporation.

Joe Smith is a short, stocky former disk jockey who enjoys a good reputation with the artists he represents. He is in his forties and perhaps, therefore, not a natural fan of rock-and-roll, but he admits to enjoying much of today's music, including that of the songpoets, a number of whom his company represents. We talked in the old Warner Brothers offices on Madison Avenue, in a little green room, on a gray day. I wanted to explore the ways in which artists are discovered. I asked him, for instance, about Van Morrison.

"We had a fellow that worked for us named Andy Wickham. I don't know if you know Andy. Andy knew about Van, knew Van. He'd known him when he was with the group, first of all, in England. Andy told me that Van was in Boston, with a band, wanting to get out of a contract he had which he considered unfavorable. And was I interested? And I was interested, so I got in touch with Van in Boston; I tracked him down.

"He had some immigration problems. And he was, in fact, under contract with somebody. Before *Astral Weeks,* he had had one or two things that he had done—"Madame George," ideas for some other things—but I felt that Van, in addition to being an important writer, had an instinct for the pop market, was the kind of person who can be a doubleheader artist, who could be bigger than some of our other people, because he could write hit singles—the strength of his writing gave him a chance for success with singles.

"Anyhow, we worked out something with immigration; we got him a lawyer; we bought him out of the bad contract. He got involved with a manager and a producer and proceeded to make *Astral Weeks,* which was not a commercial success, but an artistic triumph. He sold about fifteen thousand albums, and it was called 'The Album of the Year' by *Rolling Stone.*

"And of that fifteen thousand, I'd say about ten thousand were sold on the West Coast. Now subsequently, that album is close to about a hundred thousand. We really worked hard on that album. We faced an artist who really had not been treated well before by any group or company he'd ever been involved with. He was also suspicious of us and everybody around him, and faced this situation where everybody told him what an enormously powerful album he had written and we weren't selling any.

"So Van went into a tailspin emotionally; he became incommunicado, was feuding with the producers that he'd been involved with, and went—it was quite some time before he got it back on again, and we had talked about other producers, other solutions.

"At Newport, at the folk festival, at the same time that I'd first met James Taylor, we had a bunch of acts on that show, in 'sixty-nine—the Everly Brothers, Joni Mitchell, Arlo Guthrie, Van, Jack Elliot—a marvelous festival, and a very important one for us. We had a funny dinner there one night, at a posh hotel, the Viking, and we took over the dining hall. We had it just for our acts. Everybody came with their families and groups, and it was fun. We had the Pentangle there. It was a nice party, and everybody really had a good time.

"It's interesting. We just did this in the course of a month or so. We had a bunch of our artists in town: James Taylor, Van Morrison, Randy Newman, Joni Mitchell, Neil Young. We invited John Stewart and Dave Mason, who were in town, and Phil Spector. No press, no radio—just a party. We really have that kind of feeling about our artists. And they enjoyed being with each other, too. It's interesting that Randy Newman was the hero of that evening. He was more respected than any of the others. At that party, again, we discussed with Van the fact that he felt he could make his own album best, and then we went through whatever machinations with the record company we had to go through with. He made his own album, which was *Moondance,* which had a hit record on it which was very successful, which got on the charts and established him as a very important artist.

"Morrison's music excited me, perhaps because I'm more into it. I used to be a disk jockey. I used to be the only R-and-B disk jockey in Boston. I'd play R-and-B records, and I have a pretty good feeling for that—a personal feeling, I mean. Our roster reflects the personal tastes of two people, Mo Ostin and myself, who have signed everybody in the last seven years here.

"So I dug Van—maybe more than any other artist we've signed —because I can understand a lot of what he's doing. No electronic noise that puzzles me. Jimi Hendrix puzzled me sometimes. I realize that he was a very good guitar player. I couldn't understand what Jimi Hendrix was doing. I don't understand Led Zeppelin now.

"But Van Morrison was very easy to understand. I remember picking up *Moondance* and taking it home and playing it for my wife, who's not exceptionally hip or into music. She liked it better than James's album—they both came out at the same

time—and she thought *Moondance* was just super; you know—
happy feelings. Well, that's Van's story. He's a very happy guy,
who is now set financially, finally, after a few years of our having to provide the basic elements of his life, for God's sake.

"You don't ever *have* to do that, of course. But you feel sometimes that you *should* do it. Now, my experience with the Grateful Dead has been, I would think that if I were father to every
one of them I couldn't have played more of a part in the key
moments of their life. Buying houses, paying taxes, buying instruments, getting out of busts, all kinds of things like that. I
wouldn't expect this to be a story about me doing all these
things.

"Most record companies—you must understand that—most
record companies still operate on the theory that when you sign
an artist, you then set up an adversary relationship. He's trying
to screw us, or we're going to screw him, and who does he think
he is spending that money? But our company has always been
artist first, to the exclusion of sales and everything else. We
made some horrible mistakes financially because of that.

"Artists, because of their indecision, have spent hundreds of
thousands of dollars unnecessarily in the studio. Most cases, in
the end it's been fine, you know. The Grateful Dead once—
Brian Rohan and Bill Graham were managing them—they told
us they had once spent ninety-six thousand dollars and had not
finished an album, and they had twenty thousand dollars more
in bills. What were we going to do about it? We just had to do
it, you know. Every time somebody does that, it's an indulgence.
But Van, I think Van is on his way now; all the bad, all the
black days are behind him now, and it's straight ahead.

"I think being more oriented to the artist has helped Warner
Brothers. The successful companies, now—and you know them,
they're Columbia, they're Elektra, they're Atlantic, they're
Warners, those companies—the executives in those companies
are more involved in the artistry than any other aspect. The
financial or the sales or anything else. The executives of the
Kinney Group and the executives of Columbia are all very much
into artists and music. And many of our nights are spent with
our artists in clubs, out of a genuine enjoyment of the music,

and the artists are all different. I enjoy the music, which is a very key difference.

"You see, the way their music is presented and packaged is of vital concern to them—far more than with recording artists of the past, who were always interested in albums, but not to the degree that the young singer/writer is now. He wrote those songs. He sat through the sixteen tracks of studio, laying down those rhythm tracks for a month, putting on his vocal and then sweetening them when necessary. And those songs—for somebody like James Taylor, who is one of the least prolific of today's writers, there's one song on his new album called 'Love Has Brought Me Around' that he finished one night, and he told Peter Asher and me in the studio that this took a long time coming out. He has very big chunks of his life in every song that he writes. Others—Van, on the other hand, doesn't write as personally as James. Van can work off more songs. But even for Van Morrison, they're still *his* songs. Out of his life. I think that the treatment we give him is very important.

"At Warner Brothers, we don't aim for the single market, but hitting it is marvelous, because it opens up the AM audience to these artists, which is great. That's great. James Taylor's album was very successful before the single, but wow after the single! I think if Joni Mitchell ever hit a single hit record . . . We just missed on a couple of records. She'll make it. She'll make it."

Has your own life been changed through contact with the music and the musicians?

"You mean personally? It would be a lot harder for me to be that vitally affected by it personally, because my ethic was middle-class poor, middle-class Boston. 'You gotta make it and you gotta do it.' I will say that the association, the last five or six years especially with Van Morrison and with the music—and with my own children, who are ten and eleven years of age—make me realize that this is not *their* ethic. And even though Van Morrison is going to come in hard-driving with an attorney—you know, he wants all the things in life. I would hate to say that everybody is, you know, because they're making a lot of money. The music says one thing. The artist still surrounds himself with a lot of hard-bargaining guys. I mean, they're all going to be millionaires. I'm not putting them down for it . . .

"Oh, yeah, sometimes I find that contradictory. The biggest bullshit was the San Francisco bullshit. That was the flower children. That was flower children and love and for the people. But meanwhile, the lawyers, who were treating them like they were pro-football draft choices. You know, they need thirty thousand dollars to say "Maybe," and another twenty-six thousand dollars to go into the studio. They need twenty-two thousand . . . well, it's all bullshit.

"What's all that about? And they're trying to rip off the record industry for everything they can get. I found that very disturbing. I don't object to anybody's doing anything, really. James Taylor wants to do Madison Square Garden for twenty thousand people. That's cool. Bill Graham says he shouldn't do that. He should come to the Fillmore and do it for three thousand, but Bill Graham owns the Fillmore! Maybe if Bill owned Madison Square Garden, he'd think differently.

"In my own life, I realize now that I've got enough; that's all I want, in terms of money. And my kids aren't really going to want that much from me, and even if I had it to give them they might not even want it. I've opted for a life-style of my own, and this has all been very much influenced by this counterculture. I'm not part of the counterculture. I'm still very much in the mainstream, I guess; but once I get enough, the quality of my life is much more important than the game of making a lot of money. And I enjoy my work.

"I can't imagine life without some kind of work. If you've ever met Ahmet Ertegun and Jerry Wexler—men who are very wealthy, who've done it all, started their companies, made their records, promoted them, sold them, sold their companies for a considerable amount of money . . . Working as hard as I do, as hard as anybody works. Because I don't know how you can be fulfilled. I don't know how anybody can be fulfilled by dropping out.

"Obviously, Van Morrison hasn't dropped out. He works. That amount of energy he pours into his music is equivalent to what a hardhat is doing building a building in New York. I don't know any of the musicians, or the kids making music, who've dropped out of a 'work ethic.' Maybe Joni Mitchell doesn't want to work because she just doesn't want to get up in front of a lot of people. She'd be inclined to write and sing in front of friends all the time, all small groups of people. She'd do that. It's not that she's opting out of work. I think that anybody who says they're dropping out of work, well, that's a lot of bullshit. They're the people who have nothing going. They're just lazy, and whatever.

"I've been startled by the real greed of some artists, which is opposed to their public image. And not that they should be denied all the profits that come from their work. But wanting more than they really deserve. And we faced that most of all with the San Francisco groups, that San Francisco thing, which always started from that Haight-Ashbury thing: 'We love the world, man.'

"Warner Brothers has an approach to advertising that evolved out of Stan Cornyn (v.p. of Creative Services) and out of, I think, the whole philosophy of our company. Very seldom do I do interviews like this where I say, 'Wow, dynamite.' We do put ourselves down; there is a lot of self-deprecation. We take shots at each other.

"I am the company Don Rickles, and we put each other down. We know now that we represent a very attractive company to an artist, and to the press it's an interesting company. We have Frank Sinatra at one end of the company and Tiny Tim at the other; Frank Zappa and Beefheart, then the Taylors and the Mitchells—which makes it an interesting company, and we're proud of that.

"You can't say it in advertising. You can say that in the *Billboard/Cash Box* kind of advertising, because that's all scam anyhow. When a consumer's reading it, especially someone perceptive who's into the rock press, a soft sell, an undersell, a talking about our own people—our Mr. West, our treasurer, our accountant—that's Stan's humor. He writes with a lovely touch, and the first ads were his, and many of the ads are his.

"Now Stan's writing less of them, and Pete Johnson is writing some; Judy Sims is writing some, and that's a pretty clever group of people. That advertising has been a major factor in attracting artists. They love that advertising.

"Oh, we've had some artists it's kicked back on. And sometimes it gets very cutesy. Sometimes it just doesn't come off.

"Would you want to always put up a picture of the artist and the name of the record and say 'Smash hit on RCA' every week? Then you don't try anything. Then you don't come up with the Van Dyke Parks ad that you still remember from three years ago. Or an ad about Joni Mitchell as ninety-percent virgin, which she objected to strenuously. Or Van Morrison with a black mask across his eyes, saying, 'This man scored last night.' Van was not thrilled about that.

"Oh, there are cases where it doesn't come off. And cases where it comes off and the artist doesn't like it. But in the end, every manager, attorney or artist sits down just the way we're sitting down and they talk about our advertising.

"Tell me another company where people talk about their advertising. Not how much, but the quality of it. And on the general bottom line, our advertising is far more effective than ineffective, and we get a lot more hits out of it than we do misses. And if Joni Mitchell is unhappy with the ninety-percent-virgin line, it's for personal reasons, not that the ad was ineffective. It was a damn good ad; she was just maybe not happy with the connotation that she was a virgin."

TWO CRITICS—GLEASON AND MARCUS

During the late '60s a vast plague of amateur critics swept over the music scene. Perhaps because editors were older and confused by the scene and could not themselves figure out what was happening in pop music, they delegated critical duties loosely. Or perhaps it was just that so many people were taken suddenly by the power and insistence of the new music that they felt a compulsion to write down their feelings.

By 1973, there has been some refinement, and there have emerged a small number of important critics of the new music. Many of the best have been attracted by the four serious publications on pop music—*Rolling Stone,* based in San Francisco but with offices in New York, Los Angeles and London; *Fusion,* out of Boston; *Creem,* out of Detroit, and *Crawdaddy* in New York. There are others in each of those cities and in many college towns around the country, but the big four are the most consistent and perceptive. Many publications have rock critics or commentators—*The New York Times,* and magazines like *The New Yorker* and the *Saturday Review*—another indication of how much pop music has increased its audience in the last few years.

With all of this activity, nearly every worthwhile disk released in this country is assured of some comment somewhere. Reviews are not guarantees of sales, but they are often helpful to an artist struggling to make his voice heard above the huge crowd. The feature articles often lapse into gossip, and there are many writers who have let their interest in personalities overwhelm any interest they might have in the music. In general, the present rock press seems as if it will be with us for a while.

Both the critics whom I interviewed have written extensively. Ralph Gleason, one of the founders of *Rolling Stone* and a frequent contributor both to *Rolling Stone* and to his former employer, the San Francisco *Chronicle,* is one of the few older writers who recognized the explosion of pop music in this country. He and Al Aronowitz, writing for the New York *Post* and the late *Saturday Evening Post,* have been in the forefront among the "straight" journalists ferreting out what was best in pop and presenting it to an often skeptical readership. Gleason lives in Berkeley with his family, and we talked in his living room, overlooking San Francisco Bay and the city beyond. He is youthful-looking man of about fifty, and he was enthusiastic about discussing songpoetry, songpoets and most especially Bob Dylan.

Greil Marcus, who is currently completing his second book on rock, is a former editor of *Rolling Stone* and, in my opinion, one of the most perceptive of the rock critics. During his tenure at *Rolling Stone,* he provided his readers with introductions to some of the best artists we have, and his record reviews are reprinted in the *Rolling Stone Record Reviews,* a useful collection. Marcus, who is in his late twenties, lives with his wife on a high hill above the city of Berkeley and, when we spoke, was teaching and studying political science at the University of California at Berkeley. His home, like Gleason's, is dominated by records and sound equipment.

Gleason's living living room, where we spoke, has two huge speakers, each nearly five feet tall—the kind of big black boxes one sees huge rock bands using to project their sound.

RALPH GLEASON

I asked Ralph Gleason when it had first struck him that something exciting was happening to pop music.

"Well, I'd have to go back and read my articles over to remember the precise moment. But I was in a peculiar position. In the 'fifties I was in the eyes of the public as a jazz critic; I had begun writing once a week and then it increased to seven, covering both jazz and popular music. So, back around the early 'fifties, I was doing things like interviewing Hank Williams. And going to see Chuck Berry, Fats Domino and Bill Doggett on one of the Phels Brothers concert tours.

"I was writing about the songs in the top-forty thing all the time, invariably from various points of view. There was a whole run of suicide records; people got killed in them, and stuff like that. There were hot-rod records, surfing records—so I was always fascinated with the phonograph record and its instant mass communication. I was not a folk-music fan particularly, although I reviewed all the folk-music concerts, because nobody else was doing it. I was motivated to do that out of curiosity and also out of economics, because if I wrote extra reviews I got paid for them.

"Part of what I did was to review all the Hungry i shows, for instance, from the beginning. So I reviewed Peter, Paul and Mary when they were at the Hungry i, which was the second or third gig they had. Barbra Streisand and everyone else would show up there. Now, basically, I hated Peter, Paul and Mary, including 'Blowin' in the Wind.' I still don't like them, although I've come to the realization that many of the things they were saying—not singing, but off of records, in interviews—concerning popular music had some truth to them. But I heard Woody Guthrie and Leadbelly and Big Bill and all those people in person. And Peter, Paul and Mary—two rabbis and a hooker —just didn't make it for me.

"I heard Dylan at the Monterey concert in 1963. When I first heard Dylan, to me he was a bum Woody Guthrie. It didn't do anything for me at all. Then he was coming back in here on a concert tour—he came back to play a concert at the Berkeley Community Theater—and the second album had just been issued at this point, and I sat down and listened to it. I mean, I really listened. The first album sounded to me like something I was very familiar with: young white kids trying to sing New Orleans blues—we had millions of them around here, but nothing happened with it. The second album I got turned on to. Songs like 'The Times They Are A-Changing' really hit me.

"It's impossible for me to separate the impact of that music and the emergence of the whole political youth movement in the Bay Area. They came simultaneously, and they fed each other. To discover that the most interesting thing at the Berkeley Folk Festival was not what was going on on the folk-music platform but what was going on with the kids sitting around the fountain playing the harmonica two and a half hours later: it was really a gas! Some of the early songs turned me on, and still turn me on, like 'Do You Believe in Magic?'—that was a very important song. Just as 'Eve of Destruction' was an important song, despite the fact that Pete Seeger criticizes it still, probably as a song.

"I don't know further than that what particular songs were important at that time. It was the whole thing. And that summer the Dylan concerts were incredible experiences. In the spring of 'sixty-six we had Beatle music all over the place, we had Dylan all over the place, we had the Byrds in one place, the Lovin' Spoonful in another. It was just insane! They were in crummy clubs, working for scale. Then that fall, the San Francisco thing exploded. Well, somewhere along there, it became obvious to me that the real folk music in terms of expression of people's ideas of the current culture was not in the Tom Paxton kind of thing at all, but in rock-and-roll.

"I went to the second Big Sur Folk Festival, and I was on a panel with Joan Baez, Mark Spoelstra and Allen Ginsberg and somebody else, about the importance of rock-and-roll, which I thought was more important than what Joan was doing, and still do. Well, she listens to all of it. Luckily, she's figured out that she can't do it. There was a time when she thought she could do it, and that didn't work. So the lines of these songs began to assume a role as part of the currency of expression, and it all sort of happened at once. It would be very hard for me to sit down and figure it all out sequentially. My reaction at the moment is that it all just exploded. It did, but I'm sure it probably took a long time.

"You could listen to the top-forty songs at the end of the 'fifties and beginning of the 'sixties and find songs that were interesting, songs that evoked all kinds of sentiment. There were hillbilly songs that were coming along then, and antiwar songs. Those were the kinds of things that I thought of as urban folk music, in a very non-folk-festival kind of way. And I'd always had an objection, and still do, to the preciousness with which the folk-music people surround what they do. I was yelling and screaming at them at the Berkeley Folk Festival, the Monterey Folk Festival and the beginning of the 'sixties that real folk music was a lot more likely to be found in top-forty radio than would be found in digging out the remnants of the culture of the 'twenties that was still ambient in the Virginia hills. Not that they shouldn't do that—that was a good thing to do—but it wasn't enough: the pure, only thing against which everything else ranked badly.

"But it really turned me on to see Dylan singing songs that were more than *Sing Out!* or *Broadside* message songs, that were poetry of some unspecified kind, and to find that the thing communicated instantly to whole groups of people. To discover that Dylan could sell out the Berkeley Community Theater all on his own, by virtue of one announcement in the paper.

"The genius with Dylan was to create a body of work—and without being facetious—like the Bible and like Shakespeare, which spoke to an entire generation of people so openly that they could fit into it whatever they brought to it. And so if you're convinced that 'Tambourine Man' is a song about a pusher, you're never going to be unconvinced about it. I've had to dismiss all the drug things, because the general stance of the drugger towards the music is that it can be neither understood nor accepted by someone who isn't on the drug. Well, I've never used speed, or LSD, or grass in the course of listening to any of this music, and I stand on the record. I know you don't have to do it.

"The thing that happened, I think, historically is that in a certain sense the workers took over the means of production, and the audience began to make records for itself. At one moment it changed from where Carole King sat in that music-publishing company grinding out songs with Goffin for a hundred and fifty dollars a week to where people were writing the songs they were interested in singing, and there's no doubt that that came from the folk-festival/radical-folk-music tradition in this country, or there would have been no opportunities for them to do it at all.

"They found out that there was an audience for this, and this audience suddenly became a mass audience, motivated to a considerable degree by the fact that the Beatles were able to demolish the standard formula for writing songs. And I think that the Beatles and Dylan running in tandem, and the dialectic running between them, opened up the idea in the minds of millions of people that they too could express something of what they felt about what was going on in music, and they did not have to think of it in the same terms that people who wanted to write Cole Porter songs had to think of it. So all of a sudden, you get people doing it.

"That plus many other factors in the society, including the demise of Hollywood, the destruction of the Hollywood image —all that sort of thing—came along to where you didn't want to grow up to be a movie star, hike to Los Angeles, get a job, hope that Sam Goldwyn would discover you, and neither did your old lady. The road to fame and fortune was to make a record and have your voice coming back to you out of all those radios and off all those jukeboxes all over the country."

Do you think of some of the new songs as prophetic of changes in the youth culture?

"Well, I don't think that Dylan's 'Subterranean Homesick Blues' or 'Like a Rolling Stone' or those new songs were prophesizing or anything like that at all. What they were was an excellent description of things as they were. They were written in January of 'sixty-six, and I called them Bob Dylan's State of the Union Messages, because that's what they really were. They were descriptions of the culture of the United States of America at that time. He managed to do two things simultaneously. With 'Subterranean Homesick Blues,' he was doing it in the language of the people to whom he was speaking. In 'Chimes of Freedom,' he wasn't necessarily doing that. I mean, all that is in there, but the rhetoric is more classical, and he went on with that. He became more and more out-front poetic, leading to songs like 'Sad-Eyed Lady of the Lowlands,' which were straight-out poems.

"Dylan did in a certain sense prophesize with 'Like a Rolling Stone,' because that is what has happened. It had to happen, and it wasn't yet happening. And another thing. I don't think he had to know it was going to happen. There's one mystical view of songs that is fairly prevalent in the San Francisco area, where there's a good deal of pseudoreligious mysticism involved and a lot of drug mysticism involved, and so forth, in which the musician doesn't create the song, he's only the instrument through which it's transmitted."

I asked Gleason how he perceived my generation—especially since, as I told him, I'd heard him referred to as its "oldest member."

"Well, I've been able to turn some members of my own generation on, and unable to turn others on. I know I was able to turn a lot of people within the circulation of the *Chronicle* on to Bob Dylan songs. They weren't being played on the radio at that time. The FM underground did not exist. They weren't being played on top-forty radio when I wrote about them.

"I had a position, whether it was earned or accidental at that point, of being 'respectable,' appearing in the leading morning paper. So if I spent a lot of time and effort in writing about them, and if I did it well and communicated, people would listen to it. And they did.

"I had two kinds of letters that were very encouraging. The first kind of letter was from sixty-year-old housewives saying: 'Jesus, you know, it really isn't all that noise I thought it was. Thank you for introducing it to me, and Simon and Garfunkel and other pleasing things.' And the letters from young people saying: 'My God, I can't believe it. I never thought anyone would understand. Wow, too much!' As a result of some of those pieces—and I must have written fifty columns over the course of three years about him—a Catholic high school in Sacramento started to teach Dylan in an English class. Things like that.

"I think this is a good thing to the degree that it interested people in him. All those things are a pain in the ass in one sense, but in another sense, at that time, there was a certain amount of validation that needed to be given to it. We now accept all that as a very real and valuable contribution to American culture, but we didn't accept it in 1964 and 1965.

"I think that in order to get to that, some things like that had to be done. It was necessary to yell and scream at the folk festival people that Ray Charles was more important than folk music, or whatever kid who had written four bars of blues from something in the paper. The *Broadside* thing is okay as far as it goes, but basically Ray Charles is more important.

"I don't know how I got hung up on this music except, as I say, I was already writing about popular music. I was involved in it in a way that, as far as I could see, no other adults were, except disk jockeys who were really in another bag and some people who were making records. Nobody else in my generation was paying any attention to it. But this goes back even further than that. Do you remember *Dig* magazine? That was fantastic. I remember in one issue they had a whole spread about haircuts, the different kinds of haircuts. My friends would come to visit me and I could talk to their kids about *Dig* magazine, which their parents wouldn't let them have in the house; they had to hide it out in the garage. I used to feel real foolish, 'cause here I was, all grown up, with kids of my own, and what the hell's the matter with me?

"Many jazz musicians in the 'forties and 'fifties couldn't listen to Bessie Smith and Ma Rainey blues because the records were so old and rickety and had such a tinny sound. They couldn't hear it. That always disturbed me, because I'd always encountered something in those records for myself as I grew up. So once I was able to get past my prejudice against electric guitars—which equated with Arkansas, Jim Crow hillbillies for me—once I got past that I was able to expose myself to a different kind of sound and not be turned off by definition.

"And once that impact got to you . . . and Dylan made that impact. He got to me first, before the Beatles did. The Beatles came on as fun and games, a kind of entertainment, and then became something much greater than that. In fact, I think that's what actually happened to them. And it was possible then to accept that, and listen to it, and hear what they were saying. In addition to having the visceral experience of listening to them, you could actually hear the words.

"The music expresses the necessity of becoming individual. It goes back to the 'lonely crowd' and all that. It's one of the few remaining unexplored methods of achieving a kind of reality in a world that's gone beserk. And it's not surprising to me that it took a poetic form, because however you want to define poetry, it's really fruitless to deal with this world in precise scientific terms.

"You take *The Making of the President,* or one of those books, and they're full of accurate, provable details, and they don't tell you anything at all. And the poetic, the Norman O. Brown thing—to understand the reality of politics we have to go to the poets—that was certainly true in the past, and it's true in the present, except that the poets have become something that the academic poets don't want to think of as poets.

"Louis Simpson has a gig being a poet someplace, but that's no good. It doesn't make any difference what he says. Very few of the poet-type poets have worked up any energy to have any effect on the world whatsoever. Robert Lowell had a little, maybe, but I don't think it makes any real difference.

"The United States of America, the reality of that thing out there, would not be altered if you removed most poets from existence, removed every word they ever wrote. But it would be altered if you removed Dylan.

"Dylan and the Beatles opened the door. They did it. And the great thing about them is that they not only opened the door but they showed that you could go on doing it. It's easier to do it once; it's hard to do it and keep on doing it. It goes all over the place: John Sebastian; Crosby, Stills and Nash; Joni Mitchell to some degree; and the Dead, and Neil Young, Rod Stewart, Leon Russell . . .

"Dylan is surely the most important, though, and I think he may very well be one of the most important people who have lived in my lifetime. It doesn't mean he's not subject to the ordinary human frailties, like writing a bad song because he has a boil on his ass, or whatever.

"One of the things that has been so freaky about all this is that never before in the history of any nation, or any culture, has such great power and wealth been accumulated by people so young, who, regardless of the truth of their perceptions, have got, by necessity, a limited body of experience on which to draw. And it's bound to turn them, and twist their heads all over the place, and frighten them, and panic them."

Do you believe that when an artist, especially a young rock artist, becomes rich and successful, he no longer shares the life of his audience and is therefore less able to communicate with them?

"That's the trick, to be able to do it. Mick Jagger doesn't have to be on the demonstration line to write 'Street Fighting Man.' In a way, you don't have to explain it. That's why he's an artist. That's why he isn't a hack. You don't have to break your arm to be able to write about it. He's able to do these things, which doesn't necessarily mean that he is the things he writes about.

"It could mean that, and sometimes they're written—with him and the Beatles and anybody else—out of direct personal experience, but not necessarily. That's the gift they have. Maybe that's the song that's out there in the air that they're the transmitter of, the machine through which it's done. I don't know.

"The thing is to be able to live like Mick does, isolated from the street, and to live like Bob does, isolated from the crowd, and still be able to project yourself out there somehow, and obviously, they can do that.

"How could John Fogerty sit on this hill, a mile from here, and write songs about the Mississippi Delta when he's never been out of California? That shows you what television and radio and records do to transmit the fabric of culture. There's a piece of mine in Jon Eisen's first book, *The Age of Rock*, where I talk about looking to the black blues singers as protest music and as poetry and as saying something, and then we went through that period of rock-and-roll and R-and-B on almost to right now, where the black writers were not saying anything. It's not that they weren't saying anything; they were *attempting* to not say anything.

"Because they were doing something else. In a way, the whole role of blacks in the culture, and the movement and their own current struggle and revolution, preoccupies them in areas that formerly did not exist, and the talented tenth now is drawn off in many more areas than it was in the 'thirties and 'forties. There's some truth to that.

"It's still the quickest way to get rich, as Sly Stone proved, and it's easier for the black performer to be successful if he's politically neutral, because it's a racist society. It's possible for David Crosby to go on stage and talk about Tricia Nixon as the kind of chick who'll give you bad head, but I doubt very much if Sly Stone could get away with that. It was an astonishing thing for B.B. to do all those songs that year that really did say something. I don't think it could have been done if he hadn't been such a part of the concept of blues. He's really, in a certain sense, an old-fashioned blues guitarist.

"The blues was essentially protest. It was white people who made those records successful, and then that thing fed back into the black community, and B.B. now has an audience of young blacks that he didn't have a few years ago. Because, you see, he had an audience of young blacks in the 'fifties who grew up, and their younger brothers or sons he did not have, and now he's got some of them. I don't know to what degree, but I don't think Taj Mahal has a black audience. And neither did the Chambers Brothers.

"You know, Sammy Davis keeps talking about this—the problem with all black performers, that the black performers have had to function in a very restricted area, by the definitions imposed upon them by the white society. They haven't broken down. The great comment that someone said years ago at the Fillmore was that at the Fillmore the only black people on the stage are our cops.

"Blacks didn't go to the Fillmore. Not after Graham got it. They went for twenty years before, but after they put on the rock bands they wouldn't have anything to do with it. They went to see Aretha, and some of them went to see B.B., and I know they went to see Otis, but by and large, they're not into that. You see, there's a way, I think, in which—I don't know how to explain this—in a certain sense, the white jazz musicians of the 'forties and 'fifties, the beboppers, the junkies and the poets —these people achieved a kind of psychic blackness by virtue of being outcasts from white society by the road of junk.

"And when you get down to the bottom, all junkies are junkies, black or white. Race disappears from it, because the only thing that matters is junk. Okay, now the black community has not got the time, I don't think, to afford the luxury of the Grateful Dead. It's that young people are either too busy surviving, or trying to do something to help the rest of them, to devote their energies to something that appears, for whatever reason, to be as trivial as that. They simply don't relate to that. Now, it may be the heaviest thing in the world for some nineteen-year-old kid from Sheboygan. And in a way, those people are obeying Stokely Carmichael's admonition to go back to Berkeley and change the white community.

"They didn't go back to Berkeley to change the white community in quite the way he had anticipated, though it's perfectly obvious that they did in fact change the white community, since they elected a black mayor. But it took a little bit of time for a number of things to happen. I don't think they can get into this thing except in terms of economics, and as long as they can make money for themselves and for their own group, and that's what Stokely's been doing, when that music is cast in a certain mold it goes out past that group and is attractive to both a certain sort of liberal element in the white community, but also to the general element.

"Then I think it becomes the huge financial success, like he's had, like Marvin Gaye has. Marvin Gaye is involved, in that latest song 'What's Going On?' Now, you take somebody as militant as Nina Simone, who has moved over and adapted Bob Dylan songs, and Roberta Flack, who's singing Leon Russell songs . . .

"I don't think that the black community got into the rock-and-roll possibilities until Jimi Hendrix. When he got over here, Jimi Hendrix became a folk hero to young blacks. But the black audience began to dig him. What I mean is that guys like Miles Davis went to see him. Just like they went to see Sly.

"I think that a fallout from the rock thing is going to be some kind of poetic expression that is not hung up, as the Beat poets were hung up, with a special thing, and as the avant-garde poets are now, in using words as musical sounds, and ringing changes on those sounds regardless of the meaning. I think that you get people now writing poems and you see them cropping up not just in *Rolling Stone* but all over the place, in which they do the same thing that the rock poets do, which is to speak about things that everybody's concerned with. Whether it's Lenny Bruce, or Jimi Hendrix, or Miles Davis, or Billie Holiday, or what, like Julian Bond's poem in Howard Zinn's SNCC book—you know, the Ray Charles–Billie Holiday poem. I'm looking forward to some poets I can read."

GREIL MARCUS

Do you find yourself really hearing the lyrics only of songs you get off on?

"Pretty much. There's nobody in music that has meant more to me than Dylan. Nobody's music has meant more to me than Dylan's, nobody's records or performances, and every time he's

had an album out, like from the time his first record was released, I'd get it and play it a whole lot, and I loved it and all
that, with the exception of *Self Portrait*.

"But there have been songs that I just didn't dig. 'Tombstone
Blues' never really got to me, and it's not because I think it's
a bad song or anything. It just didn't have a beat that I like or
something. I never really liked it that much, and I was never
aware of what the words were; I never paid attention. I wasn't
going to sit down and pick them out. Whereas some other songs,
like 'Ballad of a Thin Man,' I think I must have, without trying
to, memorized the words to that song after hearing it twice,
because it was just so powerful. The music, the way he sang it,
the words—it was just automatic. It certainly took no effort to
know what those words were.

"But on *Nashville Skyline,* which is an album I really love—
I think it's a wonderful album—I'd be really hard put to quote
you two lines from any song. It just isn't that kind of record.

"With the Stones, their words are very hard to understand—
on purpose, I mean. It's very intentional. There are numerous
Stones songs where I sing them along to myself, sing the words,
but I'm sure I've got them wrong, and that's really central to
rock-and-roll, this sense that a priori the words don't matter
much. You know, they might, but that's the assumption you go
by. So in many cases, they just can't be heard and so the
listener is forced to improvise, to make up his own words."

Bob Hunter of the Dead told me he's reluctant to have his
lyrics printed at all.

"Well, he's right. I wrote a review of *Let It Bleed* and I
quoted some of the lines from 'You Can't Always Get What You
Want,' and I got it wrong. I didn't think so at the time, but I'm
pretty sure now. What I quoted was: 'I sang my song to Mr.
Jitters/And he said one word to me/ And that was: Death.'
That's what I printed. Well, two years later I heard the song
on the radio and I suddenly flashed that what it was was: 'I
sang my song to Mr. Jimmy'—I like Jitters better, but, you know
—'And he said one word to me/And that was: Bed.' In other

words, what that song is about is a homosexual putting the make on Jagger, which is really nice; that's really a powerful image. And so's the other one. They both exist simultaneously for me.

"The thing is, all these people who print their lyrics on the back of the album, for lack of anything better to put there, ninety-nine percent of these are not worth reading; some of them aren't worth hearing, either, but most of them sound all right in the song, but they're not worth reading.

"I saved something for this discussion. This is a press release I got two days ago for a new singer/songwriter named Kent Morrel, who's got an album coming out called *Dreammaker*. There's a lot of nonsense about how he thinks dreams will save the world if people start dreaming more, and everything groovy like that. Then there's some quotes from some of his songs. He's a poet, that's how he's presented: songpoet.

"Let's see. 'In the land of hate and fear and fright/There dwells a dragon/And the dragon's name is War.' That's from 'The Dragon.' And then from 'Paradise Lost': 'Today the sun will rise to brown and dusty skies/But no songs of birds are heard from factories.' And then here: 'Hail to the dreammaker/Where has he gone?/Drowned out by take-side children/Singing all their lonely songs.' There's one thing in that last couplet that's really hideous and that's that line 'take-side children.' That's awful; that's really vile. Anybody who knows anything about writing would never use that. This guy's being presented as a poet, and he knows nothing about words.

"It seems to me that one of the fashionable things now in the music business is for a guy to come out as a poet, and one of the nice things about rock-and-roll is that anybody can do it. Even somebody with no talent, like the Stones. They can make a pretty good record. I like them, but I think they don't have any talent. Or the Troggs. 'Wild Thing' is a great record, and God knows, they don't have any talent. But you can't sit down and write poetry without having some feel for the language, for how words go together, for what you want to say. You don't have to know what you're going to say, but you have to know what you *want* to say.

"Anybody can sort of draw out a good beat, but that's a little different from writing poetry. I don't know if writing poetry is more important, but it's different. And so the image has come across that—that nonsense about how every man has a great novel in him, or every man's a poet in his heart. It's bullshit. Utter nonsense. The novel that that cliché refers to is obviously that guy's life story, which refers to another piece of bullshit, which is that all novels are autobiographical. Right, *Moby Dick* is really an autobiography. Sure. That's bullshit too. And it's sort of a romantic democratic view of the world.

"There's a few people I like: I like Whitman; I like Blake; I like Shakespeare; but I'm not a great fan of poetry. It's harder for me to read than almost anything else, and so when people started talking about songwriters as poets, like when Ralph Gleason began to talk about Dylan as a poet, or for that matter, when Allen Ginsberg began to talk about Dylan as a poet, I started to wonder about that. So I wrote a few of his songs on paper, to see whether they would make it, and they all fell apart with one exception, which was 'Visions of Johanna.' It's an incredibly tight, beautifully worked-out poem, where the images are very carefully followed through and set up. The purpose of the obscurity of the song is very clear: there's nothing in that song that can't be seen, that can't be understood. In fact, the images force you to go deeper into it. I mean, to me that's a great poem; that really works."

My theory is that these writers aren't poets, but something different that fills a similar function: songpoets.

"You can approach the whole subject of songs and poets simply by saying what is, or what was, the function of a poet in society; what role did he play? If the songwriter seems to be playing an analogous role, then you can start talking about it. But then there's the other problem: poetry instantly summons up this whole tradition, which starts with Aeschylus and Homer and goes on all the way to now.

"Ginsberg's a part of that tradition. He's read all that stuff, and he's conscious of being part of that tradition. He would recognize that. And it seems very doubtful to me whether

Robbie Robertson in any literary sense ought to be considered part of that tradition, although Robertson's role in society is probably a whole lot closer to what Aeschylus' role in Athens was than to what Whitman's role in America was, or closer to Shakespeare's role in Elizabethan England. Because basically Shakespeare and Aeschylus were popular culture. That's fact. It's very obvious. Shakespeare was writing all these incredibly commercial plays, and not only that, but people really dug it. They didn't just dig them because they were good stories. They really dug watching Hamlet go through those terrible torments, and they really got off on King Lear out there on the heath. I mean, they were picking up on what was there. Same with Aeschylus. Those people found their culture so beautifully captured in this small artistic, cultural event, and it really made them feel proud to be part of their city.

"One of the things Robertson is doing is he's trying to figure out what it means to live in this country, what possibilities there are, what things have been closed off. He's trying to affirm certain things that people tend to dismiss; that song about the Civil War basically says, 'There's more here than you thought.' And just about everybody responds that way. Robertson is dealing with his audience in a very direct manner. He's speaking to these same concerns about what kind of community they're living in and all that. And not only that, but he's able to do it. He's working in a form of media that's very direct. He can communicate with several million people at once just by cutting an album, whereas Whitman was trying to do that, and he was probably much more of a genius than Robbie Robertson—which is hardly a put-down of Robertson—but he published his books and nobody bought them, and everybody said they were shit. He was failed popular culture. He wasn't popular. That's one of the things about popular culture. You always have to figure out why something's popular.

"There's a whole image when you say the word 'poetry' that that word summons up. It's a deep word with lots of resonances. It summons up lots of things, one of which is Edgar Allan Poe in a garret, drunk out of his mind, shooting up and scribbling out some magnificent poem. And that's really the image that a lot of people carry around with them. Whereas God knows where most poetry is really written, but that's certainly not the way rock-and-roll poetry, if there is such a thing, is written.

"There's a thing about rock poetry. I think Rod Stewart writes really good songs. I love Rod Stewart, but I also think he writes good songs. However, I don't think any of the songs he writes can by the farthest stretch of the imagination be called poetry. But it's an interesting thing. How do you separate, differentiate, the poets from the nonpoets, like that song 'Every Picture Tells a Story.' That's a really good song, but it's got some lines in it that are really atrocious, like 'My body stunk, but I kept my funk.' That's like saying, 'Gotta rhyme it, gotta rhyme it.' That's terrible. But in the context of everybody playing, and Rod Stewart screaming, and the drummer bashing away, it's just fine. It's not poetry; it doesn't do anything that poetry does, and it shouldn't."

Aren't there songs where the words interfere with the musical thrust? For instance, "Tell Me, Mama" by Dylan?

"Oh, I don't think so. I've heard that song enough times so that the words are very clear to me, and there are times when the unity between what the music is expressing and what Dylan is expressing through the words is so astounding. He and Robbie wrote a great rock-and-roll song there. Whereas something like 'Ballad of a Thin Man,' it's much more a matter of setting up a scene musically that Dylan can act in. But that song 'Tell Me, Mama,' that's a rock-and-roll song in a way that 'Ballad of a Thin Man' isn't, not in the same way.

"The only times the words get in the way are when the words aren't any good. I don't think 'Sad-Eyed Lady' is any good. I think the harp playing in the beginning and the end is really wonderful, but the song is just a load of nothing, and there's no music there at all. Now, a song like 'Absolutely Sweet Marie,' which is just covered with all these really tangled, involved images . . . God knows what the story line is, but those images jump out. They make sense. The idea of a Persian drunkard following you. You don't have to know what kind of story's taking place to know that that's really creepy. And he gets that across with no trouble. That's really a rock-and-roll song. If he sang it slow: 'There's a Persian drunkard following me'— that wouldn't make it, but with him singing, and everybody clanging away, it's great.

"'Like a Rolling Stone' is not a great piece of poetry. No, I don't think it's a great piece of songpoetry either. I think it's just a lot of shit with something at the end of every single verse that just knocks you dead. It just obliterates everything else. Like the first verse, 'Once upon a time . . .,' is a brilliant beginning, and then he goes on—well, I can't even remember how the first verse ends, but the way the second verse ends is that you're going along, and there's all this la-de-da stuff, and then suddenly 'You're staring into the eyes of the mystery tramp/ And he's not selling you any alibis.' That's just incredible. And then at the end of the third verse, there's been all this stuff about Siamese cats, and that's just fine, and then he says, 'He wasn't really where it's at/After he took from you everything he could steal,' which is incredibly powerful. He's constantly going back and forth like that. He's said in an interview that he sometimes has to use a couple of bad lines to set up a good one."

A lot of the songpoets seem to be furthering the work of imagist poets like Pound and William Carlos Williams. Dylan, in particular.

"You know, it's strange. He still does weird things with clichés. All through his best songs, he'll walk right into a cliché, stare it in the eye and then kind of slide around it. As though he were saying, 'Ha, I beat you again.' As on 'New Morning'; on that song, he has a line 'Automobile coming into style.' Well, now, anybody in his right mind would have expected Dylan to have said, 'Automobile coming into view,' but automobile coming into style? What does that mean—the new cars are arriving in the showrooms? Well, God knows what it means, but it's a fantastic image. It has this great sense of novelty and excitement. 'Oh boy, new cars.'

"I don't know if there's any specific context he meant it to have, but it really does something for that line in a way. He walks up to the cliché again and he slides right past it. It's like in 'Love Minus Zero,' he's got a line where he says, 'The country doctor rambles.' Now, what's so incredible about that line is that it's close to what a country doctor does, but it isn't what a country doctor does. A country doctor does not ramble. A country doctor gets into his buggy and he goes out and visits sick people, and he isn't rambling. Not by a long shot. But Dylan's country doctor rambles.

"Here is this guy out there, and the wind's blowing and it's cold, and he's so into what he's doing that he's just digging it. He's not worried about getting anywhere; he's just gliding along. That's really amazing. That's what is really poetry about that— not some of the more complex images, which are really interesting too, but they're not doing with language and with expectations that are in people's heads what that line does.

"'My Love She Speaks in Silence' is too obvious for me. It's like, 'She speaks in silence'—so, a paradox. I mean, that to me is just a guy trying to write poetry, but 'The country doctor rambles' is a guy doing it.

"You're talking about songpoetry, and you take a song that in terms of its words is, in your terms, worth talking about as poetry, and it seems to me you really have to start wondering if the music is different—if it were sung by a different guy, in a different way, whether it would have any impact on you, or as much, or any that's worth talking about. Because I've got another version of 'Visions of Johanna,' which Dylan cut with The Band—a studio version—and it's done very, very differently. It's basically gorgeous, is what it is: beautiful. It's like 'Turn, Turn, Turn' by the Byrds, or something. And the words are just not as important to the impact as the version he put on the album. Now, I've heard Dylan do 'Visions of Johanna' with just an acoustic guitar, and it's a fucking bore. It really is."

CONCLUSIONS

$\mathbb{S}$ OMEONE once told me that books get written when a prospective author gets tired of searching futilely for a volume, and this book is no exception. For years I've been prowling libraries and bookstores waiting for the right volume that would recognize and credit the songpoets. The new form is a skillful amalgamation of intelligence and energy—the wedding of rock-and-roll and guts and brains. Added to this is an extraordinary willingness to examine and expose one's own experience. Even in this time of popular revelation, people spilling out their intimate secrets on television talk shows, it is remarkable to me that these songpoets have found it in themselves to be so uncompromisingly honest and intimate in their writing. They do not hesitate to put themselves down for vanity or hatefulness. But at the same time, they reveal their joy, feelings and kicks.

As a group, they represent one small part of rock's second generation. There are other currents—some exploring the use of theater and others progressive sounds. Each has its innovators —Alice Cooper and David Bowie in theatrical form, and artists such as Miles Davis and John McLaughlin in the progressive form. The seven artists I have chosen are the innovators in their

217

form. They share, among many other things, the courage and the ability to take us where no songwriters have taken us before.

Bob Dylan is, unquestionably, the original in the form. His willingness to confront his critics again and again is well documented. Constantly moving and constantly evolving, his music captures the essence of a generation. It is hard to remember always how big a step Dylan took when he injected electric music into his work, and what tough resistance he met—and that at twenty-four he abandoned a style of writing and performance in which he had made it big, as well as a tried and true audience, for a new mode and ultimately for a broader audience. With a single album and a few personal appearances, he single-handedly altered the image of rock-and-roll. Rock, which had been a subject for scorn or closet listening, became the form with which a generation related to the world. The Beatles, of course, contributed greatly to this, but I do not think they could have produced much of what they did without the influence and leadership of Dylan.

There is a tendency among many critics and many listeners now to dismiss Bob Dylan as exhausted and musically ineffective. There has been a definite change in the direction of his work, and a loss of the surrealistic effects and the mad energy that initially attracted much of his audience, but it would be shortsighted to dismiss a thirty-year-old genius. There has been no diminution of Dylan's talent with words or his ability to make strong music that is entirely his own. He will surprise us again, as he has done in the past.

If Dylan has abandoned surrealism, at least one of his followers has not. Don McLean, who broke on the rock world with his long, despairing look back at the '50s and '60s, "American Pie," has in later songs found a new way to use the imagery of surrealism. A shallow use of ambiguity is boring and phony, but McLean seems to be fairly successful with the imagery of surrealism and the ambiguous paradox. His songs are passionate affairs, often angry; his sense of the language is strong, and his insights often get through to us. He has gained by adding his own strengths to rock.

Humor, only sometimes present in popular music, runs all through the work of these young writers. It is not a humor of obscenity or guffaw, but of subtlety and gentle or bittersweet surprises. Randy Newman is perhaps the most comical of the songpoets. He spends a good part of his time hiding out in his Los Angeles home, watching television and reading, and is a very special case. His songs are apparently simple, full of complicated analysis of deceptively simple individuals. When he writes of a rapist, as in "Suzanne," we are all out there with him, making obscene phone calls and lurking in the bushes. When he talks about a young man confronting his dying father whom he does not know very well, there is no sentimental cop-out. I'd like to see Randy Newman give a concert before the joint houses of Congress, for he could give the politicians a lesson on the sterility, the confusion and the odd innocence of our times.

Laura Nyro is a different cup of wine. She is the songpoet of urban passion, capturing the seaminess and the bright flashes of joy of the city street. Her music is intense, both in concert and on records—it scorches; her lyrics are simple and musical. She has absorbed a lot of black city music and flashed her own light on it, using everything from her own strong piano-playing to some of the best arrangements rock has. She steps delicately between the fine lines of economy and overstatement.

Joni Mitchell has always been an extraordinary songwriter, but with *Blue* she is in the first rank of performers—a tasteful and moving actress. She is innocent-looking and shy, and her wise and caustic lyrics surprise. In a time when love songs are too often quick, facile and insincere, her emotional songs stand out like diamonds among cut glass.

Van Morrison and Bob Hunter of the Grateful Dead are prime rockers. Morrison can deliver a rock lyric with more passion than a hundred of his imitators combined. In the midst of Black Sabbaths and Grand Funk Railroads, his voice and writing are representative of the best in rock. He writes short hit singles with twists, as well as long, intricate songpoems full of images of childhood and loss. On stage, when he is on, he gives a show that leaves you breathless. His ensembles, although frequently subject to shuffling, are all first-rate, and like Dylan before him, he seems to have the ability to draw out the best his musicians have to offer with his own energy and professionalism.

Hunter, the only one who never steps on stage to perform, is anyhow part of the Grateful Dead, which is finally being recognized as one of the great bands. I believe that this is partly due to Hunter's ability to lend poetry to their fierce beat. The characters who populate Hunter's songs, whether workingmen or sophisticated ladies, are very American. They are strong and innocent rebels hinding behind normality. The Dead are filling stadiums with their fans now. They may be boogeying in the aisles and testing out all the drugs, but if his teen-agers listen, they will come away wiser.

These seven are very individualistic, but they share a great deal. All are children of the middle class—some from more comfortable backgrounds than others, but all essentially with backgrounds of television, literacy and comfort.

All seven are young, and have been rewarded for their talent in their twenties. They are what baseball writers call young veterans. They have had time to absorb the intricacies of surviving in the record business, have succeeded where many have failed. Their best work is ahead of them, since none has shown signs of flagging and nearly all have improved steadily.

For the most part, they are self-taught musicians who at one point or another picked up a guitar or sat down at the piano. This has been to their advantage, since it appears to be a source of freedom. Experimentation comes naturally; they have integrated a number of musical influences into their work, including rock and jazz and folk music and, in the case of Randy Newman, quite a bit of that forgotten American art, movie music.

Yet there is a problem inherent in being self-taught. Self-imposed limitations are not always visible, and such a craftsman may find himself bogged down in repetitiveness. Some sneak off for lessons in arrangement and composition, and others seek out people who are well versed in these things. Too often they are surrounded by businessmen and sycophants who want nothing more from them than the same repeated successes.

One of the most important things the songpoets share is their ability to integrate rock into their work. Not only has this added to the breadth of their work but, for nearly all, it has put them in positions of public success and material security. They are free to experiment, free to write and perform and make a good living while at it. Many who have excluded the energies of rock have fallen by the wayside, unable to sell records or draw an audience because they failed to acknowledge that their lyrics alone were not strong enough to draw. The songpoets have realized it and prospered, musically and financially.

All the songpoets are basically apolitical. Politics, whether it is Democratic or Republican or the politics of the street, is simply not what works for them. They don't trust political activism.

Finally, what unites these seven is a deep and nearly instinctive humanism. Each writes of people with great care and love. They do not compromise their criticism, but they rarely fail to make it clear that it stems from a deep affection for people. Their honesty is a testament to it. So is their concern for the lost, the lonely and the despairing.

Personal involvements are important to their songs, as if they were models of larger struggles and larger problems. When Bob Dylan wrote, "How does it feel to be on your own?" he was speaking not to one lost girl but to a generation. When Van Morrison examines sweetly his own roots and the lost joys of his Belfast childhood, he is speaking of all the lost childhoods. When Joni Mitchell writes, "I'm afraid of the Devil/ But drawn to those who aren't afraid," she is talking about how people stumble into lives of drugged uselessness.

Each, drawing on his own limited experience, creates a small world of justice and poetry that often expands into a vision of greater scope. The vision is profoundly humanistic.

Working independently, and within a business that one record executive has described as having the "morals of a rhino in heat," they have still managed to hang on to their visions.

Now that they have made their mark, perhaps those who control the media will recognize this and begin to play their music more and more. If their work spreads out through records and radio, we will have more of them—maybe even more honest and exciting songpoets.

CITADEL UNDERGROUND provides a voice
to writers whose ideas and styles veer
from convention. The series is
dedicated to bringing back into print
lost classics and to publishing new
works that explore pathbreaking and
iconoclastic personal, social, literary,
musical, consciousness, political,
dramatic and rhetorical styles.

Take Back Your Mind

For more information, please write to:

CITADEL UNDERGROUND
Carol Publishing Group
600 Madison Avenue
New York, New York 10022